Titles in the
Business Analysis Professional Development Series

This series is for those interested in developing a career in business analysis. Each book within the series will help practitioners develop the knowledge, skills, competencies, and capabilities needed to master the typical business analysis career path. These instructional texts are designed for use in professional training, continuing education courses, and self-learning.

Successful Business Analysis Consulting:
Strategies and Tips for Going It Alone
by Karl Wiegers

Mastering Business Analysis Standard Practices:
Seven Steps to the Next Level of Competency
by Kelley Bruns and Billie Johnson

Mastering Business Analysis Standard Practices Workbook
by Kelley Bruns and Billie Johnson

Seven Steps to Mastering Business Analysis, 2nd Edition
by Jamie Champagne

Mastering Business Analysis Versatility:
Seven Steps to Develop Advanced Competencies and Capabilities
by Gina Schmidt

Agile Business Analysis: Enabling Continuous Improvement
of Requirements, Project Scope, and Agile Project Results
by Kevin Aguanno and Ori Schibi

Mastering Business Analysis Versatility

Seven Steps to Develop Advanced
Competencies and Capabilities

Eugenia C. Schmidt, PMP, CBAP, PMI-PBA

ISBN 13: 978-1-60427-157-7

Printed and bound in the U.S.A. Printed on acid-free paper.

10 9 8 7 6 5 4 3 2 1

Library of Congress Cataloging-in-Publication Data is available in the WAV section of the publisher's website at www.jrosspub.com/wav.

Phone: (954) 727-9333
Fax: (561) 892-0700
Web: www.jrosspub.com

CONTENTS

PREFACE

PURPOSE

Many books prescribe an approach to business analysis or speak to specific challenges; however, *Mastering Business Analysis Versatility* is a guide to assist business analysis professionals in finding their own path—making their own choices for needed activities, techniques, and tools that are the *right-fit* approach based on different initiative variables and situations. To have the confidence in making these choices, business analysts (BAs) must also advance their competencies beyond the fundamentals in their management and analysis skills, knowledge of life cycles, and techniques. In other words, this book is intended to support the needed versatility of the BA and the tailoring of the work that they perform.

AUTHOR INSIGHT

As a novice BA, early in one's career, the focus was always on the deliverables to be produced. If the client wanted a project charter with the scope defined in it, they got it! If the client requested to use their template for a requirements specification, they got it! Responding to client requests seems to be the right thing to do. Have you ever been in this situation? Having completed templates as requested, were you confident of having done it *right*? Over time, your own ability and confidence to deal with a greater breadth of business analysis activities and your experience with more predicable outcomes advances you to another level of proficiency. Instead of being driven by the templates, there will likely be more focus on understanding stakeholders—listening more and digging deeper. You may realize that to gain a greater understanding of how things work at the enterprise level, there needs to be a better understanding of how projects are actually helping the company. How did this project connect to the rest of the projects or the company strategy? The love of continuous learning may encourage you to seek out more challenging opportunities, as it did for me.

Using this drive to find new challenges, I successfully landed a position as an internal consultant at the phone company, where I was assigned to a *rapid-delivery* group within the technology organization. This enterprise-level group was responsible for sharing internal knowledge within the company, and we were charged with actively looking externally for best practices in the industry. My role constantly changed to fulfill the enterprise's immediate need for implementing multiple strategic initiatives quickly. The business world was changing fast—and versatility was the name of the game. The role changes sparked additional learning experiences, ultimately posing the question: What were my responsibilities? How do activities change in this new role? What existing knowledge can be leveraged? How do behaviors need to be modified to be successful? How do stakeholders see me? Should my communication strategy change with them? How does the approach to my work change? As success in a constantly changing environment grew, so did my confidence, and vice versa. The ability to adapt grew exponentially during this period in my career. But it didn't end there. The next career move was on the horizon—becoming an external consultant.

As an external consultant, the ability to dig in deep on prior experiences and adapt to a client's environment quickly were the keys to consulting success. But it wasn't just about adapting, it was about *preparing* to adapt. Seeing the bigger picture wasn't just about utilizing different techniques or activities, it was also about how to help others make decisions and motivate them to accomplish their goals. As my skills and expertise in the field grew, my accomplishments were being recognized by others in the profession. However, what was most important to me was having the ability to share the knowledge that I had acquired with others to further the profession that I was, and still am, most passionate about.

Mastering Business Analysis Versatility is about making thoughtful adjustments based on a variety of different views, perspectives, industries, initiative types, conducted retrospectives, etc. In this book, you will find illustrations for a variety of ways to improve your ability to quickly assess the environment for what will influence your approach, how to pick and choose the right-fit approach, and how to adjust your approach based on risks. Advancing business analysis capabilities is about refining the abilities we have (and possibly adding a few new ones), which will help us navigate changing environments to result in successful outcomes and successful careers.

INTENDED AUDIENCE

The intended audience is experienced professional BAs or managers of BAs who have the passion to continue their learning. These analysts may also have other specific titles, such as: business systems analyst, agile BA, data BA, process BA, enterprise BA, operations BA, or requirements analyst.

Others may also be interested if they occasionally perform business analysis activities and would like to add more breadth and flexibility to their non-BA role or to understand how business analysis activities might integrate with their own activities, such as: user experience designer, process engineer, business architect, data architect, project manager, ERP consultant, business consultant, Scrum Master, product owner, trainer, quality assurance manager, developer, release coordinator, or solution architect, just to name a few.

BOOK ORGANIZATION

Chapter Overview

There are eight chapters in this book—an introduction that sets the stage with some fundamentals and seven additional chapters representing the seven steps to business analysis versatility. These seven steps will provide insight and knowledge, allowing the reader to master their versatility for applying various business analysis approaches. The goal is to advance competencies and capabilities in this discipline.

Chapter 1: Introduction

The *Introduction* provides some fundamentals, such as the purpose of business analysis and the need for organizational support. In addition, this chapter will provide some specific advanced behaviors—or *soft skills*—that are critical for implementing many of the recommendations provided in future chapters.

Chapter 2: Step One

Move to an Enterprise Mindset requires the BA to expand the breadth of their thinking beyond the boundaries of projects and organizations and consider strategies at the highest levels that influence tactical activities.

Chapter 3: Step Two

Adapt to the Life-Cycle Approach moves the BA role toward that of an advisor and consultant by gaining an understanding of three life-cycle approaches (predictive, hybrid, and adaptive) and by providing insight into why planned activities may be influenced by the life cycle, why adjustments may be needed, and where flexibility may exist.

Chapter 4: Step Three

Consider Uniqueness looks beyond the life cycle to the many different types of initiatives or projects that make them unique (e.g., vendor packages, process driven, user focused, etc.), influencing the business analysis approach. Various types will be evaluated while offering business analysis work breakdown structure tailoring considerations.

Chapter 5: Step Four

Adjust Based on Risks identifies different risk classifications that may require the BA to modify either the business analysis approach or the overall project approach. Various responses to the risks are recommended depending on the approach.

Chapter 6: Step Five

Always Focus on Value looks at business and stakeholder value from many perspectives and levels. It also looks at how the BA can provide value to the organization by always looking for opportunities.

Chapter 7: Step Six

Bridge the Capability Gap assumes proficiency beyond the basics focusing on both individual competencies and organizational capabilities. Recommendations to close gaps between current and future targets are provided.

Chapter 8: Step Seven

Build Up the Tool Chest assumes that BAs can improve their own efficiencies by using the *right-fit* techniques and tools for the approach. Many example applications will be provided in this chapter.

Supporting Information

Although many books about business analysis use a single case study throughout, this book will use a variety of situations to increase each reader's ability to become more intuitive and versatile. Each chapter has a summary and questions to reinforce the content of the chapter. An appendix provides examples and templates, ultimately helping the reader to advance professionally. A website link provides electronic versions of templates and additional supporting material for educational purposes.

ACKNOWLEDGMENTS

It is difficult to write any book without the support of others. Many thanks to my business associates, friends, and family for providing valuable assistance with illustrations and editing: Stathia V. Sylvester, Jimmy N. McNally, Mary E. McNally, Edith Assaff, and SuAnne Sharef.

I would like to dedicate this book to my mother who never had the opportunity to attend school or work in the business world, yet her perseverance in life taught me to face any challenge courageously. And finally, to my husband, William, who was more supportive than he will ever know throughout this long process.

ABOUT THE AUTHOR

EUGENIA C. SCHMIDT, PMP, CBAP, PMI-PBA

Eugenia (Gina) C. Schmidt, founder and managing partner of VITINAR, is a well-known expert, consultant, instructional course designer, and trainer in business analysis, project and program management, project recovery, program/project office setup, information systems, and life-cycle methodologies.

Ms. Schmidt worked in various management and technical roles—such as project and program manager, business process manager, risk manager, business analyst, systems analyst, and enterprise and systems architect—for a number of firms, including AT&T, Coopers & Lybrand, Price Waterhouse, and Lighthouse Consulting Partners, before forming her own business.

Gina has successfully managed information technology implementations and methodology rollouts in multiple industries and has trained thousands of students and practitioners in business analysis, project management, and other professional services. She has instructed in classrooms, online, and through webinars for over 25 years.

In addition to providing services through her own company, Gina also contracts with various educational institutions and training companies to develop and conduct intermediate and advanced business analysis and project management courses. She recently developed a new Business Analysis Master Class Series program for ASPE Training.

Ms. Schmidt received her B.B.A. in computer management from Northwood University. She has received multiple achievement awards in consulting, including the "Woman of the Year" Award by the American Business Women Association. Gina is a published author and a sought-after speaker for many professional association conferences, seminars, and other events held by the IIBA, PMI, BA World, and Women in Technology.

She resides with her husband, William, in Fraser, Michigan.

 Web
Added
Value™

This book has free material available for download from the
Web Added Value™ resource center at *www.jrosspub.com*

At J. Ross Publishing we are committed to providing today's professional with practical, hands-on tools that enhance the learning experience and give readers an opportunity to apply what they have learned. That is why we offer free ancillary materials available for download on this book and all participating Web Added Value™ publications. These online resources may include interactive versions of the material that appears in the book or supplemental templates, worksheets, models, plans, case studies, proposals, spreadsheets and assessment tools, among other things. Whenever you see the WAV™ symbol in any of our publications, it means bonus materials accompany the book and are available from the Web Added Value Download Resource Center at www.jrosspub.com.

Downloads for *Mastering Business Analysis Versatility: Seven Steps to Developing Advanced Competencies and Capabilities* include:

Templates in Microsoft Word Format:

These files can aid the business analyst in creating deliverables for larger initiatives:

- Feasibility Study Template can help create a deliverable that provides an assessment of solution alternatives and if those alternatives are technically possible within the constraints of the enterprise or organization [A2.1]
- Business Case Template can help create a deliverable that proposes larger initiatives requiring justification by showing how the enterprise or organization will get a return on their investment [A2.2]
- Requirements Management Plan (RMP) Template can help create a deliverable that provides a common understanding of how requirements will be addressed throughout the life cycle [A2.3]

Workbooks in Microsoft Excel Format:

These files are tools for assessing business analysis competencies of both individuals and organizations [based on Appendix C content]:

- Business Analyst Competency and Capability Self-Assessment provides guidance to the individual business analyst in determining their current competencies and goals for improvement based on both individual and organizational needs
- Business Analysis Organizational Capability Assessment assesses the organization's ability to support business analysis activities for successful outcomes through its people, processes, and technology

Bonus Checklist:

200+ Business Analysis Questions is a bonus file not included in the Appendix of this book but is provided in WAV. It gives business analysts over 200 sample questions that helps them probe for:

- Understanding stakeholder environments, their needs, and what they value
- Understanding problems and the current or future state
- Movement from business requirements to stakeholder and solution requirements
- Different types of initiatives, such as Business Process Improvement, Business Intelligence, Technology-driven, etc.
- Project trade-offs

Additional valuable, customizable BA spreadsheets, slides, and activities can be purchased at www.jrosspub.com/wav.

1

INTRODUCTION

PURPOSE OF BUSINESS ANALYSIS

Business analysis is not a new discipline, but it is one that can challenge even the most seasoned analysts. Many companies today define individual career paths for those who are performing these activities. Professional associations provide business analysis certifications, and universities provide educational certificates and degrees. The reality is that for those who pursue this career, there may be no a single road to success or a special recipe, but there are many different paths that can lead to success as well as to the mastery of the profession.

Being an Expert

So, what does it mean to be an expert in your field? Consider the difference between a cook and a chef. The chef is the expert in the kitchen, and he or she is just as concerned about a successful outcome as the cook who is preparing the meal. They both want to achieve a pleasant, delicious meal for their customer. However, a chef has the experience and ability to adapt and adjust to changing circumstances, while the cook may have a more limited ability to do so. The chef not only knows about the inner workings of the kitchen, but also understands the importance of the vendors who supply the fresh ingredients, the need to follow the community's food service regulations, the obligation to know the tolerances of the restaurant owner, the significance of the geographical location, and even the cultural impacts of taste preferences, etc.

Although the chef and the cook both start with an initial recipe, the chef's expertise allows for the creation of a full menu by making necessary changes and adaptions based on elements such as customer feedback and tolerance for changes to the menu, customer cost constraints, the need for innovation, available equipment, etc. The chef must have a good understanding of how changes will be managed. Some changes may require the involvement of the owner for reviews and approvals, a full revamp of the menu based on customer feedback, and refinement of kitchen processes. In other words, some changes may have a large impact and several risks. But the owner and chef may identify many smaller changes that can be done incrementally, such as modifying a menu item each week to check the reaction with a small focus group of patrons. If a vendor runs out of a needed ingredient and it will be unavailable for months, how does this impact the processes and value to restaurant patrons? As the *chefs*, we as business analysts (BAs) should have the confidence to adapt and make changes, to make substitutions if needed, and know what we have available to us to make it work. We may have even predicted this and have a backup plan. Our advanced preparation in anticipating change gives us the courage to make the needed adjustments without a fear of failure because we are ready to improvise. We are willing to take on the risks for the rewards.

To be a master chef is to go beyond the doors of the restaurant. It is about looking at food trends and new opportunities; constantly reviewing our menus, cooking processes, and techniques for potential improvements; evaluating the customer's response to changes in our menu items; and making the needed adjustments to provide more value to not only the restaurant patrons, but to the restaurant owner as well. A true master chef networks with other chefs to share ideas, pursues new certifications and award opportunities, and writes and shares recipes with the community. Finally, in order to be that master chef, the chef must mentor others in their mastery by ensuring that they at least know the basic techniques of food preparation and that they can grow to be creative and innovative in combining different techniques and even creating techniques of their own—all in an effort to keep their knowledge fresh and to be innovative in their passion.

Similarly, as we experience the implementation of our business analysis activities, we learn to perform retrospectives and adjust. As we gain valuable experiences, we determine what information is valuable to retain and use in other roles. We prepare by understanding all the situations that might occur and we work to have the necessary tools in our tool chest as we navigate challenges. We learn to foresee signs of problems and find ways to circumvent them. We see the smoke *before* the fire.

Business Analysis as a Process

Business analysis is all about knowing how to help the business achieve its goals. It's about identifying your stakeholders and helping them get to the right solution by understanding their structure, processes, policies, and operations. It's about helping to produce a quality solution that provides value while staying within the constraints of time, money, and resources. Eliciting requirements by using proven methodologies can reduce rework and will result in business confidence. An in-depth understanding of the business needs enables the translation of needs into solution options. Utilizing a repeatable requirements process will not only facilitate and present a professional image of service delivery, but also a true quality product. However, keep in mind that these requirement processes must also be versatile enough to address the uniqueness of the organization and their initiatives. Consistently evaluating and improving requirement processes will increase the likelihood of a business partner reaching out to the BA earlier in the idea generation phase—this is when the BA can become a trusted advisor. If an organization is looking to lower solution delivery costs, consideration should be given to bringing in business analysis best practices and then continually improving them.

With so many sourcing options in the industry, it takes deliberate workforce visioning to set sourcing guidelines that enable goal achievement. Whether an organization decides to work with external vendors or an in-house workforce structure, it is important to manage the risk of knowledge leakage. This can be done by retaining and improving capabilities within an organization while also improving individual competencies. Who knows their businesses as well as BAs do? They know how work really gets done, how decisions really get made, and what will really work within the constraints of business culture and the project. In order to advance these capabilities, competencies must improve, and the organization must allow for the application of business analysis best practices in their environment.

THE NEED FOR ORGANIZATIONAL BUSINESS ANALYSIS CAPABILITIES

Business needs must be anticipated by understanding the complex business challenges and the impact that technology advances can have on the company's ability to deliver products or services. Producing solution options is a unique value that BAs provide. Without these knowledgeable resources, organizations would be forced to depend on external service providers to bridge the gap. So, when is it critical to have these knowledgeable resources in-house? Organizations should consider improving in-house business analysis capabilities when:

- There is great effort and money expended with little results
- It is unknown if a feature or function was implemented
- Meetings continue to produce solution ideas without implementable requirements
- Frequently only one solution option is provided
- Rework is accepted and is common in environments where there are frequent vendor or internal organizational conflicts—especially disputes over who is paying for rework costs
- Scope disagreement continues even after validation of the solution has already started
- Stakeholders feel they are not receiving the value expected in return for their investment

What do business analysis knowledgeable resources look like? How can they help the organization address issues such as those in the previous list? A competent and knowledgeable BA should be able to:

- Reduce product risks by using methods, tools, techniques, and checklists selected specifically for the initiative that is being undertaken
- Drive to the right level of requirement detail, determine the right models to use, and identify the best questions to ask based on who is providing and receiving the requirements

- Ensure business analysis activities are properly identified, estimated, well justified, and incorporated within the overall planning process so that appropriate time is allocated
- Capture the complete set of requirements so that solutions address all stakeholder needs, not just those with specific or hidden agendas
- Know how to drive out effective requirements when given a solution idea, a preference, a high-level requirement, or an ambiguous requirement
- Define, communicate, and manage expectations around solution scope—early and often
- Know the status and take ownership of every requirement throughout the life of the requirement
- Uncover and validate assumptions by eventually turning them into questions or specific requirements
- Look for opportunities to assist in solution idea generation
- Easily switch between roles, communicate role changes, know how to prioritize role activities, and address role conflicts
- Recognize the effect of rework and help reduce unplanned rework by effectively conducting business analysis activities
- Share knowledge to improve team and organizational competencies in business analysis

That is quite a list—and it would be difficult to accomplish without the support of an organization. Just as a BA can help an organization, an organization can impact the ability of the BA to perform their role. Chapter 7 will address both individual competencies and organizational capabilities. Most of this book will focus on the BA as an individual, which includes identifying seven steps (each in its own chapter) that can help the BA become more effective and confident in both a strategic and tactical setting, in various governance environments, and in applying different life-cycle approaches.

BEHAVIORS TO ADVANCE PROFESSIONAL CAPABILITIES

Which business analysis behaviors are needed to advance our career? How are these behaviors different from the ones we currently possess? How can current behaviors be changed to make us and our organization more successful? What do we need to do more proficiently? How can we be more versatile? There are many desired behaviors that are defined by business analysis associations. These behaviors, as elaborated upon in the upcoming paragraphs, are ones specifically needed for more advanced competencies. They can be applied in many other roles, but the focus will be specifically on the performance of business analysis activities within each chapter of the book for maintaining versatility in an advanced business analysis role. These behaviors include: be a leader, build trust, exhibit courage and confidence, promote collaboration, and accept change.

Be a Leader

What does it mean to be a leader in the business analysis profession and in different situations? There are various definitions of leadership, but one simple perspective is that leadership is about encouraging a group of people to work together. Leadership could be measured based on how clearly the group sees the shared strategy, mission, or goal so that group members are all heading in the same direction and on how likely they are to make changes in their path in order to work together. Do members influence one another to consider the shared objectives?

Unfortunately, leadership isn't that easy, and there are many factors that can affect how we lead. One of these is the leader's position of influence. BAs are rarely in a position of power in the organization. Typically, BAs are positioned either at a tactical level or at a strategic level (see Figure 1.1). At the tactical level, BAs work within project or program environments. At the strategic level, BAs will work within enterprise-wide initiatives or other more global interactions. Yet, leadership can occur within any of these environments. According to John C. Maxwell in *The 360 Degree Leader*, there are five levels of leadership.[1] The BA may likely be at the lowest level of influence based on Maxwell's model. The *position* level gives you the right to lead, and often people follow because they must (otherwise, it might hurt their career). Maxwell's four other levels—*permission, production, people development*, and *personhood*—show how influence can increase through individual relationships, achievements, helping others, and earning respect.

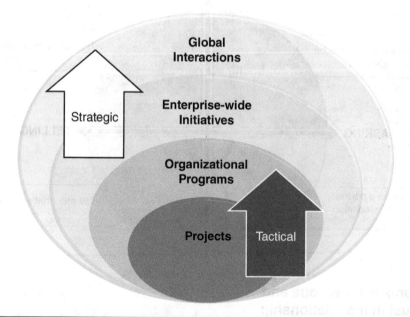

Figure 1.1   Understand BA leadership environments

Although a BA may typically be placed at the lowest level of the spectrum, there are roles that would allow for an expanded use of leadership skills. For example, a BA may serve as a *contractual worker* or take on a *consultant* role, with many roles that fall in between (see Figure 1.2). In my experience as a contractor—hired to fill a role and to perform certain activities that were assigned—I found my activities were closely managed. The pay was not as lucrative as working in a consultant role. However, even after moving to a consultant level, the *contractual worker* assignments often continue to be a BA's bread and butter—these positions are often easier to obtain and fulfill. As you can imagine, the expectations are also very different when you are brought in as an expert to provide advice versus as a facilitator to help a group make a decision on the selection of a solution. Some roles require using more advanced behaviors such as leadership skills, but even at the contractor level, you may find the same skills can be applied. Pulling from your own experiences, imagine this situation: you are hired to come into an organization to interview stakeholders with specific survey questions. Even though there is some leeway in the questioning process, this specific task is managed closely. How can you display leadership skills in this scenario?

You may be thinking: how could I be a leader when I am not leading anyone? Keep in mind, based on the role, the expectations of the role, and the situation at hand, your level of influence as a BA may change. Leadership does not always require managing others. Sometimes it requires

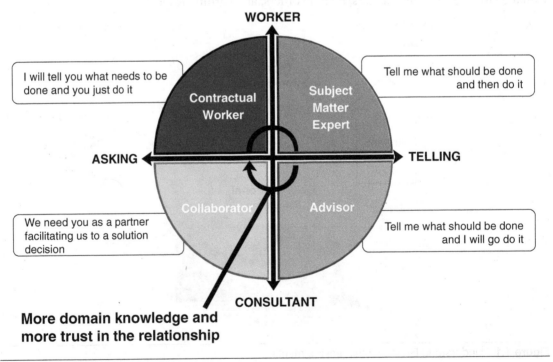

Figure 1.2   BA role expectations

displaying characteristics that good leaders have. As Maxwell notes in his book, a leader must be able to self-manage at any level or role. He describes seven areas that should be focused on for effective self-management: (1) manage your emotions, (2) manage your time, (3) manage your priorities, (4) manage your energy, (5) manage your thinking, (6) manage your words, and (7) manage your personal life. So even within a contractual assignment, you can demonstrate self-management skills. In my experience, managing time and priorities were particularly critical to the task at hand when working as a contractor. Influencing stakeholders to schedule time with me in order to fit the constraints of the project was one of my biggest challenges—along with being able to work that schedule within my own time frame and personal life. By navigating this successfully, I was able to build my trust with my manager and stakeholders. Building trust is a critical leadership skill, which we discuss in more detail in the next section.

Build Trust

Depending on your role, you may not have the luxury of time to build up trust with all stakeholders. Building up trust quickly is a critical skill for any personal and professional relationship. Early in my career while training to be a consultant, I found myself dealing with external and multicultural clients. Relationships had to be established quickly because of project time constraints, yet it was challenging due to distance and cultural differences. Building these relationships required exhibiting the following characteristics:

- *Care* and *curiosity* **about the relationship**—what each individual brings to it:
  "Can you tell me more about the process you were thinking of improving?"
- *Understand* **yourself first**—recognize weaknesses that need to be overcome:
  "Could you draw me a picture or list those points out on the white board? I am having a problem following along verbally."
- *Listen*—learn each other's concerns and shared interests and remember them:
  "I found some templates that might help you with that problem you shared yesterday."
- *Take* actions—they are worth more than words:
  "What can I do, right now, to address that issue?"
- *Identify* **individual skills**—where each can help to improve the relationship:
  "Would you like me to facilitate a meeting with the other stakeholders to help your group reach an agreement?"
- *Value* **what each provides to the relationship**—and vocalize it:
  "I really appreciate the time you have allocated to clarifying the existing process for me."
- *Achieve* **credibility**—follow through on realistic promises:
  "I realize that you have a constraint of a fixed date, but we are receiving many scope changes that will impact the allocation of our resources. Can we work together to resolve this?"

- *Tailor* **communications based on each other's style**—gain a common language: "Would you prefer that I put the business rules in a table or a flow chart format?"
- *Encourage* **open and truthful conversations**—and be willing to model them yourself: "Would you mind sharing why you seem to be getting upset about this conversation?"

CULTIVATE (the acronym derived from the first words of the bullet points) the relationship when trying to build trust quickly! These characteristics, applied daily in my personal and business life, were reinforced by Stephen M. R. Covey in *The Speed of Trust: The One Thing That Changes Everything.*[2] Covey provides some interesting statistics on how trust in an organization can save money in the long run. This was witnessed in my own career repeatedly with external clients. As a vendor, contracts with clients were required. Nothing was done without a written agreement, but that piece of paper meant little without trust. Trust is needed so that listening takes place, particularly when changes need to happen. Agreements can be volatile and may require changes. If trust is lacking, successful negotiations will not occur.

To develop trust, you need to act ethically. A colleague of mine once told me of an ethical situation she was faced with. She went to her manager with the situation and her manager said, "Your ethics are getting in the way of us making money!" Pressures and sales goals had to be met. The situation required her to be truthful about an implementation timeline and the impact it might have on client operations. She mustered up the courage to tell her boss that while she *could* push and sell the timeline to the client, she *would not*, then she proceeded to explain why. Ultimately, she was truthful to the client and, thus, the manager had no choice but to support her decision. In fact, this colleague went on to write her own book on leadership. According to Michelle Pallas in *Pack an Extra Pair of Underpants: Leadership Inside Out,*[3] there are seven acts of leadership: (1) know where you are going, (2) broker capability, (3) connect, (4) be a role model, (5) care, (6) have courage, and (7) live right. Courage is a critical element of leadership. According to Pallas, to have courage is to "act without fear after thoughtful consideration." Acting in an ethical manner can sometimes require displaying both courage and confidence, which are skills required of good leaders.

Exhibit Courage and Confidence

Have you ever had to deliver bad news to shareholders? Present to a hostile audience? Question a decision? Probe for requirements when stakeholders are uncooperative? Make a change that isn't popular? Challenge unrealistic expectations, such as deadlines? Admit mistakes you've made? BAs need the ability to persist when they are fearful of uncertainty, risk, or change. You can't have leadership skills without courage! Here are just a few ways to gain courage:[4]

- Build confidence by building up your expertise or connect with a mentor.
- Define why the action is so important to you. (What is your story?)
- Make the *big push* to action, don't just get paralyzed in your thoughts.

- Have the information to defend your point of view.
- Build up your influence and negotiation skills.

My mentor for courage was my colleague and past business partner, Michelle Pallas. We built a successful consulting practice together, and the reason it worked was because our leadership skills complemented one another. In the areas where I was weak, she was strong—and vice versa. Her strongest asset was her courage. When facing a fearful business situation, she became my sounding board. Even though my homework had been done, the situation had been analyzed, and supporting information and documentation had been gathered, taking the next action—the next step—required an often-needed push from my business partner, my *courage mentor*. We all need that little shove occasionally, and it is important to have someone there when things don't go right—to help us work through the situation and be courageous while doing so. We should all tap into the support system we have, whether it be colleagues, siblings, a spouse, a best friend, and/ or a network of resources. While you may find one person who can be supportive in most situations, you may also find that you need a collection of mentors to help when you are encountering different difficult situations.

Whether or not you decide to bring a courage mentor on board, make sure you define why the action you want to take is important to you. Take the time to:

- Define the situation and explain it in terms a mentor will understand
- Assess the impact to you and to all others
- Provide evidence that you have looked at the situation from all sides
- Do a pro/cons list or a force field analysis (assesses strength of helping or hindering forces)
- Envision the desired best outcome
- Consider your actions for the worst outcome

Once you have the courage to confront the situation clearly, you can use influence and negotiation skills to promote collaboration, particularly when the situation involves conflict among stakeholders.

Promote Collaboration

How can I promote collaboration by using influence and negotiation skills to address stakeholder conflicts? Regardless of the methodology used to deliver solutions, a BA must be an excellent facilitator when dealing with multiple stakeholders. Stakeholders often need to agree on the requirements for a solution (baseline), which of those requirements are most important (prioritization), and which solution to select when provided with alternatives (decision making). This type of business analysis facilitation requires techniques such as negotiation and influence to help the stakeholders collaborate. What is collaboration? My assumption when going into any project was that stakeholders had different perspectives and agendas. These conflicts are normal. Collaboration needs time in order to work through disagreements (*groan* period) and allow for venting time. This means time for exposing diverse views, listening, and probing before there is agreement or a decision made.[5]

My training as a facilitator taught me that it was important to encourage others to explore views by asking for further clarification. To understand their perspectives, put yourself in their domain. When there is trust, this groan period moves much faster. To converge these views quickly, influence and negotiation skills must be used in order to get to agreement. Shift from strong positions. Make problems into opportunities by bringing in more information. Silence is *not* agreement. It will haunt you later. Have the courage to deal with it now.

Influencing others is something we all do every day. There are several options. You can influence by conveying who you are, what you have done, what you can do, and what others can do. Let's just say that a team from work wants to meet up for lunch and each member of the team tries to influence the rest as to which restaurant to go to. The BA of the group suggests they all try to eat healthier (that wasn't me, by the way) and recommends a Mediterranean restaurant (proposes value gained). The product owner wants them to go to a top-rated local eatery (leverages external references). The quality assurance analyst suggests the restaurant next door because it is the quickest and they have meetings to go to right after lunch (gain efficiencies). The project manager (PM) suggests they just go to the place they always go to because they've had a great time there before (shows previous successes). The project sponsor says they should go have pizza since he is buying (leverage position). The systems designer wants to go to an old family restaurant across town because the owner is retiring and it is closing within the next month (show scarcity). The business subject matter expert who has been putting extra time in to help solve a problem for the team suggests everyone go to her favorite Chinese restaurant. Everyone immediately agrees with the subject matter expert since they feel a sense of indebtedness (gain favors)! This example shows some of the various influence options that can be used. BAs may need to use many different influence techniques to help with stakeholder collaboration. Figure 1.3 is another way to look at influencing techniques based on: (1) who you are, (2) what you've done, (3) what you can do, and (4) what others can do.

As a formally trained facilitator early in my career, I ran Joint Application Development (JAD) sessions in my role as a BA. The experience gained by applying my new negotiation skills became valuable throughout my career, but especially during my first big billing system initiative—the phone company's transition to a competitive environment. As in any collaboration, time is needed to understand different views. Often, we think we are negotiating when what we are really doing is haggling. Haggling is when you state your demands, usually starting with unreasonable offers to see how much the other party will tolerate. It is usually a take it or leave it mentality. Someone does win, but someone also loses. Haggling clearly happens every day for those one-time and low-value types of transactions. No one cares about the relationship—probably won't see them again! Haggling differs from negotiating, in which the focus should be on truly understanding where the other party is coming from. When negotiating, everyone agrees that the goal is to accomplish

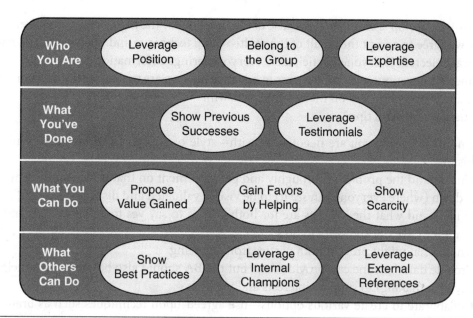

Figure 1.3   Consider leadership influence options

a win/win, requiring a willingness to take the time to probe and understand, to build a long-standing relationship, and to establish trust.

Another observation in negotiation is that often we confuse *positions* with *interests*. Think of interests as varying by each party as to why each party is taking a stance or position. What comes to mind is a business analysis situation in which the sponsor takes a position that states we must purchase a package as a recommended solution because it can be delivered more quickly and more cheaply, yet another business partner insists that we build an in-house solution because it would address 100% of the requirements. They have been arguing for over 20 minutes, continually restating their positions. As a BA and facilitator, it is my job to help them address this conflict by introducing probing questions to gain a deeper understanding of their reasons for taking that stance. Let's say I just happened to be prepared with some data that the packaged solution addresses only 50% of the high priority requirements and 80% of the medium and low priority requirements. We discuss the requirements that the package does not address and the resulting impacts to all stakeholders. We decide to take the time to brainstorm other solution options. As a group, we determine that there are three other options that could help get to a win/win. One option addresses the purchase of two add-on packages. The add-ons include the additional features that are high priority. Another option is to custom build just the portions that are missing. The final option is to wait, there is another package out there that may address more of the requirements, but because it is so new, it lacks client references. We don't want to be the first. The having-to-wait option is eliminated because of the timeline for the high-priority requirements. As a group, we agree to accept the result of the multi-voting technique and the two add-on packages option was selected. Everyone participates, everyone brings information to the table, everyone asks numerous questions, everyone agrees in advance how we are to decide (the decision-making process) and everyone agrees on the result. A win/win!

Negotiation hints and tips:[6]

- Know the people you are negotiating with—style of communication, state of mind, and history
- Understand the problem thoroughly and get agreement on that understanding by writing it down (where everyone can *see* it) to be visibly validated and discussed
- Understand what the benefits are for both parties to say yes to an agreement and assure that they have the authority to do so
- Know what might prevent both parties from agreeing
- Provide data (anyone can provide data, but the BA should also be prepared to help in the decision making) to support interests and position
- Collaborate to create various options—use agreed-upon techniques such as brainwriting and multi-voting
- Pick your battles to get to the win/win
- Don't be afraid to ask for help in the negotiation
- Know and communicate alternatives if an agreement cannot be reached
- Know at what point parties may walk away

Negotiation and influence techniques will be tapped into daily regardless of role and business environment. But as BAs, we are in the best position to apply these techniques when needed to promote collaboration among stakeholders. Another area requiring strong influence techniques and collaboration skills: acceptance of change.

Accept Change

It is hard not to discuss change when this book is about versatility. In Chapter 2 we will address the BA in a change agent role. A key function of that role is getting stakeholders to accept change. But how can we convince others to accept change if we can't accept it ourselves? Having experienced my share of company mergers, acquisitions, divestitures, an exorbitant amount of reorganizations, outsourcing, new methodologies, and huge advancements in technology, there is no question that a negative response to change and displaying fear of change is not uncommon.

With any change, you should ask yourself: "What am I afraid of?"—and then look into yourself to see how you can best deal with that fear. It displays a sense of control when you can plan out how those fears can be addressed. Transitioning from working with the phone company to joining a consulting firm was a huge step in my career. But it was also a big change—resulting in experiencing many fears. Earlier in the chapter we discussed having a courage mentor. This was a time when relying on a mentor was important to me. Talking through my fears with someone was extremely valuable. Discussing my apprehensions made it easier to accept the change and forced me to move forward with a plan rather than be paralyzed. This ultimately resulted in one of my best career moves. Accepting big change is not easy, but it does get easier. Now instead of fearing change, I look at it as an opportunity and prepare to adapt. I am always looking ahead and wondering—what's next?

It should be clear by now that there are a few special behaviors needed for mastery and advancement. What lies ahead for your journey to mastering business analysis versatility are these seven steps: (1) move to an enterprise mindset, (2) adapt to the life-cycle approach, (3) consider uniqueness, (4) adjust based on risks, (5) always focus on value, (6) bridge the capability gap, and (7) build up your tool chest. In Chapter 2 we will show the importance of having an enterprise mindset.

SUMMARY

- Have the courage to lead; leadership can happen at any level in the organization
- CULTIVATE relationships to build up trust quickly
- Promote collaboration by allowing time to expose diverse views, using negotiation and influence techniques
- Influence techniques are based on: (1) who you are, (2) what you've done, (3) what you can do, and (4) what others can do
- Accept change by asking yourself: "What am I afraid of?"—and then have a plan to address those fears
- There are seven steps to mastering business analysis versatility: (1) move to an enterprise mindset, (2) adapt to the life-cycle approach, (3) consider uniqueness, (4) adjust based on risks, (5) always focus on value, (6) bridge the capability gap, and (7) build up your tool chest

QUESTIONS

For the following scenarios 1–4, determine which leadership skills will help you prepare. What should be your course of action?

1. You have been following your business analysis approach and have finished eliciting the requirements from over a dozen stakeholders. You have captured the statements, but still must conduct some analysis activities to ensure you didn't miss anything and that stakeholder conflicts are resolved. This will take another week, just one day more than

estimated. The PM, Suzzy, wants you to stop now since the designers and developers are ready to start—and the PM feels you are just analyzing too much anyway. You set up a meeting to discuss this with Suzzy.

Leadership skills: _____

Course of action: _____

_____

2. Jamie is one of your stakeholders for a major strategic project and has volunteered to represent all the customer representatives. Based on some initial research, you found out that Jamie is new to the organization and has only been active with the customer representative organization for a few months. But, you also know that this stakeholder does have extensive industry knowledge from another company. You fear Jamie does not have the organizational and business domain knowledge to represent that group as the key business owner and decision maker. Additionally, fearing that assumptions will be made regarding how processes are performed here, Jamie has agreed to meet with you to validate your concerns, understand how important this assignment might be for her, and ensure the proper representation of a very important group.

    Leadership skills: _____

    Course of action: _____

    _____

3. During initial stakeholder meetings, you noticed a lot of resistance and a lack of cooperation from your key stakeholder, Terry. You recently worked up the courage to confront the issue and find out why. It took a while, but after discussions with others, you found that in prior experiences working with IT, the customers were disappointed—promises not kept, lack of user involvement, IT didn't listen, etc. Without solid customer cooperation, this project will have a very limited chance of succeeding.

    Leadership skills: _____

    Course of action: _____

    _____

4. You have been working for seven months on a project that is doing very well. But, last week after an acceptance testing validation walk through, Lambra, the user group representative, suggested how the software could be improved. In your opinion this was outside the scope of the defined requirements for this project. This scope increase would require

rework and would delay the project by 30 days. You thought you were done with this project and have already been assigned to another project in a few days. Lambra asked to meet for further discussion.

Leadership skills: _____

Course of action: _____

_____

5. I am trying to influence a client to select my solution by convincing them that the economic conditions will change and that the solution will help stimulate business under those conditions, but they need to act now in order to be ready in time. What is the influence technique I am trying to use?

_____

6. True or False

a. Be *flexible* with your interests and *assertive* with your options.   _____

b. Scarcity is an influence technique that should be used often.   _____

NOTES

1. Maxwell, John C. (2005). *The 360 Degree Leader: Developing Your Influence from Anywhere in the Organization.* Nashville, TN: Thomas Nelson Inc.
2. Covey, Stephen M. R. (2006). *The Speed of Trust: The One Thing That Changes Everything.* New York, NY: Free Press.
3. Pallas, Michelle. (2013). *Pack an Extra Pair of Underpants: Leadership Inside Out.* Michelle Pallas, Inc.
4. Niland, John and Kate Daly. (2012). *The Courage to Ask: Cultivating Opportunity in the New Economy.* Leicester, UK: VCO Global.
5. Kaner, Sam. (2014). *Facilitator's Guide to Participatory Decision Making.* Second Edition. San Francisco, CA: Jossey-Bass Business & Management Series.
6. Lum, Grande. (2005). *The Negotiation Fieldbook.* New York, NY: McGraw-Hill.

2

STEP ONE—MOVE TO AN ENTERPRISE MINDSET

"The chef not only knows about the inner workings of the kitchen, but also understands the importance of the vendors who supply the fresh ingredients, the need to follow the community's food service regulations, the obligation to know the tolerances of the restaurant owner, the significance of the geographical location, and even the cultural impacts of taste preferences, etc."—Chapter One

The strategic level of business analysis is where the business analyst (BA) must deal with governance entities and higher levels of management along with having a greater focus on the alignment to strategies. When BAs are at this level, their role is often expanded to deal with external teams, conduct benchmarking with other companies, and bring in best practices. Also, at this level, BAs may be in positions of authority if assigned to enterprise level governance entities, such as project/program management offices (PMOs), or in management positions having BA direct reports. But it is more likely that their leadership skills will require them to *lead up*. This is where they need to find ways to help their leaders manage heavy workloads and find ways to keep from wasting their leader's time—know when to push and when to back off.

ENHANCE ENTERPRISE OR STRATEGIC MINDSET

How do we go about thinking more strategically and with more enterprise breadth regardless of our BA role? Enhance your enterprise or strategic mindset by:

- Expanding cultural understanding
- Collaborating with executive-level management
- Strengthening vendor relationships
- Conducting benchmarking and competitor research
- Addressing enterprise risks
- Building governance relationships and sharing domain knowledge
- Considering strategic outcomes

Each of these will be discussed in more detail throughout this chapter.

Expanding Cultural Understanding

To have a cultural understanding of the enterprise, you must look under the covers. For example, is the enterprise:

- A globally or geographically dispersed organization (structure)?
- A private or family owned company versus a public company (structure)?
- Aligning service business units within other business units or are they centralized (as it relates to structure, service business units such as Human Resources, Information Technology (IT), etc.)?
- Using multiple languages internally with employees or externally with users and customers (diversity)?
- A result of blended cultures through acquisitions or mergers (diversity)?
- Only adopting proven solutions versus being on the forefront with technology (risk tolerance)?
- Going through rapid economic changes, either loss or growth, and providing predictions for the future (competitiveness and forecast)?
- Heavily regulated (extent of external influence)?
- Consistently making decisions by consensus or using other decision-making methods, such as autocratic or democratic (how decisions are made)?
- Operating each business unit as its own entity with different processes and financial reporting, such as a franchise versus operating each as a centralized unit with consistent processes and financial reporting?

These questions are important because the devised approach and the solution must fit within the enterprise's cultural environment. By using the sample questions provided, my roadmap for an initiative might consider a release structure because the company is geographically dispersed with a low risk tolerance. If one of my solutions was to implement a package, I would validate client references so that the solution is successful at many different installations. Assuming the company is also heavily regulated, quality checkpoints are critical, with an emphasis on identifying and validating business rules. As demonstrated by these examples, a better understanding of the culture provides a better approach and solution fit.

Collaborating with Executive-Level Management

Large initiatives typically have executive-level stakeholders who are involved and are impacted. BAs must gain courage and confidence to collaborate with high-level stakeholders in an organization in order to do their work successfully. The ability to communicate succinctly is essential to building up that confidence. Being prepared with *data at the ready* to support summarized information fuels that courage (as addressed in Chapter 1 when describing leadership skills). Having the ability to speak the same language, such as strategy terminology, also builds trust between the parties. Stakeholder analysis techniques, which we won't cover in detail here, often address the political power and influence that executive-level management may have and how they can be leveraged. This foundational knowledge of how to analyze your stakeholders is critical to building executive-level relationships.

Strengthening Vendor Relationships

Just as building trust with executive management internally is a valuable strategic mindset, it is just as valuable to understand our relationships with vendors. In today's environment, we frequently purchase and outsource products and services for the enterprise. Organizations are spending more time looking for solutions and commercial packages as opposed to building or utilizing internal resources. It may make economic and strategic sense to do so. The BA is often put in the position of dealing with multiple vendors, whether the vendors are providing solution alternatives or currently supporting the operational environment. In either case, an understanding of the relationships and the boundaries of those relationships impacts how we conduct our business analysis activities, especially in the way requirements are elicited and communicated to external parties that are responsible for building and/or providing these products and services.

Business analysis activities and estimates often involve the external providers of products and services, which creates the need for requirements to be more robust and surrounded with more context. As a result, requirement management activities are rarely outsourced. As an internal BA, strengthening relationships with vendors improves communications, increases collaboration, builds up trust, minimizes rework, reduces oversight, etc. Understanding the different vendor relationships allows the BA to tailor activities most appropriately. These vendor relationships tend to fall into five general categories based on contractual agreements: (1) staff augmentation relationship, (2) turnkey relationship, (3) integrated team relationship, (4) managed partnership relationship, and (5) enterprise partnership relationship. Each of these has their own business analysis uniqueness.

Staff Augmentation Relationship

The staff augmentation relationship is based on a vendor-sourced relationship that is at the individual level—one in which the individual is selected based on his or her skill to conduct specific tasks and is directly managed by an internal resource. The internal client resource has control of when, what, and how the vendor resource activities are conducted. The relationship is typically that of a contractor who is paid for time and material and defined at a manager's functional level. For the BA, it is often a vendor resource that is brought in to help build a solution. At the tactical level on individual projects, these vendor resources may not know the company, its culture, the terminology, or the business domain. They may be brought in for a few months to perform tasks and leave, yet they must still translate requirements to build the solution. Business analysis estimates must consider the extra time it takes to communicate and continue to collaborate regarding requirements. This can also hold true for any newly hired employee who doesn't have company or domain knowledge. Vendor resources at the staff augmentation level are most often on projects that are run by internal project managers (PMs). Having been in the role of a PM, I know that BAs often have challenges with vendor resources. Either the resource has limited understanding of requirements management or, as stated earlier, a lack of business domain knowledge to understand the context around the requirements. But as a PM, I valued the fact that the BA brought those challenges to me so that we could collaborate on solutions to address them. For a staff augmentation relationship, that is the correct action to take for a BA.

Turnkey Relationship

The turnkey relationship is based on a vendor's team that is managed by a vendor's PM, having responsibility for delivering a specific outcome as agreed to in a contract with a client. The vendor's PM has control of all team resources and the *what-and-how* aspect of the team's performance. The relationship is defined in contractual terms at a project level, usually stating a fixed price that may or may not include other expenses based on a specified deliverable. As in the staff augmentation relationship, more context and robust requirements are necessary, but a key difference is the limited access to the vendor team by any internal client resources, even the BAs. A formal deliverable is typically provided by the BA, which is then handed off to the vendor with little ongoing collaboration. With such a high risk for miscommunication, it is necessary to elaborate on assumptions (scope, solutions ideas, etc.) and constraints within the business analysis deliverables. There is less transparency from the vendor's team, so during contract negotiations, decisions should be made as to whether there will be interim validations along the way—such as a prototype or other demonstrations to ensure that requirements are being properly interpreted before the final contractual solution delivery. The more that quality and time are constrained, the more the need for interim validations and possibly more visibility into how requirements are traced to solution components by using a shared traceability matrix. The earlier these can be provided, the better the results.

In a turnkey relationship, compared to all other relationships, the BA has the least visibility and control internally. The vendor uses his or her own methodology, so managing expectations regarding handoffs must be addressed early, especially since business analysis terminologies and methods vary in the industry. The more business analysis standards—such as *A Guide to the Business Analysis Body of Knowledge (BABOK® Guide)*[1]—are accepted across industries, the easier the communications will be with vendors. But because vendors can contractually use their own methods, the BA will have to adapt. How to handle issues with the vendor is usually described within the agreement. In my experience, issues are formally documented and sent through the vendor's project manager. If they do not get resolved or require escalation, they go through the enterprise procurement group. As a warning, having been in the position of the vendor providing the turnkey solution and reviewing other turnkey teams, I found that clients tended to put too much trust in the vendor. Be involved in the agreements. To state a cliché—trust but validate!

Integrated Team Relationship

The integrated team relationship is based on a combination of internal and external resources with one common goal, likely to be bound by a defined project. The PM is assigned by the internal organization and has influence over the team. Teams run in a collaborative manner with co-responsibility for phased deliverables. The contractual relationship is often at the organizational level, in which an organization will partner with a vendor to supply a pool of full-time equivalent (FTE) resources in a budgeted year. These resources are on-boarded and often trained in internal methods and terminology—and may even go through a knowledge transfer process. Often this method is used for working with offshore teams. A small team may be assigned in combination with an internal team (30% vendor and 70% internal). In this integrated relationship, the team must sync up their differences in methods, templates, standards, and tools.

In this type of a relationship, the BA must get consensus on the business analysis approach by the integrated team. Having been assigned to many integrated teams, not only as a BA but as a project and program manager, I found that syncing up methods is critical. As we will discuss later, a valuable business analysis deliverable in this integrated team is a project level requirements management plan (RMP) that can help communicate and get buy-in on how requirements and business analysis activities will be conducted (see Appendix A2.4). Because of the importance of collaboration in this structure, the BA has the influence to promote an approach that will work for the team and the project outcomes.

Managed Partnership Relationship

In a managed partnership relationship, the vendor has a relationship at higher levels in the organization and may cover multiple functional areas. The contractual relationship is typically a master agreement (umbrella agreement) that goes through a formal procurement process. This type of agreement is more dynamic and clarifies the accountability of both organizations with shared goals and measures—a balanced two-party agreement. An example application for this type of relationship is the implementation of business process outsourcing (BPO) when a business process is to be outsourced and that business process becomes a vendor-supported operational process at the vendor site. At this managed-level relationship, there is an expectation that business analysis standards already exist at a cross-organizational level documented through an RMP and that the vendor accepted those standards for how they will conduct business analysis for all future changes (see Appendix A2.4).

Business analysis challenges include addressing data integrity, privacy, and intellectual property business rules. All activities, including business analysis activities, need to add more formality to measures and identify how those measures will be monitored for work performance, process performance, and quality of the outcomes (products) for this managed partnership relationship to be successful. These measures can also be stated in agreements that align with the master agreement, such as a service-level agreement.

Enterprise Partnership Relationship

The enterprise partnership relationship is like the managed partnership but with added overarching structure—an alignment to enterprise strategies with a financial investment at the enterprise level to move more non-core capabilities to vendors. The investment includes infrastructure, and other software and hardware tools, that can automate and make the vendor relationship much more effective. One of my technology clients staffed an enterprise global sourcing center whose function was to implement their outsourcing strategies. Their plan was to move from a 30/70% model (externally outsourced/internally sourced), to the reverse over the next few years. At another financial client, BAs needed to participate in the knowledge transfer process by sharing current state models and helping vendor resources to build use cases of the current state functions that the vendor would eventually support.

By having the vendor create the use cases, vendors not only gain business domain knowledge of the current functions, but both client and vendor have documentation that becomes the baseline for future changes. There was also a huge financial investment in software that included configuration tools, virtual collaboration tools, repositories with global access, and special security software. An enterprise relationship such as this requires a huge executive level and financial commitment.

Communicating Requirements to Vendors

Regardless of the type of relationship, there are several other items to address when working with vendors. Textual requirements should be supplemented with use cases or other forms of documentation (models, matrices, etc.) to help clearly define scenarios for acceptance testing—especially when documenting *what-if* scenarios that mostly internal resources, such as super users, can uncover because of their past exposures. Requirement priorities must be clearly communicated because of the internal politics involved to resolve any conflicts. Assumptions around project context and business knowledge must be made visible because context provides better understanding of the meanings behind the requirements that vendors may not have the knowledge to probe or ask about. Requirement reviews need time allocated to provide some history, set the level, explain the process, clearly define entry/exit criteria for the review, and share risks. Last, there should be awareness of how vendor cultures may deal differently with the way risks are communicated to their clients.

The RMP gives the team a common understanding of how the requirements process will work, who is responsible for what, how it will be controlled, what tools will be used, what information should be captured, and which templates should be used. This plan may be created at an enterprise level to establish standards, but exceptions and variances may need to be communicated to the team requiring a project level plan. It is important to tailor the plan and not be too strict about using every section in the template. Again, the focus is on *syncing* up the requirements management process across the team(s) for a successful outcome. There are two key plans in addition to business analysis activities when dealing with an integrated, managed, or enterprise relationship. The RMP is one of those plans, the other is the requirements communication plan (R122CP).

The RCP is necessary for large, complex projects in addition to projects that require heavy communication with external resources. It is structured the same way as a project communication plan but focuses on business analysis components. There are three tables (Tables 2.1, 2.2, and 2.3) that reflect different examples of the RCP. The main content for an RCP includes: (1) what needs to be communicated; (2) who communicates the information; (3) who receives the information; (4) how the information will be conveyed; and (5) how often or when. Other content can elaborate on how the communication will be managed; for example, Table 2.3 has an extra column to identify if there is an expectation of a response within a certain amount of time. Notice, this more elaborated RCP (see Table 2.3) has more detail compared to other industry

Table 2.1 Simple business analysis communication plan

What to Communicate	Source	Receivers	Dependencies	Frequency	Mode
Initial business needs	Domain SME will document within the project charter	PM and BA will review and confirm understanding	NA	At project initiation	E-mail
Requirements for request for proposal (RFP)	Domain SMEs	BA will document during 3 weekly facilitated workshops	Approved project charter from PM	Weekly by domain area	Live meeting
RFP deliverable	BA (consolidation from workshops)	Short list vendors	Short list from RFI, sponsor, and procurement approval	Once with possible addendum for answered questions	Formal procurement process
RFP responses	Short list vendors	Evaluation team	Review of RFP responses	RFP deadline	Facilitated workshop
Contract review updates	Procurement	BA and PM	Vendor selection	Every Monday starting with draft contract to final contract	E-mail
Use case scenarios status	BA	Vendor	Signed contract	Weekly review from signed contract to installation of pilot software	E-mail use case scenarios as being developed
Pilot software status	PM	BA	Installation of pilot software		
Transition requirements and configurations	Implementation SME and vendor	BA will document during facilitated conference calls	Approved solution design from system analyst	One month prior to implementation based on rollout plan	Conference calls

Table 2.2 Mid-level business analysis communication plan

To (stakeholders, including team members and vendors)	From (stakeholders, including team members and vendors)	Information (Both project and product deliverables or other informal communications)	**Restrictions to Communication and Information** (if intellectual property, confidential, need to know, etc. Who can/cannot be copied or forwarded)	Frequency (milestone or date triggered, project checkpoints when frequency may change)	Mode (how it will be communicated, such as conference call, video conf., etc.)	Expected Response
Customer sponsor	Client PM	Milestone status on project timeline and forecast	No restrictions Cc to client PM	Every Monday by 1 p.m. EST	E-mail	None
Client PM	Vendor team lead	Task status on project timeline and forecast	Restrict from other vendors Cc to vendor engagement manager confirmation	Every Friday by 1 p.m. EST	E-mail use standard status form	Receive
Vendor engagement manager	Vendor team lead	Burn rate sheet	Engagement manager only	Every Friday by 1 p.m. EST with teleconference review every other week	Lotus Notes project database with Notify	Receive confirmation
Vendor team lead	Client BA	Business requirement updates	No restrictions	At each milestone	Teleconference	E-mail follow-up

examples (see Tables 2.1 and 2.2), especially when dealing with external resources. Because we need to sync up our methods with vendors and get a common understanding of priorities, this elaborated RCP with additional columns is especially useful. To emphasize, the RCP can be very simple for smaller and less complex projects or may even be an informal work product just for the BA, but it can also be necessary for larger and more complex projects to help manage expectations with stakeholders.

Conducting Benchmarking and Competitor Research

Another strategic mindset that deals with external resources is benchmarking and competitor research. Although benchmarking can be used internally by comparing metrics across organizations within an enterprise, it is most often used to determine how we are doing in comparison

Table 2.3 Complex business analysis communication plan

	SME	SA	TRN	SI	IAS	QAT	PRC	BA	PM	SPR	VR
Business Case and Feasibility Study	CL	CL	CL	CL	CL	CL	CL	MT	MT	X, T	
Project Charter, Initial Plan, Lessons Learned		CL	CL	CL	CL	CL	CL	CL	X, T	PR	
System Requirements Specification and Business Results Validation	MT, T, R CL, W	CL, W	CL, W	CL, W	CL, W	MT, T CL, W	CL, W	X	MT, T CC, D	EM	
Product/Vendor Research List, RFI/RFP	EM	EM	EM	EM	E	EM	X, T	EM	EM	MT, R	MT, R
Signed Contract, Warranty and Support Validation	EM, R			EM, R			X, T	EM			
Usage and Test Scenarios, Test Cases, Acceptance Test Results	MT, T CL, W	CL, W	CL, W	CL, W	CL, W	X	EM	MT, T CL, W	CL, W	EM	CC, W
CRP Results	MT CL, W	CL	CL	X, T	CL	MT CL, W	EM	MT CL, W	CL, W	EM	MT CL, W
Preliminary Design Specifications	TBD	TBD	TBD	TBD	TBD	TBD	TBD	TBD	TBD	TBD	TBD
Prototype Results	TBD	TBD	TBD	TBD	TBD	TBD	TBD	TBD	TBD	TBD	TBD
Installed Product Module List	TBD	TBD	TBD	TBD	TBD	TBD	TBD	TBD	TBD	TBD	TBD
Proof of Concept Plan and Results	TBD	TBD	TBD	TBD	TBD	TBD	TBD	TBD	TBD	TBD	TBD
Transition and Training Plan, Awareness Sessions Schedule	TBD	TBD	TBD	TBD	TBD	TBD	TBD	TBD	TBD	TBD	TBD
Updated and Implemented Procedures	TBD	TBD	TBD	TBD	TBD	TBD	TBD	TBD	TBD	TBD	TBD
Training Materials	TBD	TBD	TBD	TBD	TBD	TBD	TBD	TBD	TBD	TBD	TBD

MT = Face-to-face meeting
CC = Conference call
CL = Collaborative tool
EM = E-mail
PR = Presentation

D = Daily
W = Weekly
T = Toll gates
R = Response required

SPR = Sponsor
BA = Business analyst
SA = System architect
QAT = Quality assurance tester offshore

PM = Project manager
SI = System integrator and builder offshore
IAS = Information architect and security
TRN = Trainer and change champion

X = Responsible for communication
TBD = To be determined

PMO = Project management office
VR = Vendor PM
SME = Subject matter expert/business owner
PRC = Procurement manager

to others in our industry (e.g., banking), within a function across industries (e.g., security of information), in the use of new technology regardless of industry (e.g., cloud solution), or for a core capability (e.g., eLearning delivery for a training company), etc. The information can be obtained from many different sources: government studies, paid research companies, non-profits, professional organizations, etc. Benchmarking provides that baseline to measure against and to assess gaps. This can be shown visually using various tools. Figure 2.1 shows the use of a radar chart that benchmarks information security. By comparing the benchmark to others in this example, you can see the gap in the fraud metrics. This shows there is an opportunity to fill the gap by using an industry best practice software package. Another approach is to show the metrics within a specific process. Table 2.4 shows an external benchmarking measure used in a process form. Benchmarking is a way to always be thinking about what our enterprise can do to continue to improve and move forward.

When conducting competitive research, information must be captured to help with decision making. A good place to start is to understand each competitor's strengths, weaknesses, and differentiator—i.e., the factor that sets them apart. You can classify competitors into three main categories. (1) those that directly impact you, such as selling the exact same product; (2) those that indirectly impact you, such as those selling a product that meets the same needs; and (3) those that are emerging and that you need to watch. To have a strategic mindset you need to be aware of these external influencers.

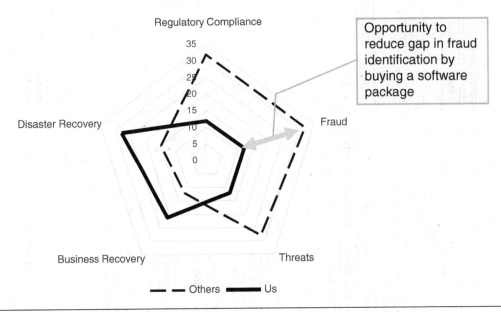

Figure 2.1 Radar chart example for information security capabilities benchmark

Table 2.4   Example process benchmark metrics

Function:	3.1 Post-workshop feedback
Process ID:	3.1.3
Process Title:	Manage class evaluations
Description:	Notifying, pulling, organizing, summarizing, and distributing evaluation summaries from each workshop delivery
Trigger:	Scheduled instructor-led workshop delivered
Metrics:	Percent of online evaluations completed per workshop
Baseline:	45%
Baseline Date:	25 Aug 20XX
Industry Benchmark:	70%
Industry Benchmark Date:	15 Mar 20XX

Addressing Enterprise Risks

By performing benchmarking and competitive analysis, you may also expose risks that must be managed at the enterprise level. The BA has an important role in managing risks that may affect the full breadth (multiple business units) and depth (multiple organizational levels) of the enterprise. Because of the extent of impact, the BA must have the right strategic mindset to recognize and help manage those potential risk events, in addition to understanding the enterprise's tolerance for risk. It is important to know that boundary of tolerance—not only with your individual stakeholders, but within a corporate culture. This is not a one-time activity. Constantly changing internal and external environments, including changing culture, introduce new risk events that need to be addressed.

When exposing enterprise risks, trade-offs must be justified. Managing risks at the strategic level will require more resources and capital in order to be effective. The impact to value (not just financial) needs to be thoroughly investigated. There are five asset categories that can help identify potential future event risks[2] that are associated with what an enterprise would value:

- Physical assets (what we own)
- Customer assets (who we serve and those providing our income)
- Financial assets (what we have saved in money or investments)
- Employee/supplier assets (who we can leverage, resource talents)
- Organizational assets (how we do things, our knowledge, our brand, our intellectual property)

In addition to these assets, the business model and operating model that we will discuss later in this chapter can also be used to identify enterprise risks. Not having a business model or accurate and consistent information about the five asset categories will affect how quickly or effectively we uncover risks. Responses to enterprise risks may include introduction of new policies, changes in processes, new technology, and other actions to protect assets.

Risk management should be an organizational capability, and business analysis can contribute toward improving that capability; but it can also make business analysis more difficult if that capability does not already exist at the enterprise level. If an enterprise is in constant crisis management, it will be much more difficult for the BA to follow a formal approach without a champion or other enterprise support, such as a PMO or other governance entity.

Building Governance Relationships

Governance, as a general definition, is an entity that can be found at many different levels within an enterprise providing consistent processes and policies. The governance entity uses these processes and policies to control and provide direction for the way decisions are made. They can also provide standards for addressing how information is provided to help with decision making. Characteristics of a governance entity include:[3]

- Extraction of information for proper decision making (such as deliverables from projects or project reporting)
- Dissemination of shared information for process guidance, policy guidance, clarity of responsibilities, tolerance levels (risk, time, money, quality, etc.) and standards
- Oversight of the fairness of policy to all stakeholders and timeliness in its communication to stakeholders
- Efficient use of their own resources
- Ethical conduct, providing good examples to stakeholders

BAs need to build relationships with certain governance entities that will impact their approach. Equally important, they need to find opportunities for sharing their knowledge with these entities. There are four main types of governance entities that require BA involvement. At the enterprise level, enterprise architecture governance manages and controls the architectures (business, information, and technology). At the organizational level, project governance groups—called PMOs—are often established to help manage more complex initiatives in *projectized* environments. PMOs may also be at the enterprise level, as referenced earlier. Business unit governance is structured for centralized functions in the enterprise (such as IT). Finally, portfolio governance is established to categorize and rank investments at any level within the organization based on how budgets are established. I have helped establish many governance entities in my career, and they all had a similar goal—striving for consistency to drive successful outcomes for their investments. Keep in mind the *garbage in, garbage out* cliché—for management to make good decisions, they need good information!

Enterprise architecture governance provides the BA who works on more predictive types of projects with architectural standards for creating conceptual models, helps to identify architectural design constraints impacting solution options, and provides views of conceptual models from both business and information architectures. For projects that are more adaptive (see Chapter 3), the momentum and informality can give the adaptive project team a false sense of autonomy, missing needed enterprise viewpoints. Someone on the team, preferably the BA, who has the strategic mindset and breadth of systems knowledge should be asking questions that can help benefit the enterprise. For example:

- How can this new information we are creating contribute to the overall information architecture?
- How can we use existing infrastructure identified in the technology architecture to reduce costs?
- Should we check to see if we already have processes in place that address these user stories in another business unit (business architecture)?

Enterprises need to prioritize ways to best spend their finances, so they will require proposed initiatives to go through a process of justification and approval. Whether this happens at the highest enterprise level or within the business units depends on the allocation of budgets. These portfolios are categorized to help in ranking them. Four main portfolio categories are: (1) research investments, (2) long-term investments, (3) investments to reduce legal risks (i.e., regulatory), and (4) discovery investments (e.g., use of new technology). Discovery investments would require a feasibility study and a formal presentation of the results to management for approval in order to continue to a business case (see Appendix A2.1). Multi-year, long-term investments require a rollout of a large product or service and are considered a program because they hit multiple budgets across time and impact multiple business units. Since they are value based, these long-term investments would require a business case (see Appendix A2.2). Other portfolio categories would require a simpler form—for example, a project charter or product description form—depending on the amount of the investment the approvers are willing to risk. The BA may be assigned the responsibility to create the business case or project charter together with the sponsor or project manager. The business analysis activities in the creation of those deliverables focuses on the solutions scope and the measurement of value (discussed further in Chapter 6). Standards for both are needed to more effectively categorize and rank during the portfolio processes and are usually managed by the PMO.

Interaction with a PMO can make a difference on whether the PMO's goal is accomplished and whether the BA can also be successful on his or her own project(s). Types of BA/PMO interactions that can contribute to project successes include:

- Providing feedback on which project processes (e.g., change control procedures) or policies (e.g., when to obtain approvals) work/don't work depending on specific project characteristics
- Reporting realized benefits and other measures of success to the PMO or steering committees

- Providing plans (work breakdown structures, RMP, RCP) for sharing across projects
- Identifying those business analysis factors that influence estimates
- Contributing business analysis templates (assets)

Table 2.5 shows a PMO's list of business analysis assets used within an enterprise that were contributed by a specialized group of BAs. Note that Table 2.5 reflects a predominantly predictive approach with major phase deliverables consisting of work product components and the use of various tools. It also identifies which assets should be created, dependent upon the size of the project (small, medium, or large). PMOs may tailor their processes and policies based on risk, business impact, and complexity, or other scoring methods to set the appropriate level of control. When reviewing Table 2.5, consider the fact that projects may vary by the criteria being used to prioritize. Although one initiative may be inexpensive and require minimal resources to implement, if not tracked and implemented successfully, it could result in huge penalties to the enterprise. Impact to the business must be considered as part of the criteria. The point is that a large-sized project may be a lower priority with less risk. It depends on how you make the determination of small, medium, or large. If the determination is based only on cost or number of resources needed rather than risk, ability to execute strategic goals, or other defined value, then the table's intent should only be to guide the BA in determining the right approach to take—even though the governance process may make a different determination.

Here are a few characteristics that may influence governance determination and/or the BA's approach:

- Risk tolerance of the organization
- Constraints of the project
- Breadth of impact across the organization
- Project financials (return on investment, total cost of ownership)
- Resource commitment
- Number of stakeholders impacted
- Number of business processes impacted
- Number of interfaces
- Position of decision makers in the organization

Every effort should be made to deliver the outcomes as initially agreed to in business cases and to manage expectations if there are variances. The BA should track and report on benefit realization, create business analysis deliverables based on standards, and abide by approval processes for their deliverables used in decision making. Again, BAs may need to go beyond what the governance entity directs them to do, especially since they also know more about the specifics of the project than anyone else.

Business unit governance is structured for centralized functions in the enterprise and is created to manage large portfolios of projects requiring use of centralized resources in addition to

Table 2.5   Example PMO business analysis asset list

ID	BA Asset	Category (Life-Cycle Phase or PM Process)	Status/Version	Project Size			BA Responsibility			
				S	M	L	A.D.	B.B.	E.S.	E.D.
A0001	Vision or problem statement	0 In all phase deliverables		X	X	X				X
A0002	List of exclusions and assumptions	0 In all phase deliverables		X	X	X				
A0003	Solution constraints	0 In all phase deliverables		X	X	X				
A0004	Business requirements	0 In all phase deliverables		X	X	X			X	
A0005	Stakeholder profile	0 In all phase deliverables			X	X				
A0006	Business case	1 Justification phase deliverable				X				
A0007	Feasibility study	1 Justification work product			X	X				
A0008	Value proposition	1 Justification work product				X				
A0009	Solution statement	1 Justification work product				X				
A0010	SWOT analysis	1 Justification tool		OPTIONAL						
A0011	Benchmarking	1 Justification tool		OPTIONAL						
A0012	Project charter	1 Initiation phase deliverable			X					
A0013	Scope definition statement	1 Initiation work product		X						X
A0014	Context diagram	1 Initiation work product			X	X				X
A0015	Opportunity assessment checklist	1 Initiation tool		X				X		
A0016	Requirements management plan	2 Planning phase deliverable				X			X*	
A0017	Business analysis plan	2 Planning phase deliverable		X	X					X
A0018	Business analysis approach	2 Planning work product			X	X				
A0019	Guiding principles	2 Planning work product				X				
A0020	BA work breakdown structure	2 Planning work product			X	X				
A0021	BA communication plan	2 Planning work product				X				
A0022	Stakeholder involvement plan	2 Planning tool				X	X			
A0023	BA process responsibility chart	2 Planning tool			X	X			X	
A0024	Requirement risk analysis	2 Planning tool				X				
A0025	Gap analysis table	3 Scope tool		X	X	X		X		

providing standards and direction for that business unit's functional capabilities. Using an IT centralized business unit as an example, the BA may need to follow a systems development life-cycle methodology defined by the IT governance organization in addition to following portfolio management policies. Business units are usually defined by functions performed within the enterprise. Business units can also have their own budgets for projects that fall within their functional areas. But for technology projects in enterprises that have a centralized IT organization, the business unit will contribute a certain amount for maintenance of the software and hardware, for the development of new systems, and for systems that cross business units. IT receives these funds and they, in turn, will prioritize the portfolio(s). Portfolios are groups of initiatives that need to be considered, usually based on budget allocation. Once prioritized, a line is drawn to establish funding for the projects. There may be additional negotiation to obtain more funds from the business units. This is just one example in which portfolios can be structured quite differently within an enterprise depending on how business units are organized, how funding and budgeting processes work, and who is making the final investment decisions.

Finally, governance at the lowest level—the business analysis level—is not an official governance entity, but there still is a need for consistency, especially in a non-projectized environment. This level of governance requires the commitment to establish processes and policies for how decisions will be made about requirements and designs without a formal resourced entity. The RMP would be a quick and efficient way to convey the information and gain agreement.

Considering Strategic Outcomes

BAs must consider many other elements to select the appropriate approach and to determine the right set of deliverables (final outcomes for review and approval), work products (interim outcomes of tasks for review), techniques (different ways to address a task), and tools (items that help to improve the efficiencies of the tasks). Because we are focusing on the enterprise and strategic mindset in this chapter, we will also focus on how certain strategic outcomes influence the business analysis approach. There are four major strategic outcomes that a BA must consider when building any product roadmap or business analysis approach: strategy alignment, business model, operational model, and business architecture.

Strategic Alignment

Without linking to strategy, there is no way to know whether a project has successfully accomplished the goals defined in the strategy. Business analysis activities must include activities that align high-level requirements to the strategy. There are multiple ways to see that the vision gets executed. We can check as to whether: (1) business units have similar objectives in their strategy, (2) the portfolio of projects is prioritized based on alignment to this vision, (3) each project's business requirements enable the vision, (4) each elaborated requirement and solution options align to that vision, and (5) measures and metrics are defined and implemented to make that vision operational. As you can see, each major level aligns to the next: strategic level (1 & 2), to tactical level (3 & 4), to operational level (5). As we move from the strategic level to the operational level, the strategic vision becomes less ambiguous. It is necessary to have a good understanding of the outcomes from that first strategic level to properly align to it.

Business Model

One strategic outcome is the business model that tells us how the business works today. When performing strategy analysis, BAs perform gap analysis—looking at current state versus future state. This can be performed by using business models. One such visual model is the business model canvas. According to Alexander Osterwalder and Yves Pigneur, "A business model describes the rationale of how an organization creates, delivers, and captures value"—and the business model canvas is "a shared language for describing, visualizing, assessing, and changing business models." They believe that you can visibly describe the business model using nine basic blocks that cover four key areas: customers, offer, infrastructure, and financial viability. The nine building blocks are: key activities, key partners, key resources, cost structure, customer relationships, customer segments, value propositions, channels, and revenue stream.[4] An example application of the business model canvas, using a training company, is shown in Figure 2.2. A set of questions adapted for Figure 2.2 is included in Appendix A2.3 based on the nine building blocks. That model is the current state. In my experience, a good use of this model is for an initial impact assessment of any new initiative or vision statement. For example, Figure 2.2 presents a training company that exclusively conducts instructor-led training. This current-state model was done in facilitated sessions with business management. Do we all have the same understanding of the business? Many times, I have interviewed management and found they have very different views or silo views of the business. How does that impact the information we try to gather and the affect it has on decision making?

The training company strategy for the next two years was to convert 50% of their business to eLearning. Reviewing the current state, what would be impacted? How might the business model change? Would the customer segment change? Would the value propositions be different? The business model canvas is an excellent tool to start at the highest level for gap analysis and to help guide these discussions with management.

How the canvas is used can vary by industry. A public sector organization may apply it differently than a small entrepreneurial company or even a university. The canvas can also vary in scope and level. I have seen it used at a business unit level. Instead of the training company in the scenario, think of the same model used for the training division of a larger company. The canvas can be applied to reflect current state and future state—and then multiple future states! As a consultant, it was an extremely valuable tool for me to gain a better understanding of my client's business. Although the business model may capture many components of the business, another view of the business is how it operates based on the integration and standardization of its processes.

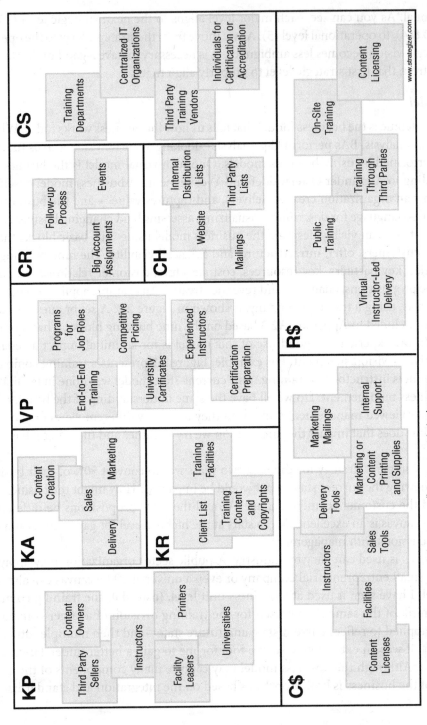

Business Model Canvas under creative common license, www.strategizer.com

Figure 2.2 Business model canvas example: training company

Operational Model

By understanding the operational model of an enterprise, the BA can better understand which solutions are the best fit and can determine the right set of competencies needed to match the environment. An operational model has four quadrants that apply to an enterprise's business processes: diversification, replication, coordination, and unification.[5] If an enterprise is more diversified today—meaning that they have independent business units with unique products and customers having a limited need to communicate among each other—then solutions are likely to be unique. In this environment, the likelihood increases that service organizations (such as IT) will be decentralized and aligned with the business units. Funding approvals may still occur at the business-unit level for all projects.

I observed an example of a diversified operating model when working with a manufacturing company operating as separate plants in the Midwest. The company started acquiring many different plants supplying parts to the automotive industry. This rapid growth triggered some issues with IT. Each plant had their own enterprise resource planning (ERP) system supported by multiple vendors. They realized how the cost of supporting these different vendor solutions would impact them greatly in the future, not only for the maintenance but for having the ability to react quickly with new products for the constantly competitive automotive industry. The diversification operating model worked fine when they were localized with different clients but it no longer served their needs.

Now, with the acquisitions, they had to transition to a replication operating model, where many of the acquired plants needed to operate similarly with centralized support of the systems, yet allowing for the fact that management would still need to remain autonomous. Solutions required more standardization of processes, thereby more process modeling techniques used by BAs. This also required heavier facilitation and leadership skills to gain consensus on those processes across many more stakeholders. In the diversified model, the manufacturing company did not have a need for BAs. A few IT resources at each plant did everything. But the need for consistent processes required new skills. Coming in as a coach, I was brought in to help get a newly assigned group of BAs up to speed and to prepare them for this new environment.

If the operating model requires a high level of business integration, while still allowing for independent processes (opposite of the replication operating model), then it is considered a coordination operating model. An example of this coordination operating model can be found in many banks. Each business unit may share customers. For example, I have a business account, an individual account, and an investment account at the same bank. The processes for managing each account may be different and not standardized across the business units, yet those processes would need to share my information. One Midwest bank client of mine got along fine within the coordination operating model for some time. Business integration was high. Financial transactions needed to be shared. Standard interfaces—such as EDI (Electronic Data Interchange—a computer-to-computer document exchange system), ACH (Automated Clearing House—a bank-to-bank payment system), and many others—were the focus of BAs at the enterprise level. All other process work was more at the tactical, individual business-unit level. Competencies were focused on business rules analysis, data requirements, and transition requirements, especially when mergers with other banks started to happen. My exposure to this client took place over 20 years. As a contractor, I was brought in to evaluate vendor packages to improve workflow processes. As a trainer, I was brought in to train their PMs and BAs. As an advisor, I was brought in to assess their outsourcing strategies.

Over time, this Midwest bank transitioned from a coordination operating model to a unification operating model. Within the unification quadrant, not only is business integration high, but in this case the bank also invested heavily in business process standardization to ease the transition to an outsourcing model—for both maintenance and development of systems. Being within the unification quadrant requires centralized management, assigned process owners, and centralized data. There is not only a greater need for more advanced business analysis capabilities as an organization (especially if services are being outsourced) but there is also a greater need to have architectures in place.

As shown in the previous examples, models can help the BA by knowing how an enterprise operates today versus how they plan to operate in the future, whether or not this is explicitly stated in a strategy. Note that operating models may be more of a cultural observation rather than a formal assessment in many enterprises. The operating models prepare the BA with the appropriate mindset when determining the right approach and best solution fit. The more the operating model moves towards unification (a higher need for business integration) and business process consistency, the more the enterprise needs a business architecture to get to that strategic outcome.

Business Architecture

The business architecture is part of the overall enterprise architecture that provides a holistic view of various organizational components and the relationship between them. It shows the way these components are integrated and standardized for the enterprise. These components are often grouped into three architectures within the enterprise architecture (architecture frameworks vary in structure). The one we will focus on is the business architecture, looking at the enterprise at a conceptual level. The business architecture adds visibility to the functions, capabilities, and the organizations of the enterprise for better decision making that is influenced by the business model and strategies of the enterprise. The second architecture from within the enterprise architecture is focused on the data and the rules around that data—information architecture. The third and final architecture is focused on the applications, services, and infrastructure—technical architecture. For a BA, the focus would be on the business architecture (see Figure 2.3).

Figure 2.3 provides a broad look at business architecture. Starting at the left of the figure are the various assets and tools that can be used to show the knowledge of the business. Most organizations have some assets that can be leveraged with knowledge captured conceptually in diagrams or matrices, such as hierarchy diagrams (organization charts), process maps (value streams), models (data models—information is often included in the business architecture), etc. These can

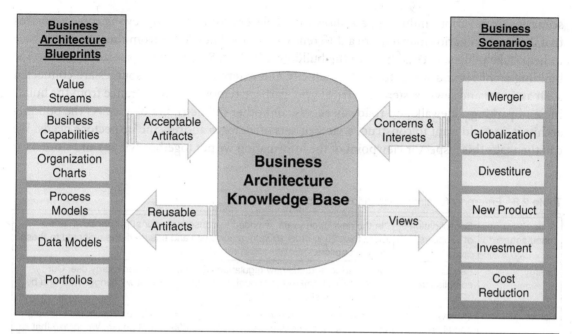

Figure 2.3 Business architecture

all be used to communicate the knowledge of the business. Think of the various blueprints used to capture the knowledge of a building. But what if it is an old building with no blueprints? As the architect making changes to that building, the architect would have to: (1) interview the owners or others with knowledge of the structure, (2) walk around to evaluate the existing structure, (3) use tools to look *under the covers*, and (4) create blueprints of the existing building before making any major changes to it. How detailed will the blueprint need to be? What determines the scope of blueprints the architect creates? How much information is out there, but not in a usable format? This challenge exists with the creation of business architectures today. Where does the knowledge exist today, and what shape is it in? Is it usable?

In the center of the diagram is the knowledge base where the data coming in becomes relevant information for stakeholders. It goes through a process like the creation of a data warehouse. The data may need to be cleaned up and relationships will need to be built between the different components that exist within the blueprints. For example, you may want to know which business capabilities relate to a process that is documented within a value stream blueprint. The relationship between these three components (business capabilities, process, and value stream) can be shown in a matrix or diagram.

A good understanding of the business is needed when building and applying a business architecture. On the right side of Figure 2.3 are scenarios—the concerns and needs from stakeholders requiring enough information to help in resolution and decision making. Example enterprise scenarios from various industries are shown in Table 2.6. Note when reviewing these scenarios that different scenarios may require a different view of the knowledge from the knowledge base to help stakeholders. Let's go back to the building architect. Say the city inspector comes to the building architect and wants to see how all city and external supplier resources are connected such as: water and sewer system, electrical grid, garbage removal, exits/entrance from the building and parking, sidewalk and roadway access, and other public rights-of-way. As the building architect, I would want to construct a view or sets of views to address the inspector's needs. We can then take this inspector viewpoint of the information we put together (views) and store it for

Table 2.6   Enterprise business scenarios example

Auto manufacturer	Consolidation of suppliers	"In the next three years, we need to consolidate our suppliers down to no more than 50 in order to reduce our costs and ensure risk is reflected to these larger suppliers."
Energy	Regulatory compliance	"We need to address new regulations and incentives for energy use. Our systems must be flexible enough to adapt to these new changes now and be ready for new changes in the future."
Bank	Improve operational efficiencies	"We are going through several acquisitions and need to consolidate our data centers. Our data centers occupy over 50,000 feet of space. We realize that our network architecture will be very diverse in the types of software platforms that we will be using."
Government	Improve data and process efficiencies	"Our county needs a solution that will break down the boundaries that currently exist between information and applications by providing us with much greater ability to efficiently manage the enormous amount of data currently maintained sometimes two, three, four, or more times over within the individual units of the county. We need consistency in delivering information to our citizens and employees in addition to providing them with one entry point for getting that information." http://www.oakgov.com/it/egov/Documents/portal_strategy_final1.pdf
Insurance	Improve market position	"Long-term customer relationships with those customers who have the potential to purchase more products and services are critical to our future success. We need full accessible portfolio information about our customers. Today we have to go to several systems to get that information."
	Improve operational efficiencies	"We need to replace our current financial systems to maximize our operational efficiencies, accommodate business change capability, and enable merged and detailed profitability reporting by segment and to facilitate our executive management reporting. Our vision is to also include data warehouse and decision support capabilities. To emphasize the risks and impacts, there are 70+ feeding systems that just feed information into the GL system. The current technical environment is a mainframe VSAM-based system that is over 30 years old. The server portion of the infrastructure is HP UX and using SYBASE for the DBMS. We would like to send out an RFP to narrow the selection of a package."
Hospital	Regulatory compliance	"There is a law in congress that is expected to pass in the next few months. Once it is passed, we only have 6 months to be in compliance. We need to figure out the impact to our processes."

Continued

Healthcare	New product	"It is important to provide a way to present information on multiple devices used by physicians—PDAs, laptops, iPads, etc. We currently have several projects in progress to move us to electronic medical records."
Legal firm	Improve market position	"We handle very large clients under contract. Many of these clients are large technology firms. We need to retain these clients and show future clients that we can leverage technology in the courtroom and throughout our firm."
Manufacturing	Improve process efficiencies	"We need to stay on top of our product defects. Our strategy for the next year is to reduce product defects by 15 percent—before our Christmas rush comes around again."
	Outsourcing a business unit	"We plan to extend our product into the international market and would also open manufacturing plants in those locations."
Marketing firm	Improve market position	"Our clients expect us to know the current market and trends for their products. That is what they pay us for. We need to improve our capability of getting the intelligence we need from data that we purchase from over 100 sources. Today, we are using about 20 different tools in different organizations to do this and it is difficult to consolidate that information by product line at the time we need it for our client presentations."
Medical records service provider	New product	"There is a law in congress that is expected to pass in the next few months. We must help our customers become compliant by introducing a new medical records product."
Nonprofit	Improve brand visibility	"We want to use new social media to reach our donors."
Pharmaceutical	Globalization	"Our long-term need is to go global with our ERP system and outsource maintenance for non-critical functionality while ensuring we comply with all regulations. Today, we are using our expert resources for maintaining these non-critical functions and would like to move them to areas that will lead us into the future."
Professional services	Globalization	"We plan to leverage resources in India to reduce the cost of the application we develop for our clients. We would also like to be more *agile* in our development process in the future."
		"Our past is haunting us. We are trying to be all things to all people. We need a competitive advantage that we can sustain over the longer term based on our strengths and still stay within regulatory constraints. Our strategic vision is to identify those capabilities and find the technology that can support us in knowing our consultant capabilities to match the right person to the right job and managing our intellectual assets for proposals and engagements while we assure that we sustain a high level of consistency and control."
Retail	Regulatory compliance	"At this time our cosmetic sales are 70% storefront and 30% online. We would like to reverse that in the next three years and reduce our costs per unit by 20%."
		"We want to be ahead of any laws and show our clients that we can improve the point-of-sale experience for the handicapped and elderly."
Telecom	New product	"Apply mobility applications to small businesses in high-growth areas."
Technology	Do the *right* thing	"We wish to provide our customers with printing alternatives that will facilitate the *green* culture."
Transportation & logistics	Outsourcing a business unit	"We need to move toward outsourcing our applications maintenance and operations to lower costs, but most important, to release resources to address new services and markets."

reuse later or for audit purposes. The views would always be linked to the overall context that it was pulled from.

If we look at the training company business scenario—"We want to create supplemental eLearning modules for our courses that can be used to enhance our customer's learning outside the workshop"—we can look at the current-state relationships in the business architecture knowledge base to assess the impacts. An example would be to look at the value stream for *Post Workshop Learning* and examine one of the processes *Schedule Instructor-led Webinar*. Can we look at our *Delivery* capabilities associated with that process to see if we need to improve this capability for eLearning? We will always have the delivery core business capability as a training company that will be stable, but we will likely need to improve our capabilities to be able to improve our processes. Often, as a BA, we focus on processes, but processes are performed by an entity, individual, or technology. Are we as an organization capable of performing those processes? We can look in more depth at business analysis as an organizational capability in Chapter 7.

The business architecture is important to the enterprise because it helps to build confidence that we are doing the right things and investing in the right things. It allows transparency into the enterprise, which supports business analysis activities such as impact assessments, identifying transition requirements, identifying capability gaps, putting a business case together, reusing current state assets, and identifying process improvement opportunities. But to leverage the business architectures, BAs must also contribute. For organizations with an enterprise architecture group, that contribution might be done through a formal process integrated into project reviews.

By having the information at hand, impacts can be assessed faster using the business architecture. A business architecture assisted me in quickly assessing an automotive leasing system that was to be implemented globally. The automotive company implementing this system wanted to assess the impact that the package implementation would have on all of its global entities. The business architecture process assets were already documented in a globally accessible tool, which made it relatively easy to assess impacts on each entity and prepare facilitators (BAs) to run requirement workshops for the package customization needs. Having this ability not only saved team effort but also improved credibility with stakeholders.

To learn more about business architecture, there are bodies of knowledge like the *BABOK® Guide*. The Business Architecture Guild®[6] is one source that provides best practices in this area through their *Business Architecture Body of Knowledge® (BIZBOK® Guide)*. Those who don't want as much depth can take advantage of their Quick Guide.[7] In any case, the more advanced BA should have, at minimum, awareness of this basic discipline.

In an organization where a business architecture already resides within an enterprise architecture group, there is a high probability that a business architect role is also part of that group. The business architect role, being established formally at the enterprise level, is a great opportunity for BAs. For organizations in which an architecture group does not exist, BAs may find themselves taking on the role of the business architect.

STRATEGIC ROLES FOR THE BA

Business Architect

Often at the enterprise strategic level, a BA may be put into other roles requiring a strategic mind-set. One of those roles is that of the business architect. As a business architect, you are the owner of the business architecture knowledge base. Not necessarily the assets that populate the knowledge base, but the processes to populate it and to access the information—more like the process owner. The information that populates the knowledge base may be owned by the domain area subject matter experts. Business architects will find ways to connect the pieces (build the relationships) in order to give the views needed that will address the stakeholder's concerns. In Chapter 7, you can find more information on business architect competencies. But one competency relating to the strategic mindset that we are advocating here is the need for architectural thinking. I think of architectural thinking as system thinking on steroids! How much architectural thinking do you need to build a shed for storage in your backyard versus a house versus a multi-story commercial building versus a campus of interconnected buildings versus a large city? That scaling up requires the ability to classify and manage the complexity of more interacting components. A common analogy is the comparison of a classic architect who is more focused on single buildings to an urban planner who is more concerned about the entire city (enterprise), including the happiness of the city's residents and politicians (stakeholders). Urban planners must interact and negotiate with a diverse group of vendors and establish standards for consistency across the city that align with government policy, while still considering the future needs of city residents.

This is not just a matter of more planning or methods. There is also more need to bring to-gether specialists so that they can help to connect the pieces. It is about creating the standards to make it easier to connect the pieces.

Change Agent

Another strategic role for the BA is that of a change agent or change champion. This role could be performed in an informal way, while performing business analysis activities (more tactical) at the project level, which we will address later. But if the initiative has a large business impact, as enterprise-wide initiatives often do, then a resource needs to be committed to the change role. When assigned such a role it is important to: (1) assess the change impact to the organization, (2) gauge the willingness of stakeholders to accept the change, (3) take actions to help stakeholders' transition to the new ways, and (4) assess the organization's overall readiness for the change. As BAs, we try to avoid activities that address the emotional aspects of change—the psychology of it. When in a change agent role, the emotional aspects of change need to be front and center. Recurring communications with positive messaging will help people who are emotionally impacted by change to adapt quickly. This can be done by addressing current-state and future-state gaps or changes needed in behaviors, skills, job competencies, organizational structure, policies, and procedures. Will people need:

- Recurring positive messaging?
- To hear from team members who are passionate about the change?
- To adjust to new procedures?
- Training in a safe environment (where trial and errors are okay)?
- To prepare for movement to different positions?

Our activities must help the users adopt the various solutions as quickly as possible.

At the strategic level, frame-bending change may occur.[8] I was first introduced to frame-bending change when working at the phone company during deregulation. Changes were implemented that had a very large impact across the breadth of the enterprise. These types of changes are used where a *big-bang* approach is necessary. It can result in a radical change to the whole enterprise. In this case, the speed in which the change had to occur was faster than people could prepare for. Because of this, the risk of instability and casualties were high. The thinking was, if culture needed to change, this approach was most effective. Bill Weiss, chairman and CEO of Ameritech in the 1990s, said at the time: "The best way I know to get people to accept the need for change is to not give them a choice. The organization has to know that there's a leader at the top who has made up his mind, that he is surrounded by leaders who have made up their minds, and that they're going to drive forward no matter what. You can't keep people from feeling scared."[9] Weiss faced opposition within the organization because Ameritech was doing well. Why change? Weiss knew the future would introduce many new competitors. There are a few frame-bending principles that come into play that we will detail in the following paragraphs, including: The Energy Principle, The Magic Leader Principle, and The Centrality Principle (Nadler 1989).

> *"Energy must be created to get change initiated and executed" (Nadler 1989).*

The Energy Principle is based on events that present a sense of danger triggering energy within the organization. AT&T deregulation triggered a huge number of events with leaders communicating the sense of urgency (and the introduction of pains) that put every single employee in motion for many years to come. The sense of urgency was generated, but often there were negative reactions to that energy, such as denial of change, which was counterproductive.

> *"Our culture had no instinct for competition . . . Finally, I decided to drop a bomb. I had to intervene on a massive basis. We had to get new, aggressive, gung-ho leaders who were willing to take fairly major risks to reshape this company" (Weiss 1993).*

The Magic Leader Principle requires leaders that embrace the vision, demonstrate the needed behaviors, and enable those struggling to change. As Weiss noted in the previous paragraph, these leaders needed to be willing to take risks. Similarly, in the change agent role, the BA must also embrace these characteristics in addition to those described in Chapter 1.

The Centrality Principle requires strategic alignment, as discussed earlier in this chapter. When working at PricewaterhouseCoopers, I was part of a quality and risk management team that required me to review projects at various life-cycle stages. I often found that the most successful teams (whether ours, the client's, or integrated) were those that could establish a very clear and transparent connection (well documented and communicated) with strategic goals and overall strategies. Generic themes that are branded or established as mission statements, such as Ford's *Quality is #1*, can help to position multiple teams across the enterprise. But, as a general rule, these themes should be consistent and limited. It is the BA's responsibility to communicate and apply these principles, especially when in a change agent role.

There was a big transformation going on at the phone company, and I was in the midst of it. My role was a combination of a PM, business process facilitator, and change agent. When acting as the change agent, I had to advocate for the new solutions that were put in place in order to prepare people for the newly delivered solutions. I did this by delivering a formal change management communication plan. Table 2.7 provides an example of a change management communication plan. It is a combination of elements from stakeholder analysis and the business analysis

Table 2.7 Change management communication plan

Change: New time-tracking system for IT to track time against system development life-cycle activities					
Stakeholder (group— such as IT managers)	**Acceptance** (enthusiast, follower, supporter, opponent)	**Influence** (high, medium, low)	**Impact** (high, medium, low)	**Message** (what must be communicated and when based on acceptance)	**Method** (how would you communicate it?)
IT Leadership	Supporter	High	Medium	Summary of benefits and impact to enterprise, weekly adoption updates	Monthly leadership meeting, formal status reports, project portal
IT Managers	Enthusiastic	High	High	Benefits, impact, and adaption updates weekly	Schedule with time during manager meetings
IT PMs	Enthusiastic	High	Medium	Explain process, benefits, and impact	Initial conference call; leverage PMO scheduled communications to PMs. Weekly status updates through project portal.
IT Leads	Supporter	Medium	Medium	Set expectations as coaches for learning process; mistakes okay during learning	Subject matter expert knowledge transfer
IT Developers	Opponent	Low	High	Process, benefits to organization, explain changes to development process, bring in team leads to process, manage the impact to their time on the job, demonstrate business value of developers' work (less likely to outsource). Ease of using the process	Direct meetings; simple demonstrations. IT lead coaches via own team schedule. Messages through project portals from change management team.
IT Quality Assurance	Resistant	Medium	Medium	Process, benefits to organization, changes to QA process, bring in team leads for QA process redesign	Direct meetings with walkthrough of flow and impacts.

communication plan but with the main objective of tailoring messages to speed up acceptance for easier transition.

You can also be a change agent informally within the realm of business analysis. Many organizations struggle with accepting business analysis as a necessary discipline. As BAs, we need to be a change agent for business analysis, especially when business analysis is new to the organization. Having your own informal change communication plan can help you structure how you might promote the discipline for quicker acceptance.

Whether you accept the different strategic roles informally as part of your business analysis function or are formally assigned to the role, be prepared for the challenges inherent in the role and have that enterprise mindset.

SUMMARY

- Ask probing questions about an enterprise's cultural environment to devise the best-fit approach and solution
- BAs must gain courage and confidence to collaborate with high-level stakeholders in an organization to do their work successfully
- There are five general vendor relationship categories that influence how a BA will communicate requirements to vendors: (1) staff augmentation relationship, (2) turnkey relationship, (3) integrated team relationship, (4) managed partnership relationship, and (5) enterprise partnership relationship
- Benchmarking and competitive analysis are ways to always be thinking about what our enterprise can do to continue to improve, move forward, and expose risks that may need to be managed
- There may be a need to go beyond what a governance entity directs BAs to do via process or policy—especially since BAs know more about the specifics of the project
- At least four major strategic outcomes must be considered when building a product roadmap, precursors to a project-level business analysis approach: (1) strategy alignment, (2) business model, (3) operational model, and (4) business architecture
- The business architecture allows transparency, helps build confidence that we are investing in the right things, and supports business analysis activities
- There are two key roles a BA may be assigned at the strategic level—business architect and change agent—both of which require additional competencies in those domain areas

QUESTIONS

1. What key elements would be in your requirements management plan (Appendix A2.4) for the following scenario?

   You are the lead BA for a large program that has three BAs reporting to you, all co-located with their stakeholders in Milwaukee. The solution designer role is assigned to an offshore liaison systems analyst. The solution designer is stationed in Milwaukee with your team. The builders of the software are in India, while the testers are in China. The solution designer, builders, and testers all work for the same new contracted vendor. This is the first major project your company has conducted with this vendor. Assume an integrated team relationship.

   RMP Elements: _____

   _____

   _____

   _____

2. a. Table 2.1 shows a simple communication plan. After reviewing the plan, what type of relationship do you think the BA has with the vendor? Please justify your answer.

   Vendor relationship options are: staff augmentation, turnkey, integrated team, managed partnership, and enterprise partnership.

   _____

   _____

   b. How might Table 2.1 look different if the relationship was different? Give an example.

   _____

   _____

   _____

   _____

3. Provide one potential risk for each asset category:

   Physical assets: _____

   Financial assets: _____

Customer assets: _____

Employee assets: _____

Organizational assets: _____

4. Table 2.6 shows various business scenarios. Select one scenario example from the table and consider what knowledge (diagrams or matrices such as organization charts, process maps such as value streams, and models such as data models) might be needed from the business architecture that would help stakeholders in decision making.

_____

_____

_____

5. Choose the best answer below:

For a staff augmentation relationship, BAs should first present challenges they face with that resource to the:

a. Sponsor or whoever is paying for the resource
b. Resource's vendor management
c. Procurement or whoever is managing the contract
d. PM or whoever is managing their work

6. Using Figure 2.2, *Business Model Canvas Example: Training Company*, and the five asset categories (physical, financial, customer, employee, organizational assets), name two enterprise risks and their impacts on this business scenario: "Currently we offer business analysis and project management training, but within two years we plan to expand our training to deliver technology organization content, such as training for software development tools (purchased or licensed)."

Enterprise risk #1: _____

Impacts: _____

_____

_____

Enterprise risk #2: _____

Impacts: _____

_____

_____

NOTES

1. International Institute of Business Analysis. (2015). *A Guide to the Business Analysis Body of Knowledge (BABOK® Guide) v3* . Toronto, Ontario, Canada: IIBA.

2. Boulton, Richard, Barry Libert, and Steve Samek. (2000). *Cracking the Value Code: See What Matters, Invest in What Matters and Manage What Matters in the New Economy*. New York, NY: HarperCollins.

3. Kelly, Eamonn V. (2010). "Governance Rules! The principles of effective project governance." Global Congress 2010. Washington, D.C. Project Management Institute.

4. Osterwalder, Alexander and Yves Pigneur. (2010). "Business Model Generation." Strategyzer Series. Hoboken, NJ: John Wiley & Sons.

5. Ross, Jeanne W., Peter Weill, and David C. Robertson. (2006). *Enterprise Architecture as a Strategy*. Harvard Business Review.

6. www.businessarchitectureguild.org.

7. Business Architecture Guild. (2017). *The Business Architecture Quick Guide*. Tampa, FL: Meghan-Kiffer Press.

8. Nadler, David A. and Michael L. Tushman. (1989). "Organizational Frame Bending: Principles for Managing Reorientation." The Academy of Management Executive. Vol. III, (3), 194–204.

9. Davis, Joyce E. [Reporter from Stratford Sherman]. (December 13, 1993). "THE NEW ERA A MASTER CLASS IN RADICAL CHANGE—Only a few CEOs have attempted corporate revolution. Meet the masters—Jack Welch, Larry Bossidy, Bill Weiss, and Mike Walsh—and learn from their secrets." Stratford Sherman.

NOTES

1. International Institute of Business Analysis (2017). *A Guide to the Business Analysis Body of Knowledge* (*BABOK®*). Chapter 3. Toronto, Ontario, Canada: IIBA.

2. Boulton, Richard, Barry Libert, and Steve Samek. (2000). *Cracking the Value Code: How Successful Businesses are Creating Wealth with New Value Ratios in the New Economy*. New York: HarperCollins.

3. Kelly, Gavin et al. (2010). "Governance Rules! The principle of 'good' policy." *Emerging Global Congress 2010*, Washington DC. Project Management Institute.

4. Osterwalder, Alexander, and Yves Pigneur (2010). *Business Model Generation*. Hoboken, New Jersey: John Wiley & Sons.

5. Kaplan, Robert W., Peter Weill, and David P. Robertson (2001). *Enterprise Architecture as Strategy*. Harvard Business Review Press.
   www.businessarchitectureguild.org

6. Business Architecture Guild (2017). *The Business Architecture Quick Guide*. Tampa, FL: Meghan-Kiffer Press.

7. Nadler, David A. and Michael L. Tushman (1989). "Organizational Frame Bending: Principles for Managing Reorientation." *The Academy of Management Executive*, 3 (3): 194–204.

8. Davis, Joyce (Reprint from *Information Week* (December 21, 1998). "THE PAY-BIG ATTRACTION OF CHARISMA IN THE TAP-CALCULUS OF MCI." "Only a few CEOs have attained the cachet of MCI's two masters — such as Jack Welch, Bill Gates and Michael Wilson — and their nonlinear success," Stratton Sherman.

3

STEP TWO—ADAPT TO THE
LIFE-CYCLE APPROACH

"Although the chef and the cook both start with an initial recipe, the chef's expertise allows for the creation of a full menu by making necessary changes and adaptions based on elements such as customer feedback and tolerance for changes to the menu, customer cost constraints, the need for innovation, available equipment, etc."—Chapter One

If you, as someone performing those all-important business analysis activities, can adapt quickly to the various life-cycle approaches and provide advice about the right-fit approach, you have progressed to having the capability of business analysis versatility. Even if leadership for the business analyst (BA) is not in a position of authority at the tactical level, the BA is viewed as an important advisor to the project manager (PM) and sponsor by having a trusting relationship with them and all other stakeholders for the project. But, first and foremost, the BA must have a good understanding of life cycles.

LIFE-CYCLE APPROACHES AND STAGES

Life cycles include stages to deliver a new solution or a change to an existing product or service. Stages include needed activities to accomplish a new solution or change goals. In some more formal life cycles, *go* or *no-go* gate decisions are included at the end of each stage that requires a deliverable review and approval. Full life cycles can start with an idea-inception stage and end once the solution has been implemented, becomes operational, and the implemented solution's value has been assessed. As a BA, you may or may not be involved in a full life cycle depending on your organizational role. An example of a very early model of a life cycle for software development was first recognized in a paper written by William W. Royce in 1970,[1] that describes a framework of phases for software development. Although Royce never mentioned *waterfall*, it has become known as the waterfall model or approach. His paper defined a simple structure of seven phases: system requirements, software requirements, analysis, program design, coding, testing, and operations. These phases have evolved over the years to be named and structured in many alternative ways. The fundamental use of phases exists in all life cycles; the variation comes with how they are applied in each unique approach.

Solution Life Cycle

For simplicity, we will refer to solution life cycle (SLC) as a generic term for a simple framework of a life cycle that satisfies business needs. Figure 3.1 shows this SLC framework from cradle to grave, meaning from concept definition to retirement within a life cycle, expanding the original Royce model. We will also refer to the Royce phases as stages, since the term *phases* can also relate to how a solution is rolled out in an evolutionary manner (such as rolling out phase I of a product, then phase II, etc.).

Generic Stages

Generic stages for the SLC are:

- **Concept definition (a.k.a. strategy analysis)**—This occurs when an idea triggers some analysis work to justify moving forward. Do we want to spend the resources on this idea? An initial sizing, costing, and benefit analysis is conducted in addition to strategy alignment. Requirements from the business perspective (e.g., vision statements, business benefits, etc.) are uncovered in addition to high-level stakeholder requirements (e.g., value propositions to specific groups of stakeholders).
- **Requirement analysis**—The BA conducts activities in this stage to uncover additional or lower-level stakeholder requirements (e.g., those interacting with the solution, those receiving outputs, etc.) and solution requirements (e.g., design constraints, data requirements, functional requirements, quality attributes, etc.). Requirements are elicited, verified, prioritized, and approved.
- **Conceptual and physical design**—These are identified as two types of design to help clarify where the BA fits into this stage. Conceptual design involves the modeling of requirements (a.k.a. specifying requirements), independent of how the requirements will be physically implemented (e.g., technology platform). Physical design specifies the *how* and is typically not performed by the BA, although the BA may be required to allocate and trace the requirements to the physical components.
- **Acquire and/or build solution**—Based on the requirements and the design, the best fit must be determined as to whether a commercial off-the-shelf (COTS) package will be selected, whether it will be built in-house, whether it will be outsourced—or a combination of the three. If acquired, the BA will likely be participating in the evaluation of the COTS

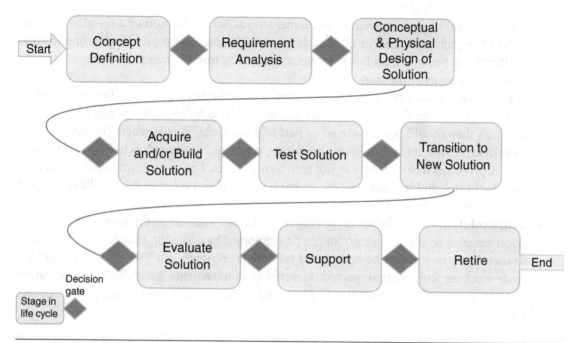

Figure 3.1 Generic SLC stages

package(s) mapping requirements to the features of the product being evaluated. If built in-house or outsourced, the BA must validate that the requirements are being interpreted correctly and traced to each component that is built and tested.

- **Test solution**—There are various tests conducted to ensure that the requirements have been fulfilled. Various types of requirements translate into different types of tests. BAs are required to manage the validation of requirements through traceability or by facilitating the validation with quality assurance resources.

- **Transition to a new solution**—Once the new solution has been identified, the BA must identify any temporary requirements, known as transition requirements, that will help in moving from the old solution to the new solution. The common transitional activities may include: running in parallel, converting or consolidating data, eliminating certain features or functions, addressing partial work, weekly/monthly events, coordination with other systems, addressing gaps in skill levels, and organizational changes. Each of these may have associated requirements contributing to a smooth solution transition.

- **Evaluate solution**—So it is implemented—aren't we done? No, not yet. Remember in concept definition, we justified the idea. Yes, we met all stakeholder requirements and solution requirements. But what about the business requirements? The vision, the benefits, and any established measures would be assessed, especially those contributing to value. This evaluation will likely happen after implementation. But, evaluation of a solution can also occur after prototypes and/or after each release. The evaluation provides an opportunity for the BA to become an advisor by helping identify improvements and prepare for the continued support of the solution.

- **Support solution**—This stage and the *retire* stage are often not seen in business analysis approaches because these BA activities are not likely to be included in any project plan, although they should be considered as part of a life cycle. This is where the BA becomes more of an advisor and consultant, supporting solutions by using tools to help identify and resolve problems that may or may not turn into projects. This stage is important to continually build stakeholder relationships, using leadership and collaboration skills to support stakeholders.
- **Retire solution**—In addition to moving from the old solution to the new solution (transition stage), a solution: may no longer be supported by a vendor, may have lost its value or usefulness, or it might be considered redundant. Business analysis activities might include working with users impacted, identifying requirements for archiving information and requirements for impacted interfaces, and communicating with enterprise architecture groups.

To emphasize, the SLC stages in Figure 3.1 exist regardless of the life-cycle approaches we cover in this chapter.

Approach Consistency

Many organizations have tried to commit to one consistent approach for all of their projects. Yes, consistent processes help in predictability, provide stability to measure consistently, improve estimate accuracy, etc. We have seen this work in many large organizations and with large clients. However, this approach assumes *consistency* in the characteristics of projects. But, wait—the definition of projects is that they are unique! So, the BA will need to use their skills and expertise to evaluate whether the recommended approach can be used when engaged in a new project. Although a consistent approach can be beneficial in most instances, there are exceptions, and if the approach is not adjusted to address these within a project, there is an increased likelihood that the project will fail. Although one consistent approach across all projects regardless of size or complexity can be attempted, it is very difficult to achieve success. As we saw in an earlier example (Table 2.5), there was an attempt to provide at least three variations based on small, medium, and large projects. Consider that the more variance in the characteristics of initiatives and projects within the enterprise, the more the need to vary approaches.

At one point in my career I was assigned to a newly established Data Warehouse Center of Excellence. Implementing a Data Warehouse solution was the newest and greatest service our consulting firm was marketing to clients, and we provided added consulting services to help clients take advantage of such a solution within their company. My job was to help build a consistent methodology to implement this new service. Why? Predictability! In addition to the sales and marketing piece, we needed to be able to propose our approach to clients and be able to estimate it as accurately as possible with a standard set of assumptions. Establishing a consistent methodology required me to interview engagement managers, PMs, and data analysts to identify the uniqueness of each client engagement that drove to a particular approach and customized solution. The result was that there was a "happy path," those common elements for all Data Warehouse projects. However, based on the assumptions made around the client environment and other variables, there were also many alternate paths. This drove our questioning when conducting our initial client needs assessments. If we could not get questions answered, we documented assumptions to make them visible so that they could be validated.

But when we say "consistency," to what extent do we mean? There is a need for some consistency, but at what depth? From a governance perspective, your internal organization may need some common elements across all projects, such as deliverables or specific content in the deliverables that are necessary to make project portfolio comparisons and investment decisions. Yet, other elements can be left flexible at the discretion of the PM and BA. Common elements might include high-level scope descriptions, business impacts, resource estimates, and budget elements. These elements can be defined formally in a project charter or less formally in other reporting templates. The objective being: consistency in the information across approaches for more effective project portfolio comparisons. Regardless of approach, budget processes still exist and need some documentation for managing the project portfolio in order to make investment decisions on a periodic basis. Also, investment decisions need to be monitored throughout the life cycle of the initiative or project. One way to do this is to ensure consistency in the life-cycle stages, as shown in the SLC in Figure 3.1. Although all life-cycle approaches have these similar stages, the stages will vary by their breadth, depth, number of iterations, and the time span of these iterations. BAs and PMs must collaborate to determine the best life-cycle approach for the uniqueness of the project and the needs of governance processes. The PM should always consider the BA's suggestions before making the final project approach decision. Are there some key life-cycle variations that we should consider as BAs? The answer is, *yes*.

SLC Variations

Table 3.1 illustrates three example variations of the SLC: the predictive approach, the hybrid approach, and the adaptive approach. Figure 3.2 summarizes those variations in a more visual way. The predictive approach is ideal when requirements are stable and have some predictability of outcomes, when quality needs are an important consideration, and when a greater business impact requires more control and transparency. The predictive approach is primarily linear and restrictive. The adaptive approach is ideal when requirements are more volatile (more likely that changes will occur), but there is more uncertainty and quality needs are relatively low. The adaptive approach is more collaborative and flexible. Most of my clients have fallen somewhere in the middle, a hybrid that is not purely adaptive or purely predictive. Hybrid approaches to the SLC are

Table 3.1   Example life-cycle approaches

Variables	Predictive	Hybrid	Adaptive
Project Scope	Work is formally planned using progressive elaboration (revisiting work detail and estimates at stage gates).	Work is defined initially at roadmap planning of releases and again before each release.	Work is defined just in time at iteration planning.
Product Scope	Functions and features are defined formally within stage gate deliverables starting at high level and then detailed (implementable requirements).	Similar to predictive initially, through formal deliverable for full project at high level. Detail level before release start for what is to be rolled out in that release. Scope is adjusted based on results of prototypes.	Product backlog defines overall functions and features at high level. Iteration backlog defines mid-level details to estimate. Conversations during iterations define more detail for acceptance testing.
Schedule	Schedule is flexible based on scope and any cost constraints but typically 7 months to 2 years. Longer than 2 years, can be broken down into smaller projects. Schedule will show milestones at stage gates for go/no-go decisions.	Fixed schedule, like adaptive, but longer (2–6 months) after analysis and design stages which include a prototype. Scheduling is usually managed in releases (e.g., product changes are packaged to be *released* every quarter).	Schedule is constrained between 2–4 weeks depending on maturity and known velocity of the team. New teams may start at 4-week iterations.
Resources	Resources are flexible based on scope and any cost constraints. Teams likely to be large (more than 10) with a combination of part-time and full-time resources. Individual performance is monitored. Performing multiple roles on the team are less likely than other approaches.	Resources are flexible for analysis and design and have fixed teams assigned to releases for rest of stages. A resource can work on multiple projects at a time (part time).	Resources are fixed at 7–9 members per team. Multiple teams can run in parallel but resources are dedicated (full time). Velocity is considered as a measure of the team's value delivery over multiple iterations before stabilized. Performing multiple roles on the team is encouraged.
Value	ROI may be defined in a formal business case. ROI not realized till end of life cycle.	Overall project objectives may still take the same overall amount of time as predictive, but more visibility and value is provided along the way. ROI realized more iteratively than predictive, but longer than adaptive.	Overall project objectives may still take the same overall amount of time as predictive, but more visibility focuses on value, adjusting, and providing value along the way. Part of the ROI can be realized at the end of each iteration.

Continued

often called iterative approaches—although that term is also used in the adaptive approach, so we will avoid using iterative and stick to hybrid when discussing the mix of adaptive and predictive approaches. Hybrid is less linear, more fast-tracking with overlapping stages, and evolutionary. Each will be discussed in detail in this chapter to provide a comparison that will prove helpful to the BA for life-cycle approach decisions and business analysis planning.

Variables	Predictive	Hybrid	Adaptive
Quality	Planning allows for quality checks and measures. Formal testing stage built into life cycle with integration of all types of enterprise-wide (system-to-system) testing. Requirement documentation allows for test strategy planning and provides information to build stable test cases. More thorough test coverage than adaptive.	A balance of formal quality checks are integrated with time and resource constraints based on release structure. Advantage of full analysis allows for test preparation. Releases allow for movement of problems to future releases if *compression* of testing occurs because of build delays. Prototypes help uncover certain defects early.	Test-driven development approach using acceptance criteria is valued. Test automation through use of tools improves quality. More extensive quality checks may be done outside of iterations in release structures by parallel teams or by separate iterations. Consideration should be given to carry integration and regressions testing from one iteration to another.
Change	Requirements and design must be stable, changes are difficult to make. Formal process is used to manage change that can impact time, resources, quality, and cost. Rework and change is controlled and not easily accepted.	Requirements and design are completed, but not stable until after prototype (baseline). Formal process is used to manage change after prototype. Changes are evaluated before each release.	Use of a product backlog and the short iterative cycle allows for frequent requirement changes to be performed to product backlog. Changes affect whether or not the change is included in the next iteration, but does not change the length of the iteration or resources (fixed). Change is an accepted part of the culture.
Risk	Risks are addressed formally and have a big picture perspective over the longer cycle. Business analysis risks are integrated into project management plans. Detailed planning allows for integrating responses into the approach. Progressive elaboration may uncover more risks.	Risk is formally addressed as in predictive, but has a *fail fast* philosophy like adaptive by introducing prototypes and the evolutionary approach with a roadmap of releases. Risks are also associated with each use case.	*Fail fast* philosophy helps to address risks early and frequently through the iterations. Product backlog grooming can uncover high risk requirements that can be moved up the backlog to address in earlier iterations. Because of the informality, teams need to be educated to communicate risks during conversations and still manage them in a lightweight way.
Stakeholders	Identified stakeholders (which can range from 6 to 100s) are elicited for requirements for the full scope of the project and are brought in for additional verification and validation as defined in the formal business analysis plan.	Similar to predictive for elicitation, but stakeholders are involved in prototyping for early verification and at appropriately assigned release for validation.	Product owner could represent stakeholders or another stakeholder (user) is committed full time during the iteration.

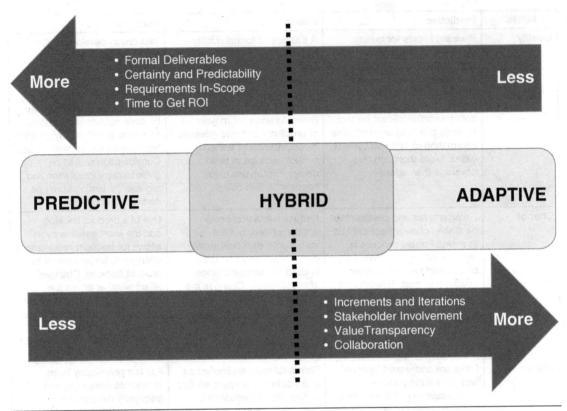

Figure 3.2 Example life-cycle approach variations

Predictive Life-Cycle Approach

In the predictive life-cycle approach (*waterfall*), the stages are very linear. For a project, the full scope of the project is addressed at each stage, but is progressively elaborated. The schedule is flexible based on the scope and any cost constraints. The BA role is well defined in this approach. Each stage of the SLC can be applied to this approach, but with some unique variations compared to the other two.

In the concept definition stage, a business case (Appendix A2.2) is characteristic of the type of deliverable you may be involved in creating or using during the start up of a project. The business case will define the return on investment and cost/benefit analysis. If the BA is in a more strategic role, they are likely to participate in the development of the business case but they are even more likely to start their involvement in the next stage—requirements analysis—in which requirements are elicited from the many stakeholders identified for the full scope of the project (stakeholder requirements). Requirements are written in textual form within formal deliverables to establish an approved baseline (assuming requirement stability) so that changes can be better managed through a formal process. Often, deliverables are split into more than one at the end of this stage. Interim deliverables may include a scope definition document, then a business requirements document (both may be done instead of a business case for smaller projects). The end deliverable for the stage is the baseline deliverable, known as the solution requirements specification (SRS)—a.k.a. system requirements specification. Some conceptual models may be included in the SRS out of the design stage.

In the conceptual and physical design stage, the full scope of the project is again addressed. Detailed conceptual models are built by the BA (these will be discussed further in Chapter 8) such as conceptual or entity relationship diagrams, functional decomposition diagrams, process models, data flow diagrams, activity diagrams, state transition models, sequence diagrams, etc. Models can reflect that current state domain to be used for analysis or used for future state stakeholder validation, simulations, reuse, etc. If there is an enterprise architecture group, the BA may not only contribute these models for inclusion, but may also pull models from the architecture's repository to reuse. Once models have been validated, requirements are allocated to physical design components.

In the acquire and/or build stage, the full scope of requirements must be allocated to a built solution, whether COTS, in-house build, outsourced build, or a combination. BAs can conduct reviews with those providing the solution to ensure that the requirements are understood and traced to components. Communicating requirements to vendors (COTS and outsourced builds) can be more challenging. This will be discussed in more detail in Chapter 4.

In the test solution stage, test strategies and test cases are developed by a testing or quality group and are based on requirement reviews with the BA at the end of requirements analysis. In the predictive approach, the test coverage is more extensive than other life-cycle approaches. All types of tests are included within this stage for the full set of requirements. Key tests that are formally conducted in the predictive approach include:

- **Unit and integration tests**—validate the internals of specific components and determine that they are *fit for use*, that the components have met design specifications and requirements, and that small groups of components can interact correctly. BAs need to review functional requirements with builders before components are built to ensure understanding.
- **Interface tests**—validate the interactions between systems. Interface requirements, such as standard protocols, are tested. BAs need to review interface requirements with system analysts or architects.
- **Operational tests**—validate compliance to the standard operating environment that relates to design constraints, a classification of nonfunctional requirements. Other nonfunctional requirements include quality attributes, which may include: usability, performance, reliability, scalability, security, maintainability, etc. BAs need to review nonfunctional requirements with infrastructure experts and validate alignment with enterprise architectures.
- **Acceptance tests**—will determine if expectations have been met with stakeholders. BAs facilitate this validation process with responsible stakeholders who will match test outcomes against their requirements and approve (or disapprove) the overall results.

- **Regression tests**—validate that an implemented change *did not* break anything that used to work in previous tests. BAs may need to assist in building and running the test bed for test cases that have already been implemented and validated.
- **System tests**—will be defined here as all-inclusive tests that validate the full set of baseline requirements, both functional and nonfunctional. However, there are conflicting definitions for this type of test, depending on what other classification of tests are included, such as those listed previously. Because of the large scope of most predictive life-cycle approaches, system tests are formally planned and become an important part of the approach, since this may be the first time that the stakeholders actually *see* results.

Methods to validate requirements are necessary regardless of life-cycle approach and some form of traceability is also necessary to ensure the requirements have been implemented—at a minimum, trace requirements to test cases.

In the predictive approach, the transition to a new solution stage requires much more extensive effort because of the size of the solution being implemented. The risks are higher; therefore, the BA must pay closer attention to the necessary business analysis activities for the transition. Once the new solution has been identified in design, additional elicitation activities will occur to uncover transition requirements. For example, in a manufacturing plant acquisition there are a series of changes applied to various software applications to accommodate additional product and service lines (the reason for the acquisition) from the newly acquired plant. That integration of new features and functions also requires the merging of customer information and accounts. Are there any special requirements needed to merge the information? What if the customer exists in both companies? When converting, how will the information be validated? There can be many questions that need to be asked to elicit the information that is necessary in order to make the transition happen successfully and in a short period of time. It is a BA's responsibility to take these requirements and go through the same stages as other requirements—but they are likely to get a later start at elicitation. They will still need to help design a solution for the transition and validate that it works based on the requirements *before* the live transition (test it). Once the transition has occurred, the requirements no longer exist in the solution—they are only temporary. Parallel adoption is a form of live validation, a more likely occurrence in the predictive approach because of the big-bang approach and complexity (see Figure 3.3) involving the simultaneous running of an old and a new system until validation deems it satisfactory. Users also learn the nuances of the new system, but the duplication can lead to many challenges, such as data integrity issues, resource issues, and defining clear success criteria (knowing when to stop).

To execute the *evaluate solution stage* activities in the predictive approach, consideration should be given to what should be evaluated. Again, the size of the solution affects the effort. The challenge comes when the effort is much more extensive than the time allocated, or when these activities aren't planned at all—plans seem to end after transition and teams move on! Planning these activities and asking for the time to complete them are critical to ensuring that they get done. This

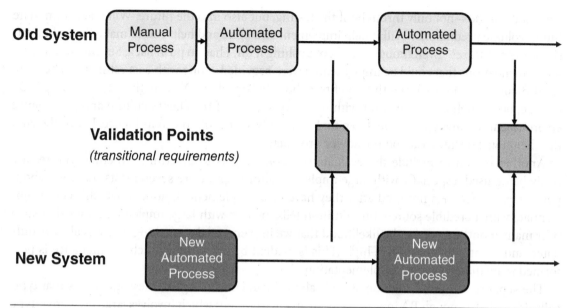

Figure 3.3 Parallel adoption

is an often-missed stage, but depending on the solution implemented, it may be a critical one to ensure that the stakeholders are getting the value out of the solution that they originally expected.

I had a client engagement in which I was brought in to conduct business analysis activities for the replacement of a newly implemented system for which business analysis activities never happened. This company, we will call Company X, had an enterprise-wide, mostly manual process that was replaced based on the recommendation of an external vendor. It was the core of this company's business, and they spent millions on this vendor's solution. It was implemented, but after two months, it already hit its limitations. Just a few of the problems included: (1) it couldn't accommodate the current volume, let alone scale up for the future, (2) executives needed business intelligence out of the system, but there was no physical database of information that could provide what they needed, and (3) there was a huge amount of redundant entry that was supposed to have been corrected. My assignment was to last for only a few months—to interview stakeholders, to uncover as many requirements as possible, and to provide some solution alternatives. None of these activities were done in the previous implementation. Several challenges had to be addressed. First, Company X was very new to project management and business analysis, so the staff had to be coached. Second, relating to the evaluate solution stage, there had to be a big push to get any measures of success. Business requirements were not very SMART—specific, measurable, achievable, relevant, and time-framed (see Chapter 6). The following message had to be reinforced over and over up to the day the contract was fulfilled, "You don't want to get into the same situation as your last implementation; you must have a way of knowing that this implementation is doing what you want it to do—not only throughout the testing, but also into the future. Will it accommodate future volume predictions? Will it help implement strategies and help you to make the right decisions for the future?" Even though they kept pushing it off, I had to push back. Several measurable recommendations that could be implemented were provided, along with cost estimates. These are the difficulties, and sometimes the benefits, of being a consultant. You are there for a short period of time, but somehow you must fit within the constraints of the client's culture and governance environment. Ultimately it came down to: I could advise, I could try to influence, but in the end, the client must decide to act on the advice provided.

Another reason to include the evaluate solution stage is to determine whether features are really being used, especially with large implementations. There are several stats out there about percentages of features not used after they have been implemented, none of which I could substantiate with a credible source. But intuition tells me that with large implementations that span over many months or years, the likelihood that we implemented something that was already outdated and eventually not used is high. This is evident based on how much maintenance is performed immediately after an implementation.

The support and retire solution stage is about maintenance. Again, these are stages that typically do not have enough BA involvement. In an environment which involves large predictive-type projects, you are likely to see teams split up into the *developers* and the *maintainers*. Developers get temporarily assigned to new projects (often defined by the large number of effort hours) that follow an SLC. The maintainers are permanently assigned as full-time equivalents to the solution for permanent maintenance (fixes, small enhancements) that doesn't follow an SLC. BAs are usually assigned to projects, but rarely to maintenance. The challenge is that many small enhancements that come through should really be combined into projects or releases and should follow the SLC. When I worked for the telephone company, our group was structured exactly this way. Over the years, our legacy (old) systems were becoming harder and harder to support. It got to the point that we either had to replace them completely or at least give them an overhaul. The constant patching created what we used to call *spaghetti* code in our systems due to the lack of having the enterprise or system-thinking mindset and not considering an overall architectural design when putting in patches. Eventually maintainers began using a release structure—a hybrid approach—and I was assigned as a release coordinator to manage changes to systems in a more coordinated way.

For each of the aforementioned stages, we describe how they may be conducted in a predictive life-cycle approach. There are two other life-cycle approaches that can provide additional insight into how much business analysis versatility is needed when dealing with the uniqueness of changes and business needs in an organization.

Hybrid Life-Cycle Approach

In the 1990's, rapid application delivery (RAD) was a discipline that my internal consulting group at the telephone company used in order to speed up delivery, which included rapid prototyping with a committed user and what was then called time-boxed scheduled iterations.[2] It was the foundation of what was to come for agile, and it was my initial exposure as an internal consultant trying to sell this new concept to management and peers. RAD continues to be used today and is considered a hybrid approach (in the middle of predictive and adaptive life-cycle approaches). During this time frame, Rational Software Corporation developed the Rational Unified Process (RUP) with a supporting suite of tools using visual modeling, which were all purchased by IBM in 2003. RUP was a specific model using RAD principles but added more of these best practices:[3]

1. Develop software iteratively
2. Manage requirements
3. Use component-based architectures
4. Visually model software
5. Verify software quality
6. Control changes to software

In addition, the application of use case techniques demonstrates how activities can overlap across stages.

Figure 3.4 is a simple illustration of the introduction of the hybrid life-cycle approach in the 1990s. The diagram shows a sample distribution of the different approaches over time, based on my own experiences as a consultant working with software development projects. As you see,

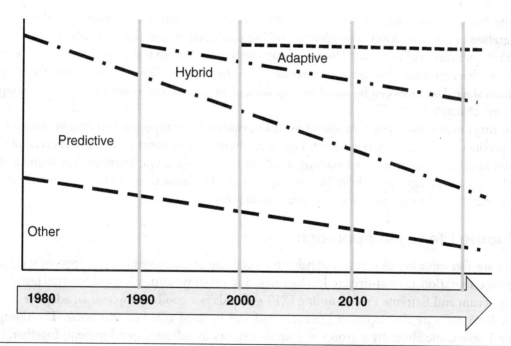

Figure 3.4   Life-cycle use over time

predictive and other approaches (custom or having no defined approach) declined over time as hybrid and adaptive life-cycle approaches increased in popularity.

For the hybrid approach, the concept definition stage and requirements analysis stage are very similar to the predictive approach, except that architecture is addressed as early as possible (in concept definition) with a roadmap of a release structure. Stakeholder and functional requirements are captured in use cases during requirements analysis (see the template and example in Appendix A3.1).

The biggest difference in the hybrid approach is in the design, build, and test stages. These stages are very iterative. Prototypes are key to making the hybrid approach more iterative. Prioritization of use cases help determine the scope and number of iterations needed for the prototype. Based on the release roadmap from the concept definition stage, requirements are packaged by release. Those not prototyped will need to go through design, build, and test stages.

The transition to a new solution stage could be completed by a release, or each release can be held in test until all releases are completed before the transition occurs. Pilots may also be part of the roadmap. Releases can be moved into a *pilot* mode, meaning that a transition may only happen for one organization or geographical area, a phased rollout. A pilot allows for another validation opportunity in a live environment. Feedback can be provided to reduce the impact for future rollouts. With prototypes, releases, and phased rollouts, the evaluate solution stage can occur multiple times.

The test solution stage can be more complex with fixed timing of releases and the possible integration of other solution dependencies rolling out together. But testing is also more efficient with the application of use cases. Uses cases can easily transition to test cases and can also be used to establish a regression testing base from one release to the next. The same is true for the support solution stage. Use cases can be saved to help document the current system and used for support of future changes.

Testing can also include *live* validations—the release of live components to demonstrate the use of a product in the user's environment. Figure 3.5 shows live releases of an alpha, beta, and final release in a live environment, but starting with a small group of users. There are key elements that would help you recognize a hybrid life-cycle approach: (1) the use of prototypes, (2) requirements documented within use cases, and (3) release structures.

Adaptive Life-Cycle Approach

There are also some key elements that help you recognize an adaptive life-cycle approach: (1) just-in-time elaboration, (2) test-driven development, and (3) show something quickly (fail fast). Agile using Scrum and Extreme Programming (XP) methods is a good example of an adaptive framework for a software development life cycle and will be used often in this book. The thoughts behind agile came about by a group of domain experts in software development; together, they

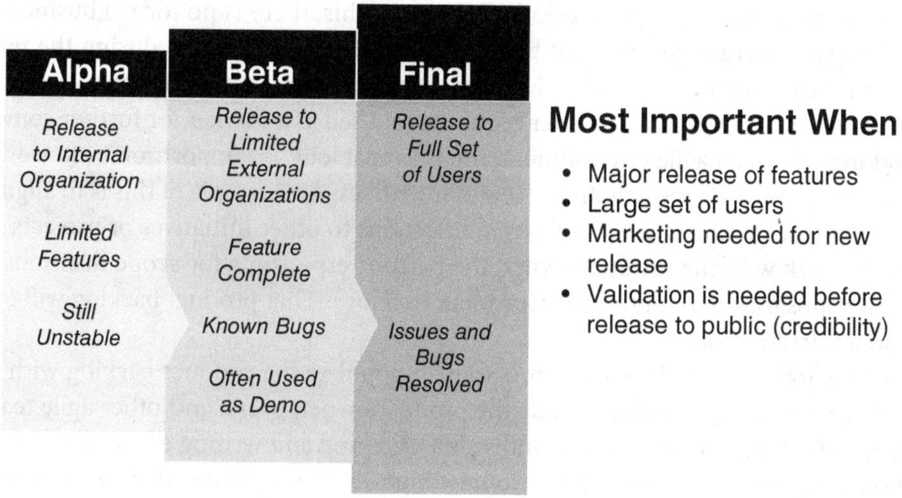

Alpha	Beta	Final	Most Important When
Release to Internal Organization	Release to Limited External Organizations	Release to Full Set of Users	
Limited Features	Feature Complete		• Major release of features • Large set of users • Marketing needed for new release • Validation is needed before release to public (credibility)
Still Unstable	Known Bugs	Issues and Bugs Resolved	
	Often Used as Demo		

Figure 3.5   Live validation

created a public declaration of what is valued for the development of software. The result was the Agile Manifesto[4]—which is listed after this paragraph. Following each statement are descriptions of BA opportunities to address each of these declarations. The bold statements that begin each bullet point are more valued than the statements that follow them:

- **Individuals and interactions** over processes and tools
  - BA opportunity: collaborating within a smaller team and with much fewer stakeholders on a continuous basis—early and often (discussion of incomplete thoughts and concepts are acceptable)—using simple tools during conversations
- **Working software** over comprehensive documentation
  - BA opportunity: understanding that scope is smaller with less of a need for formal documentation, but still balancing this with governance and other business policy or regulatory audit needs
- **Customer collaboration** over contract negotiation
  - BA opportunity: working toward a shared definition of *done*, understanding that you don't get into the detail until you must (just-in-time analysis), and focusing on business value
- **Responding to change** over following a plan
  - BA opportunity: acknowledging that changes will occur and are acceptable; think *customer first*

Agile is not just one adaptive approach, it is a combination of different adaptive flavors such as XP, kanban, lean, and Scrum (most often associated with agile). The BA role is not currently recognized formally in the agile framework. Because of this, there is no formal business analysis work breakdown structure defined, but tasks are uncovered just-in-time during the team planning session for each iteration (a 2-to-4-week agile sprint) when estimating the user story. A user story is a structured form of a stakeholder requirement used as a marker for further conversation. When working within an agile environment, the BA must look for opportunities to work outside of the iterations to ensure a more holistic view of initiatives. An example of this is to align to roadmaps, business cases, architectures, and any connections to other initiatives or projects. Another example is to work with the product owner, the person responsible for scope decisions, and the owner of the repository of requirements (product backlog). That product backlog will eventually be structured into iterations.

Facilitated workshops can be run by BAs to help populate the product backlog with user stories. The user story workshop can include the product owner, users, and other agile team members. The brainwriting technique allows individual thinking and writing of ideas on post-it notes to get a list of user stories without regard to how high-level or how detailed the user stories are. The list will be evaluated and ranked later during a product backlog grooming process. Those that rank at the top will get more discussion. Using the airport kiosk scenario, Figure 3.6 is an example outcome from a virtual brainwriting session. Note that user stories are the pointers to future discussions!

There are benefits to having a distinct role for a BA participating on an agile project because of the value that business analysis competencies bring. Benefits include:

- Quickly building up the product backlog using elicitation techniques
- Ensuring that user stories (requirements) show value
- Having the enterprise mindset to identify dependencies and align to strategies
- Facilitating stakeholder conflicts when prioritizing
- Knowing when and how to split and elaborate on user stories

Consider the concept definition stage for an SLC. Even with the adaptive approach, the BA would still need to move from an idea to justification, but it may be *lightweight*. Dean Leffingwell suggests using a lightweight business case for business epics (high-level user stories) or a vision statement.[5]

In addition to working with the product owner, as mentioned previously, the BA can be part of the agile team by helping in the sprint planning when defining the needed tasks and estimating them, facilitating the further elaboration of user stories by defining acceptance criteria, and uncovering missing requirements (just-in-time requirements analysis). Here is an example of a user story for an airline kiosk at the airport:

"As a traveler, I need to check in my luggage before going through security so that I don't have to carry more than I absolutely need to."

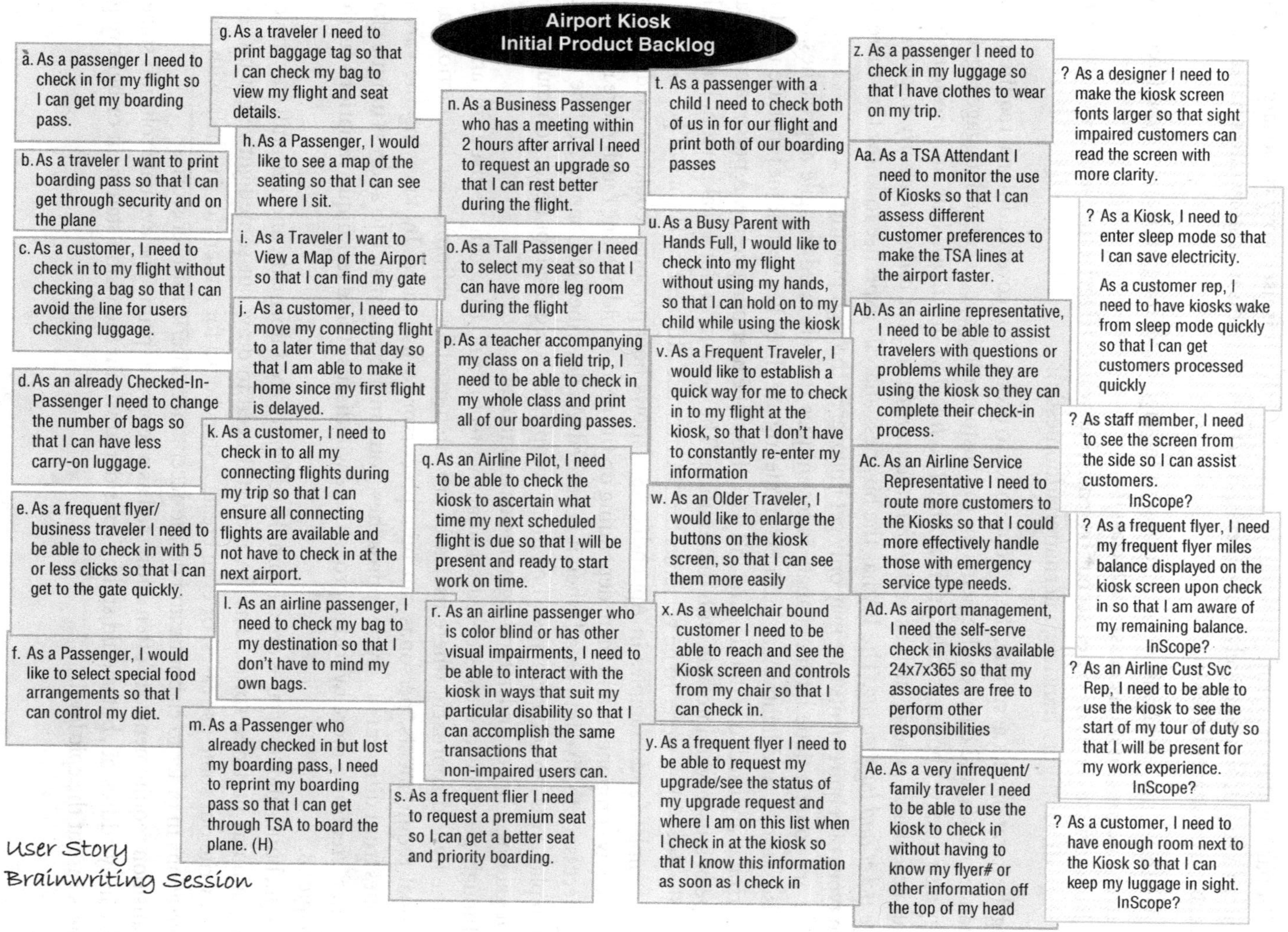

**Airport Kiosk
Initial Product Backlog**

a. As a passenger I need to check in for my flight so I can get my boarding pass.

b. As a traveler I want to print boarding pass so that I can get through security and on the plane

c. As a customer, I need to check in to my flight without checking a bag so that I can avoid the line for users checking luggage.

d. As an already Checked-In-Passenger I need to change the number of bags so that I can have less carry-on luggage.

e. As a frequent flyer/business traveler I need to be able to check in with 5 or less clicks so that I can get to the gate quickly.

f. As a Passenger, I would like to select special food arrangements so that I can control my diet.

g. As a traveler I need to print baggage tag so that I can check my bag to view my flight and seat details.

h. As a Passenger, I would like to see a map of the seating so that I can see where I sit.

i. As a Traveler I want to View a Map of the Airport so that I can find my gate

j. As a customer, I need to move my connecting flight to a later time that day so that I am able to make it home since my first flight is delayed.

k. As a customer, I need to check in to all my connecting flights during my trip so that I can ensure all connecting flights are available and not have to check in at the next airport.

l. As an airline passenger, I need to check my bag to my destination so that I don't have to mind my own bags.

m. As a Passenger who already checked in but lost my boarding pass, I need to reprint my boarding pass so that I can get through TSA to board the plane. (H)

n. As a Business Passenger who has a meeting within 2 hours after arrival I need to request an upgrade so that I can rest better during the flight.

o. As a Tall Passenger I need to select my seat so that I can have more leg room during the flight

p. As a teacher accompanying my class on a field trip, I need to be able to check in my whole class and print all of our boarding passes.

q. As an Airline Pilot, I need to be able to check the kiosk to ascertain what time my next scheduled flight is due so that I will be present and ready to start work on time.

r. As an airline passenger who is color blind or has other visual impairments, I need to be able to interact with the kiosk in ways that suit my particular disability so that I can accomplish the same transactions that non-impaired users can.

s. As a frequent flier I need to request a premium seat so I can get a better seat and priority boarding.

t. As a passenger with a child I need to check both of us in for our flight and print both of our boarding passes

u. As a Busy Parent with Hands Full, I would like to check into my flight without using my hands, so that I can hold on to my child while using the kiosk

v. As a Frequent Traveler, I would like to establish a quick way for me to check in to my flight at the kiosk, so that I don't have to constantly re-enter my information

w. As an Older Traveler, I would like to enlarge the buttons on the kiosk screen, so that I can see them more easily

x. As a wheelchair bound customer I need to be able to reach and see the Kiosk screen and controls from my chair so that I can check in.

y. As a frequent flyer I need to be able to request my upgrade/see the status of my upgrade request and where I am on this list when I check in at the kiosk so that I know this information as soon as I check in

z. As a passenger I need to check in my luggage so that I have clothes to wear on my trip.

Aa. As a TSA Attendant I need to monitor the use of Kiosks so that I can make the TSA lines at the airport faster.

Ab. As an airline representative, I need to be able to assist travelers with questions or problems while they are using the kiosk so they can complete their check-in process.

Ac. As an Airline Service Representative I need to route more customers to the Kiosks so that I could more effectively handle those with emergency service type needs.

Ad. As airport management, I need the self-serve check in kiosks available 24x7x365 so that my associates are free to perform other responsibilities

Ae. As a very infrequent/family traveler I need to be able to use the kiosk to check in without having to know my flyer# or other information off the top of my head

? As a designer I need to make the kiosk screen fonts larger so that sight impaired customers can read the screen with more clarity.

? As a Kiosk, I need to enter sleep mode so that I can save electricity.
As a customer rep, I need to have kiosks wake from sleep mode quickly so that I can get customers processed quickly

? As staff member, I need to see the screen from the side so I can assist customers.
InScope?

? As a frequent flyer, I need my frequent flyer miles balance displayed on the kiosk screen upon check in so that I am aware of my remaining balance. InScope?

? As an Airline Cust Svc Rep, I need to be able to use the kiosk to see the start of my tour of duty so that I will be present for my work experience. InScope?

? As a customer, I need to have enough room next to the Kiosk so that I can keep my luggage in sight. InScope?

*User Story
Brainwriting Session*

Figure 3.6   Example user story workshop results

As the BA participating in sprint planning, you may find that this user story is too large to complete within a sprint. You will likely probe the team to try to split this user story into smaller, more manageable user stories by asking:

- Are there any variations when checking in luggage depending on traveler type (frequent flyer category, first/business/coach class)?
- Do alternate paths or other scenarios exist that would trigger other actions (number of bags, direct flights/transfers, international/domestic)?

During the iteration (a.k.a. sprint), the BA continues to probe to uncover additional requirements, acceptance criteria, and data requirements for the customer luggage ticket and luggage tag. Probing may also uncover business rules such as *only two free bags are allowed for each frequent flyer*, or other acceptance criteria such as *verify that the transfer airport codes are clearly displayed on luggage ticket and luggage tag*. The BA has the business analysis expertise to know that there are certain types of requirements that may only get uncovered through probing.

There are some unique business analysis techniques that are used in agile approaches. Personas, user stories, and lightweight business modeling are three key techniques that are used in agile. Personas are used to better understand users from the user perspective. A persona can be an archetype of a user who interacts with the solution. The persona is not a real person, but should be described as if they were. To be versatile, the BA may use different variations of personas. The persona template and examples in Appendix A3.2 shows how personas could be used starting with just a few components and then, depending on the need, could become much more robust. It is only necessary to dive into detail when it is needed. As described in Chapter 2 in the communication plan, you can add elements when more complexity is required for better communication and for gaining a better understanding of the environment.

Although personas are considered an adaptive technique, they can be used for any project. In the hybrid approach, where use cases are often used for defining user interactions and functional requirements, personas can be a precursor to use cases. By knowing the various techniques from different life-cycle approaches, you can mix and match to address unique characteristics, creating a more hybrid approach. We will discuss these technique variations further in Chapter 8.

Design, build, and test stages are all completed iteratively, informally, and with full stakeholder participation as part of a sprint. The BA may still need to draw out some lightweight business models, write out some use cases, or even create a storyboard for a user story to help with sprint conversations in order to elaborate and define acceptance criteria for user stories.

Transition requirements are often addressed as a separate sprint. The evaluate solution stage is not formally addressed, but should still be considered within the vision statement or lightweight business case at the epic level.

PROJECT APPROACH ADJUSTMENTS

Regardless of the life-cycle approach, there are certain project challenges that a BA is likely to uncover when assessing their business analysis activities, and initial requirements they will require in facing these challenges head-on. Collaborating with the sponsor or PM to resolve these challenges early and immediately can only build up your credibility as an advisor. The following list contains some key challenges that typically surface after determining the business analysis approach and/or analysis of requirements:

- Uncovering that the project approach requires adjustments in order to be realistic and to accommodate the current understanding of the requirements
- Expectation gaps among stakeholders regarding the scope of the project and needed trade-offs
- Expectation gaps between sponsor, PM, or other stakeholders regarding the time allowed to perform business analysis activities or being asked to remove business analysis activities
- Conflicts as to which activities are performed/not performed within the defined role of a BA

Earlier in my career, I was often put into a position of accepting a project plan to which I had not contributed. However, as experience was gained, I began to believe in instincts. Instinct or intuition stems from experience. You can't quite find the reasons for why something is not right, but that information is there—often stored somewhere in your mind and you just can't seem to get to it when you need it. Without first establishing trust in a sponsor or PM relationship, it is difficult to convince these critical stakeholders to base their decisions on intuition. My approach has always been to do my research. Once I dig in to find ways of substantiating my advice with facts, I also end up finding why I trusted my intuition to begin with. Eureka! I knew it! I begin to relate those intuitions to real experiences. Similarly, this has been my approach to writing this book. My audience may not trust me, so I must point to specifics from my experiences or other references to influence them. Without trust, influence techniques are valuable in substantiating your intuitive advice. A further discussion of trust and influence is in Chapter 1.

Once a project starts and requirements have been elicited, there is better understanding of the project. In project management disciplines this is called *progressive elaboration*. Progressive elaboration recognizes that as you *progress* through a life cycle, you begin to know more about the characteristics around the project for both the work and solution scope. Checkpoints along the way help to re-evaluate the state of the project as we know more (*elaboration*). This re-evaluation includes the BA. Before the requirements are fully defined in any deliverables, or even in a product backlog for an adaptive project, the BA needs to *analyze* the requirements to determine certain attributes that will impact the business analysis and overall project approach. These requirement attributes add supplemental information to each requirement, which helps to trace the requirement to other components and assists in the analysis of requirement categories. The analysis of requirements is a critical step for not only finding missing requirements, but for providing critical information to make major project decisions. This type of requirements analysis is often missed by novice BAs.

Requirement Attributes

Requirement attributes that are captured can vary by project. For larger projects, requirement attributes may be formally documented in the requirements management plan, explaining the process of how and what is to be captured. For adaptive approaches such as agile, these attributes are frequently discussed as part of the product backlog discussions when prioritizing user stories, during sprint planning meetings, and again during sprint execution discussions. Table 3.2 includes a robust list of requirement attributes with a definition and some recommendations for when and how to use each attribute. I will cover three key attributes that are used for the overall project approach discussions with the sponsor or PM: priority, complexity, and volatility.

Table 3.2   Requirement attributes

Requirement Attribute	Also Known As or Use in Place of	Description	Application Recommendations
Identifier	Unique ID		REQUIRED: For tracing to other components or requirements. Use for any size project or initiative. Critical for referencing.
Assigned to	Author	A person responsible for initially and continually documenting the requirement; usually the BA.	REQUIRED: BA accountability.
Status/Dates		The state of the requirement.	REQUIRED: Status—stated, verified, reviewed, approved, designed, built, tested, validated, implemented.
Source		Can be a person or document that a requirement was extracted from.	REQUIRED: Know who provided the initial requirement.
Owner		A person that verifies the requirement and will provide future changes to it.	REQUIRED: Someone takes ongoing ownership of the requirement.
Approver	Signer	A person that validates and approves the completion of the requirement.	REQUIRED: Often the approver is a decision maker (sponsor or process owner) for a group of requirements to establish the baseline and to determine if the requirement has met acceptance criteria.
Priority	Rank	Priority category as established by owner and follows criteria.	REQUIRED: Determines future needed trade-offs. Criteria for values should be clearly defined. Focuses vendors and other service provider resources. In an adaptive approach, prioritization is done through a ranking process.

Continued

Requirement Attribute	Also Known As or Use in Place of	Description	Application Recommendations
Traced to/ from		Link to/from other requirements or components.	REQUIRED: Assesses impacts of changes. At minimum—trace to test cases for validation.
Complexity	Difficulty	Assess implementation difficulty.	OPTIONAL: Determines if need for proof of concept or need for more expertise on the team. Criteria for values should be clearly defined. Look at ways the requirement can be simplified or decomposed. In an adaptive approach, complexity is discussed when estimating during iteration planning.
Volatility	Or opposite— stability	The likelihood that requirements will change during the span of the project.	OPTIONAL but HIGHLY RECOMMENDED: Impacts project approach (i.e., a use of a prototype) or can impact the design of the solution so as to consider a more maintainable future structure.
Impact	Risk	Level of impact of the business requirements (goals, objectives).	OPTIONAL but HIGHLY RECOMMENDED: The larger the number of high-impact requirements, the more likely the approach may need to change to accomodate risks (see complexity).
Schedule constraint	Fixed date, urgency	The requirements must be implemented by a specific date (e.g., regulatory requirement)—use with impact to describe the impact if date is not met.	OPTIONAL: Be careful when using this as attribute requirement should be written in a way to include the constraint and the reason for it to ensure this isn't just a preference. Helps determine risks and trade-offs in order to meet the date.
Business benefit	Value	Identification of what will be gained by implementing the requirement.	OPTIONAL: Helps determine requirements with most benefits and trade-offs. If business requirements are documented and prioritized with a link to the business requirements, then this is not necessary.
Target iteration	Packaged in, release	Assignment to specific iteration or release.	OPTIONAL: Allocation of requirement. Most needed for hybrid approach.
Cost to implement		Putting a dollar value to the requirement.	OPTIONAL: Helps to identify risks and trade-offs. Costs are most often determined at a work-package level. Cost is more than human resources—equipment, software purchases, etc.
Size estimation	Effort		OPTIONAL: In a predictive life cycle, effort is often used. In adaptive, story points are often used.
Revisions/ Reason/Date		Information about revisions made to requirements.	OPTIONAL: Tracks changes. Tool dependent, but important for volatile requirements.
References	Supporting material	Information to further clarify the requirement such as procedures or standards.	OPTIONAL: Supplemental information that is especially helpful for resources that don't have domain knowledge.

Priority

Prioritization must start early, even before stakeholder requirements. I recommend starting with business requirements at the highest level. If business requirements are prioritized it makes it much easier to prioritize lower-level requirements. It aligns priorities based on the business reasons. If we don't prioritize at all, what challenges might we face later in the life cycle? In my experience, clients want everything implemented—and everything is high priority. It is the responsibility of the BA to help PMs in trade-off decisions. An agreed-upon prioritization process must be in place early, otherwise trade-off decisions become a battle at the most critical time—when resources and the schedule are constrained. Later in the life cycle, stakeholders have already committed so much of their time that without prioritization they are unlikely to agree to pull out any requirements or product features. The prioritization process should include collaboration with requirement owners, with those who are building the solutions to address feasibility, and with those who are implementing the requirement. Prioritization may change based on finding out how much something may cost. For example, during my bathroom remodel, I thought it was critical for me to have a whirlpool tub, but when I found out how much it would cost, I simply changed my mind!

There are different ways to prioritize. In an adaptive approach such as agile, ranking is an important way to prioritize. The product backlog containing requirements as written user stories will have those user stories ranked as 1, 2, 3, . . . N. N equals the total in the product backlog. How they are ranked and what criteria is used may vary based on the product owner's decision and the BA's advice. Requirements could be ranked based on several items: (1) the value defined within the user story, (2) grouping by category first (high, medium, low) then ranking within each category, or (3) date constrained user stories, etc.

In a predictive approach, there are techniques such as the *Must, Should, Could, or Won't* method (MoSCoW).[6] Again, criteria as to what falls within each priority category must be agreed to. For example:

- *Must*—might be defined as critical because requirements cause unrecoverable failures, huge legal risks (such as government regulatory requirements), or huge financial losses if not implemented
- *Should*—might be defined as high value to stakeholders but not critical and is negotiable based on cost/benefit trade-offs
- *Could*—might be defined as *pull-outs*, a lower value to stakeholders and considered optional in the launch allowing PM removal if time and resources are constrained
- *Won't*—might be defined as *add-ins*, the lowest value to stakeholders and the most likely to go in future iterations

Priorities are there to help determine trade-offs that affect the project approach. This information about the requirements can help the BA advise the PM whether a different approach may need to be used. When assessing a high percentage of critical requirements, consider:

- Effect on constrained resources or schedule
- Impact to project costs
- How dependencies to lower priority requirements may affect how they will be grouped together for iterations or releases
- Re-evaluating the criteria for what is considered critical
- Whether they are coming from the same group of stakeholders (maybe an awareness/or educational issue of what critical means)
- Bringing in more capable resources (special team) to manage critical requirements

In my experience, the benefits of prioritization always outweigh the extra time and effort regardless of SLC approach.

Complexity

Complexity cannot be assessed without going through the thought process of determining the scope of the work and the scope of the product to determine size. But also, the cost, the time frame, the number of uncertainties, the amount of business impact, and the need to be perfect—these are all variables to determine the level of complexity and will require discussion to determine if additional work or techniques are required in the approach. The most commonly used technique for estimation of complexity is based on the relationship of size to other requirements. The reason for this estimating approach is to reinforce that the team is using the more literal definition of the estimate term—meaning it is a guess. Agile does this by using a technique called *planning poker*, which is an application of *story points*. Another is using T-shirt sizes. A user (requirement) may be a small T-shirt size if it has less complexity or uncertainty than that of a medium user story initially defined by the team with certain characteristics (e.g., an average complexity user interface level with display only and information from two or fewer sources). In a planning session, the team may look at other user stories and estimate their size by relating them to the samples that were previously agreed upon. If the T-shirt size is large or bigger than large, then further discussions are needed to break it down into more manageable pieces to ensure that they can be accomplished within the constraints of an iteration's time and resources. Assigning sizes becomes easier as you assign sizes to more and more user stories.

Story point estimation uses a similar approach but has more *sizes*. Different scales can be used. Many teams use the Fibonacci sequence (0, 1, 2, 3, 5, 8, 13, etc.) on poker cards or other sequences that give teams some gaps between the number such as currency denominations (1, 5, 10, 20, 50, 100). The gaps help to establish the perception that it is a guess and make it easier to decide, rather than trying to select a precise number (such as deciding between a 10 or 11).

In a more predictive approach, because projects take longer, the challenge with complexity is knowing enough, early enough, to determine the right approach to take. Using progressive elaboration, as discussed earlier, the more you know, the more complexity is uncovered. A few complexity questions that are typically asked are provided in Appendix A3.3. Having worked on many enterprise resource planning (ERP) software implementations in the past, I have found value in the vendor's complexity assessments used for estimating. ERPs are some of the most complex software packages to implement because of their number of interfaces, amount of special configuration/customization, need for converting large amounts of data, impact to job procedures, and user skills, etc. Without assessing the complexity, it is much more difficult to estimate. Keep in mind, within the predictive and hybrid approaches, estimate accuracy improves as you revisit estimates after each stage in the life cycle.

Once complexity is determined, discussions regarding the approach should occur. Depending on the assessment of complexity, the use of different techniques to identify and respond to risks associated with the complexity may need to be considered. Complexities may warrant the use of a proof-of-concept, involve bringing in experts, or extending the time to account for learning.

A proof-of-concept is a type of prototype providing a representation of a solution. The proof-of-concept is considered a vertical prototype, one that provides less breadth but more depth than a horizontal prototype. Figure 3.7 provides a comparison of the different kinds of prototypes. I consider horizontal prototypes as a *mile wide, inch deep* because they provide a broad set of features but a narrow coverage of functionality. The opposite would be true for the vertical prototype, which would be an *inch wide, mile deep* with a narrow feature set and much depth in functionality. At the cross points could be a prototype that is used for looking at a specific feature at a breadth level—maybe using a paper-based prototype that we will discuss later. It could help resolve any design issue early and informally in a more agile way. An example from my past occurred during a project audit I was conducting in which an issue surfaced regarding two sets of stakeholders.

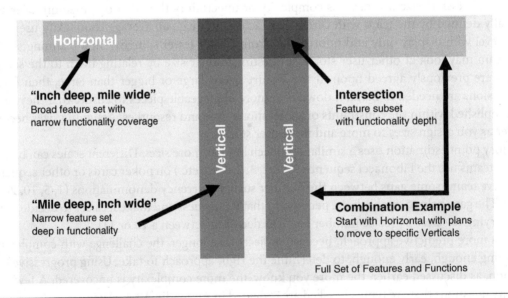

Figure 3.7 Different kinds of prototypes

They could not agree on the design of the fonts and colors. The BA finally got them in the room and did a quick prototype for the specific features they were using—in a well-lit conference room. Once it was presented, the one group of stakeholders said, "See, this works great!" The other group immediately was on the defensive, "Sure, it works in here, indoors. But our truck drivers need to see that information while in their vehicles with very different lighting—try that and you will see!" The true requirements surfaced as to why each group took a strong position on wanting the design a particular way. The result of identifying the true needs provided a win/win, allowing for different display options depending on their environment—a little more expensive, but worth it in their minds. Remember that the ultimate goal of the prototype is to *fail fast*. The sooner we find out the problems with a complex function, the quicker we can resolve the problems at a much cheaper cost.

There are also different levels of prototype presentation and approaches. A low-fidelity version (discussed further in Chapter 8) that could be used in an adaptive environment might be shown as pages taped to a board with a manual simulation navigating through the pages simulating screen shots (throw-away). A high-fidelity version might be software built on the eventual platform that it will reside on, so that users can execute it as if it was a live environment (evolutionary). Figure 3.8 illustrates the different reasons for the various combinations of prototypes.

Volatility

What most BAs don't know is that volatility is a requirement attribute that can also affect the overall solution design. Understanding there are requirements that we know have the potential to change, we should design the solution in a way to make it easier to make future requirement

	Throwaway	Evolutionary
Horizontal	One Time Product Demonstrations, Feedback on Feature Use, or to Explore Usability	Iterative Enhancements to User Classes, Use Cases, Personas, Skill Sets, or Feature Sets
Vertical	One Time Validation of High Risk Functions, Specific Feasibility, or Component Interactions	Iterative Enhancements to Functionality, Interfaces, or Technology Layers

Figure 3.8   Prototype applications

changes, especially those features and functions that may change often. A relatable example is a vendor from several years ago who was on the forefront of building an electronic medical records (EMR) system. Being on the forefront meant that the vendor knew that laws would be passed shortly requiring the medical community to retain records electronically, but the specific requirements were still being negotiated. The requirements were extremely volatile. Knowing which features and functions *might* change, they had the opportunity to design their product in a more modular fashion with external user-defined parameters. This not only allowed for quick changes once the law passed, allowing them to beat competition in the marketplace, but also allowed them to customize the product quickly depending on the type of medical practice (different user types) that was purchasing their product.

Addressing the Scope Expectation Gap

Scope discussions never, ever stop—and they shouldn't—whether it is about the scope of our business analysis work or the scope of features and functions of what we plan to deliver. It does not matter what the approach is, there is always a need to validate scope in every discussion from inception of an idea to making that idea operational. But how we manage scope varies by approach and how we manage expectations around scope may also vary. Scope changes can impact everyone on the team and the BA has a key role in helping to keep scope manageable.

Regardless of the approach, there should be a consideration of what the business perception is for scope that could be highlighted as goals, benefits, or other high-level requirements. In a predictive approach these high-level requirements would be formally documented as business requirements. In an adaptive environment, they might be documented within an epic (high-level) user story or defined informally by the product owner as criteria for prioritization.

Figure 3.9 shows the differences of how product scope is managed between different approach examples: (1) predictive, (2) hybrid, (3) adaptive. Each has its own unique way of managing changes. Each also has different ways that requirements may be structured and packaged. In the predictive approach, requirements are classified and written in a very structured way. In the hybrid approach, use cases are commonly used, and in the adaptive approach, user stories applied.

For the predictive approach, scope is defined by the written requirements within the boundaries of the project as defined by all impacted stakeholders. These written requirements are classified and written in a very structured way, as seen in Table 3.3. The predictive approach assumes an *all-in* setting for requirements until we define tolerances at the highest level and then start eliminating what can't be done because we can just go back and get more money based on what we initially budgeted in a business case or project charter. Once we determine those tolerances, "If we implemented all of what they want, we would be 40% over budget. We can only go back and get another 15%. What can we pull out and do later or not at all?" As you can see, this requires much collaboration between the sponsor, PM, and stakeholders. This is also why prioritization is so critical for making those discussions easier.

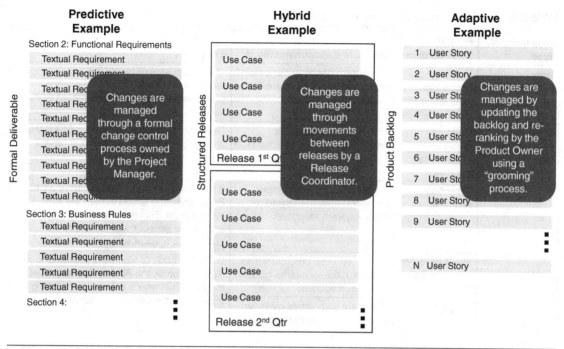

Figure 3.9   Different approaches to managing scope

Once there is agreement, we define our *baseline* for product scope and document it in a deliverable for formal approval. Once the baseline is established, changes must go through a formal process as defined at the project level, but could also be a standard across the enterprise coming from a project management office or other governance entity. Change requests go through a change control board to discuss the impacts of those changes. Because of this formality in this more traditional approach, change is seen more as an issue causing havoc to the structured plan rather than being viewed as necessary to assure an outcome that meets current needs. The BA needs to be the example to the team by still following the needed formal process, but not immediately resisting changes needed to satisfy our business and stakeholder needs as they also evolve and change. There is much less resistance as you get involved in hybrid or adaptive approaches.

Hybrid approaches can vary greatly, so my example here is based on the most common from my experiences. Hybrid approaches can be either incremental or iterative, sometimes both as applied in RUP. Change control procedures are often formal, as in predictive. But because there is likely one conceptual design, stakeholder requirements need to be flushed out for the full project or for the increments, which are more commonly known as structured *releases*. After conceptual design, these *releases* can be structured for physical design and small builds (then test and demo),

Table 3.3   Predictive approach requirement textual structures

Requirement Type	Further Classification	Structure Recommendations	Example
User (stakeholder)	User perspective (user story)	The <user> needs <user action or process> so that <benefit>.	The ATM customer needs the option to receive a receipt for a book-of-stamps purchase so that they have a record of the transaction.
Business rules (behavioral)	Policy or regulation or business constraint	<System or actor> must <condition, feature, or action>.	The ATM customer must have a BIG BANK checking account in order to purchase a book of stamps.
	Exception response	If <optional preconditions> <trigger>, then the <system> must <system response>.	If the ATM Customer does not have a BIG BANK checking account, then the ATM system must display, "You must have a checking account with BIG BANK to purchase a book of stamps at this ATM."
	Event driven or action enabled	When <optional preconditions> <trigger>, the <system> must <system response>.	When the book of stamps is provided to the ATM Customer, the ATM system must debit the ATM Customer's BIG BANK checking account by the price of the purchase.
		These are sometimes classified as a functional requirement with a restriction.	
Business rules (definitional)	Calculation	Calculate <function> of <what> by <how>.	Calculate the daily average number of books of stamps sold at each ATM machine by region.
	Facts and inferences (data related)	A <data entity> has <optionality and cardinality> <relationship> <data entity>.	An ATM Customer has one to many assigned BIG BANK checking accounts.
		If <optional preconditions>, then the <data field> is changed to <variable>.	If the ATM customer has a premium BIG BANK checking account, then the ATM card code will be set to "premium ATM customer" for access to additional options.
Nonfunctional	Deployment	The <system> will be <quality attribute type> <description of attribute with restrictions>.	The ATM System will be recoverable from system failures within 4 hours of failure detection.
	Environment or operation		
	Development environment	The <providers for the system> will assure <system> will <quality attribute description>.	The ATM vendor will assure the ATM will use bandwidth according to service level agreement metrics.

which makes changes easier to manage than with predictive approaches. Similar to the adaptive approach, there is a backlog that is prioritized, but usually it is structured according to a product roadmap with multiple releases reaching a full product release goal.

Illustrated in Figure 3.9, use cases are often the tool to define stakeholder and functional requirements in a hybrid approach. Use cases describe the interaction with the product or system solution and are structured as one goal to be accomplished per *actor*. The actor can be a person or, if automated, an application or system that does the interacting. Use cases can be easily packaged in different ways and can be structured in ways to be independent for ease of movement between releases. If we take the airline kiosk scenario, you can assume that the kiosk is used by ticketed customers (actors) to accomplish certain goals when interacting with the airline kiosk (system). Those goals could be to: check in baggage, pay for extra bags, verify reservation, choose seat, get boarding pass, etc. Each could be a use case describing the interaction in a step-by-step main flow, without exceptions. Extensions to the use case will allow for more steps to address exceptions that might occur and any alternate steps to the main flow. Further detail on the use case technique will be provided in Chapter 8.

Agile, an example adaptive approach, represents requirements as user stories. As described earlier, user stories are single statements of requirements in a structured format. User stories reside in the product backlog where they are ranked and get more detailed as they get moved to the top, just-in-time elaboration for the next sprint. The product backlog has boundaries and those boundaries are established by the product owner. The scope of the product backlog can be the boundaries of a project, a functional area, or whatever the product owner decides, and usually aligns to some established budget. When additions or changes happen to the product backlog (known as *grooming*), those changes are made continuously by the product owner—the decision maker for all changes. User stories that stay ranked on the bottom may eventually be deleted.

There is another scope boundary that is more critical, that of the iteration—the sprint backlog. Top ranked user stories are selected to be evaluated in sprint planning to determine if they can be completed in one sprint within the time (2–4 weeks), resource constraints (7–9 team members) and known velocity of the team (performance). User story size and tasks are discussed as a team, and determinations of what will be able to be managed within the sprint is a team decision. Although an agile team does not have a PM to manage trade-offs, there is a Scrum Master whose role is to facilitate team discussions. There can also be a higher-level roadmap of sprints that might require incremental builds (implementing features one by one) and iterative builds (starting with a partial feature and then building that one feature up). The product owner may structure the product backlog into *themes* to organize user stories in a way that indicates whether an increment has been completed. This kind of organization and planning is a necessity if agile must also intersect with packaged releases for other dependent product rollouts.

The adaptive approach makes it easy for the BA to accept change. Changes can happen every day with little impact because of the way adaptive projects are structured. The BA can help the most with: (1) asking value questions about new user stories to help rank them properly; (2) communicating changes to strategy, vision, or roadmaps that will affect the product backlog; and (3) acting as the liaison between other projects, releases, and governance entities to communicate impacts of changes both ways.

Addressing the Time Expectation Gap

Time is a large variant between the life-cycle approaches. Figure 3.10 provides a quick look at some typical times for the predictive, hybrid, and adaptive approaches. Each life-cycle approach iterates the stages of a life cycle differently. In the predictive approach, the life cycle is waterfall—very linear, with no iteration. This example shows a typical timeline of 7–24 months. The hybrid approach has the analysis, design, and a prototype conducted in the first few months for the complete scope, but then splits up the scope into releases that are timed every four months, during which the rest of the stages take place. Finally, the adaptive approach conducts all stages in multiple iterations with each iteration occurring within a two-week to one-month period. Now this is where versatility comes in. Notice the affect on the analysis activities. That is why the predictive approach is called *predictive*.

As a BA, the adaptive approach is much easier when dealing with time because the time is set—only the scope changes. So, you never ask for more time. You manage the very small scope to

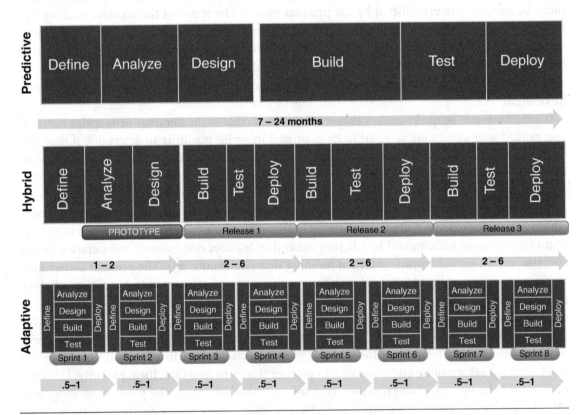

Figure 3.10   Life-cycle approach time structures

fit the fixed time frame in the sprint based on the selected user stories from the product backlog. Not much negotiation needed there.

With the predictive approach, you will consistently have to assess how long it will take you to do your activities. You must predict how long it will take to do analysis, starting with the initial estimates in a business case or charter, then again in planning, and finally at checkpoints within analysis. There is a lot of collaboration, more likely negotiation, and some influencing in order to get the time that you need. If you don't ask for it, you won't get the time you need to do a proper analysis. This is important for all predictive and hybrid approaches, although the hybrid approach may be more flexible because scope can be moved to the next release.

The following list includes some hints and tips to consider regarding time and schedule:

- Know if the integrated project plans are duration or effort driven. This tells us whether it is important to track schedule or hours.
- Ask for milestones that need to be met, including not only those you must meet but also those that others must meet that impact you.
- Account for your stakeholder time constraints and availability—those on whom you depend. If you can't interview a key stakeholder because he or she is on vacation for a month, is that going to hurt the project?
- Don't forget to account for reviews, approvals, etc.

APPROACH INTEGRATION ACROSS PROJECTS

The larger the enterprise and variances in project types, the more likely approaches will vary. This can introduce challenges for a BA who is working on multiple projects or working with other BAs using different approaches. If there is a level of coordination needed at the program level, then that coordinated effort needs to exist. BAs can coordinate business analysis activities by creating a requirement management plan at the program level. PMs are responsible for coordinating the touchpoints between their project and others. A program manager may be assigned to coordinate this effort into a high-level milestone plan. In an environment where Scrum is used, there is a Scrum of Scrums process to address that coordination across teams, but to be successful, there should only be one product backlog.[7]

We have looked at the comparison of three life-cycle approaches: predictive, hybrid, and adaptive. Each can also vary as to how we look at scope, schedule, resources, value, quality, change, risk, and our all-important stakeholders! But it doesn't end there. Next, we will dig even deeper into those things that influence how versatile we have to be—deeper into uniqueness and the special characteristics of any initiative or project we are engaged in.

SUMMARY

- The BA must have a good understanding of the generic SLC stages that are common to all life-cycle approaches and the variations of how those stages are performed within each life-cycle approach: predictive, hybrid, and adaptive.
- A predictive life-cycle approach is ideal when requirements are stable, have predictable outcomes, quality needs are critical, and the business impact requires more control and transparency. This approach is linear in nature.
- The hybrid life-cycle approach is an approach that can have varied combinations of predictive and adaptive approaches. It is less linear, with overlapping stages, emphasizes use of prototypes, and is evolutionary.
- The adaptive life-cycle approach is ideal when the requirements are more volatile and there is a high level of uncertainty with a lower level of quality expectations. This is a highly collaborative approach and more flexible to meet changing needs.
- Requirement attributes such as priority, complexity, and volatility may be approached differently in each life-cycle approach.
- The predictive life-cycle approach assumes *all-in* for requirements scope until requirements are prioritized, constraints or tolerances are applied (e.g., budget) through negotiations, and finally the elimination of those requirements that can't be done to establish a *baseline*.
- For the adaptive life-cycle approach (agile), the scope of the product backlog can be the boundaries of a project, a functional area, or whatever the product owner decides, and usually aligns to some established budget. Requirements are ranked. There is another scope boundary that is more critical in the adaptive approach—that of the iteration (the sprint backlog). Top ranked user stories are selected to be evaluated in sprint planning to determine if they can be completed in one iteration within the time (2–4 weeks), resource constraints (7–9 team members), and known velocity of the team (performance).
- The hybrid life-cycle approach is similar to the adaptive approach in that there's a backlog that is prioritized, but usually it is structured according to a product roadmap with multiple releases reaching a full product release goal.
- For the predictive, hybrid, and adaptive approaches, each iterates the stages of a life cycle differently.

QUESTIONS

1. If your project had the following characteristics, which life-cycle approach would be the best fit and why? Would you consider any variations to the approach and why?

    - Unknown legal requirements
    - Global initiative with users in five different countries and three languages

- Takes 18 months
- Has an enterprise impact

_____

_____

_____

_____

2. In the predictive life-cycle approach for the evaluate solution stage, what are some of the challenges that were identified in the example for Company X?

_____

_____

_____

_____

3. Identify the life-cycle approach that would most likely use this form of a written requirement:

a. Use case

_____

b. User story

_____

c. SMART business requirement

_____

d. Business epic

_____

e. Decision table for business rules

_____

f. Alternate paths and exceptions

_____

4. (a) Which combination of prototype types, see Figures 3.7 and 3.8, would be best for the following scenario:

   Sally is running a workshop with a small group of stakeholders from the sales team and Joe, one of the developers. She decided that it would be best to show the sales team how some of their requirements might be addressed in the new system. She plans to step through several PowerPoint drawings of web pages that she worked on with Joe.

   _____

   _____

   (b) Could you apply all four types of prototypes in one hybrid life cycle?

   _____

   _____

   _____

5. Explain how requirement volatility might affect the solution design.

   _____

   _____

   _____

NOTES

1. Royce, Winston W. (August 26, 1970). "*Managing the Development of Large Software Systems: Concepts and Techniques.*" Proceedings of IEEE WESCON. Nine original relevant pages online at: http://leadinganswers.typepad.com/leading_answers/files/original_water fall_paper_winston_royce.pdf.
2. Martin, James. (1991). *Rapid Application Development.* New York, NY: Macmillan.
3. Rational Software. (1998, revised 11/2001). "Rational Unified Process: Best Practices for Software Development Teams." Archived white paper. www.ibm.com/developerworks/rational/libary/content.
4. www.agilemanifesto.org.
5. Leffingwell, Dean. (2011). *Agile Software Requirements: Lean Requirements Practices for Teams, Programs, and the Enterprise.* p. 465. New York, NY: Addison-Wesley.
6. Clegg, Dai. (1994). Originated from Dynamic Software Development Method (DSDM).
7. https://www.scrum-institute.org/multiteam_coordination_and_planning.php.

4

STEP THREE—CONSIDER UNIQUENESS

"Although the chef and the cook both start with an initial recipe, the chef's expertise allows for the creation of a full menu by making necessary changes and adaptions based on elements such as customer feedback and tolerance for changes to the menu, customer cost constraints, the need for innovation, available equipment, etc. But the owner and chef may identify many smaller changes that can be done incrementally, such as modifying a menu item each week to check the reaction with a small focus group of patrons."—Chapter One

Business analysis experts can adjust activities performed based on many variables. Just as they must translate unique product needs into unique solutions, it is just as important to translate unique work needs into unique approaches. We have discussed the different life-cycle approaches, but to take it a step further, we must look at the different characteristics of the project or initiative to develop the best business analysis approach. In this chapter we will look at several key influencers such as different best practice models and areas of focus for business analysis approaches.

BEST PRACTICE MODELS

There are various models in the industry that can provide a checklist of items to consider when determining the best business analysis approach. For illustration purposes, it may be useful to tell you a story regarding the various best practices that I have used throughout the years.

When working as a consultant at Coopers & Lybrand, within the quality and risk management group, the director of that group (sometime in the mid-1990s) ran a brainstorming session to develop a framework that we wanted to use for clients, especially one where we were providing consulting services for their program management group to improve their project management processes. That same director was also the director of the methodology group, then called Summit-D, an internally used methodology that was also sold as a product to clients. What came out of that session was a simple framework that the director decided to call the Seven Keys to

Success™. Each key could be managed differently depending on other influencing factors that we will discuss further in this section. This framework was consistently used on all internal projects for assessments and was meaningful to management for reporting purposes. The framework was integrated into the internal methodology, which then transitioned into a methodology called Ascendant. Ownership moved from Coopers & Lybrand to PricewaterhouseCoopers (PwC) when a merger between the two took place in 1998. This framework and methodology have since been trademarked by IBM, which acquired the consulting entity of PwC in 2002. Throughout my career, this framework was used as a checklist for all proposals, status reporting, and determinations of what might influence the project approach. Over the years, I adapted the keys by forming them into questions:

1. How committed are *stakeholders*?
2. How well do *business benefits* need to be realized and managed?
3. How well do the *delivery organization's benefits* need to be realized and managed?
4. How well can you predict the *work and schedule*?
5. How predictable and realistic is the *product scope* and can it be managed?
6. Can the *team* realistically be high performing?
7. Are there *risks* that need to be responded to?

While at PwC, continuing in the practices of both business analysis and project management, getting my project management certification became a critical career choice. During that process, as with other certification process experiences, there was validation of doing the right things to progress and grow. There was also the great benefit of the certification leading to learning new things that were applied to future projects. But my real passion became business analysis, so to add to this consultant's credibility, a new certification that was available out of Toronto and offered by the International Institute of Business Analysis (IIBA®), was pursued. Continuing the learning process, a new framework was introduced by the IIBA in version 3 of the *BABOK® Guide* called the Business Analysis Core Concept Model™ (BACCM™)[1] that was similar to the Seven Keys to Success. This IIBA framework is just as important to me as a best practice model when considering a business analysis approach.

BACCM

The BACCM is a conceptual framework with six core concepts: change, need, solution, stakeholder, value, and context. They are used to consider the quality and completeness of the work that we do as business analysts (BAs). Each of these core concepts should be considered for business analysis activities and continuously re-evaluated. Each has a relationship with the others, as illustrated in Figure 4.1a. To get an idea as to how they might relate to one another, consider this statement:

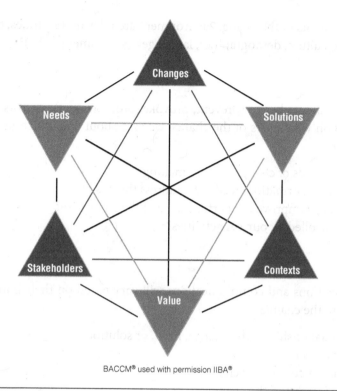

BACCM® used with permission IIBA®

Figure 4.1a   BACCM

"The improvement in our credit process of providing additional information from other sources (change) will increase the value perceived by some of our customers using the credit process (stakeholders) because they will likely want to buy our add-on features based on the fact that our competitors don't have that information integrated into their process yet (context)."

But because BACCM is conceptual, it may be difficult to understand how it can be applied to identify and manage business analysis activities. As with the Seven Keys to Success, one way to understand these core concepts is to form them into questions.

Context

This is where decisions need to be made regarding what is most important and relevant to the change:

1. What is the context that we and the solution are in?
2. What circumstances influence, or are influenced by, the change?

3. What components of the change environment are relevant (attitudes, technology, beliefs, competitors, culture, demographics, languages, governments, etc.)?

Change

Everything we do is about change (prevent, provoke, promote, etc.). As BAs, we need to adjust our activities based on what parts of the change we care about and which parts we can manage through our activities:

1. What are the kinds of changes we are making?
2. What is the transformation needed to address the need?
3. Does the change improve the performance of the enterprise?
4. Can it be controlled by our BA activities?

Stakeholder

Stakeholders' expectations and communications will vary based on their impact, influence, and interests as related to the change:

1. Who has a relationship to the change, need, or solution?
2. Who is impacted by the change?
3. Who has influence over the change?
4. Who has an interest in the change?
5. How would you group the stakeholders based on their relationships to the change?

Value

The definition and the importance of *value* will vary by stakeholder:

1. What do stakeholders consider to be of value?
2. What is the worth, importance, or usefulness to each stakeholder within a context?
3. Are there any losses, risks, or costs that would decrease the value?
4. Can the value be directly measured (tangible)?

Needs

The needs that should be addressed by a potential solution will vary by individual stakeholders:

1. What are the needs we are trying to satisfy?
2. What problem or opportunity are we addressing?
3. What enhances the value of the change?
4. What motivates the stakeholders to make the change?

Solution

Many solutions may exist to meet the needs of stakeholders. The BA must consider more than one solution and help stakeholders decide on the best solution:

1. What is the specific way to satisfy one or more of the needs within a context?
2. What problem(s) do the solution options resolve?
3. What solution enables stakeholders to take advantage of an opportunity?

These core concepts can also be addressed within each of the *BABOK® Guide* six knowledge areas (KAs). These KAs include:

- Strategic Analysis
- Business Analysis and Planning
- Elicitation and Collaboration
- Requirements Analysis and Design Definition
- Requirements Life-Cycle Management
- Solution Evaluation

Each KA represents a specific area of business analysis techniques and provides a basis for defining business analysis tasks. The core concepts are a great guide to distinguishing the depth and breadth of those business analysis tasks.

Applying BACCM

Strategy Analysis Scenario

For insight into the *BABOK® Guide* Strategic Analysis KA, we will relate to a real-life situation that involves the development of a business case for a customer relationship management (CRM) consulting practice. CRM is a category of integrated software solutions that improves how companies interact and build relationships with their customers. A consulting company wanted to build a practice to provide CRM as a service to clients by providing all the resources to design, build, and implement a solution that would meet the unique needs of their clients. Resources included the people to do the work, and the technology (hardware and software) needed to make it operational. For the Strategy Analysis KA, the focus was on defining the future state, transitioning to that future state, and aligning to other strategies.

To understand the *context* of the scenario, the implementation of a CRM practice is part of the overall strategy for this consulting firm. The strategy includes a long-term vision for an overall rollout to U.S. clients and all industries. This change would impact client attitudes toward CRM. Attitudes would need to shift from looking at CRM from a restricted view of only a sales tool to looking at it with a more extended view to measure a customer's value and ensure that all organizations have the same access to customer information for quick and informed decision making.

Interviews with executive sponsors help to refine the CRM vision within the practice and uncover objectives specifically stating how CRM will improve the client organization's decision-making process.

This *change* must be looked at from both the delivery organization's perspective and that of the client being served. The business case addresses the change from both the cost/benefit to the consulting company *and* the cost/benefit to the client to help in the proposal process. Also, the long-term vision is too large of an initiative to manage within a business case. Could they focus on what is most important in the short term to reach their long-term vision? Even though the business case described the long-term vision, the scope is being reduced to consider a more practical, phased implementation. The first phase rollout will start with the Midwest region financial industry, where there had been some successful implementations. The second phase would consider rollouts to other U.S. regions with priorities based on client profiles for the financial industries within those regions. With proven successes, the third phase would then expand into various other industries which would be addressed with a separate business case. External client stakeholders will be midsize or larger for this service offering consideration (revenue of $10 million or more). The external client company's needs, and the importance of maintaining client relationships, may introduce unique solution offerings. Assumptions need to become visible to manage expectations around changes in scope, even as early as the business case!

There were four key groups of *stakeholders* to be considered as part of the business case. The first group was the consulting company's executive team. This included the sponsor, a directing operational partner, and the management team reporting to him. They had the vision, but also represented the external client. The second group was the architecture team. They were the CRM technology and enterprise architecture experts. The third group was the solution delivery team, the CRM application experts. Because the business case is focused on the cost/benefit, the business analysis approach must focus on making assumptions visible. Rather than requirements, the key with this business case is to uncover scope assumptions made when cost estimates were provided and to make them visible for verification. These assumptions would encompass both project and product scope assumptions and later, turn into questions that would lead to more detailed requirements with a recommended solution design. Each stakeholder group has their own assumptions, but those assumptions were not in alignment, requiring stakeholder meetings to resolve the gaps. Additionally, the BA's role required that assumptions were aligned to product scope, benefit measures were more tangible, and various alternatives were clearly communicated. In this situation, enough business analysis time was allocated so that stakeholder groups agreed on the assumptions associated with each of the solution alternatives.

As presented earlier, from a delivery organization standpoint, the cost/benefit (*value*) of implementing such a practice must be addressed within the business case, in addition to the value from the client perspective. What is the consulting practice going to gain by having some standard CRM solutions to address different industries, building partnerships with software and hardware vendors, building up resource capabilities internally, etc.? What do each of our internal stakeholders value? New market entry? By when? Competitive advantage? Against whom? Revenue growth? By how much? What are the profit expectations by type of client? To answer these questions, we must also determine the value propositions (further explained in Chapter 6), the client view of value by client type, and what is needed to help sell CRM through the proposal process by connecting client needs to value. So, business analysis activities must address value from all stakeholder groups—internally and externally—within the business case. In the business case, the BA will need to look at how value can be measured in a more tangible way. Often, to make it more tangible, more detail is required. The BA can take objectives or the value propositions and identify what is to be measured, the metrics needed to measure it, and the method used to measure in order to determine if it needs to be compared to other measures and to monitor according to the prescribed method. More context needs to go around the measure for it to be tangible and useful. To illustrate this concept, think about the measurement of blood pressure. How useful is the measure on its own? What metrics are useful (diastolic versus systolic)? Is it more useful to know more about the patient (history), the time of day it was taken, whether they were standing or sitting, how it compares to others with similar histories, etc.? For the CRM business case, it was important to collaborate with all stakeholder groups to get a good understanding of what tangible items were important enough to add the cost of implementing a process to monitor. Looking at the external client, it was also important to identify suggested measures for clients that could be provided in the proposals for client solution alternatives. Warning: Don't measure just to measure. Be very selective. Once operational, it can be very wasteful if not used!

The business case requires an assessment of how *needs* are currently being met, or not, and the risks associated with meeting the requirements. In this case, a problem statement was written to elaborate on the problem in a structured way. The problem statement included the following high-level needs:

- Avoid inconsistencies in CRM proposals by standardizing the CRM process
- Reduce CRM proposal response times by proactively predicting industry needs and building standard client solution sets
- Improve CRM competencies within the organization by providing a structured CRM on-boarding process, making external coaches available, and providing a training program
- Recognize internal support for CRM—this may require a restructure of the consulting company's organization

Risks included:

- The CRM competitive environment was changing with new players increasing competition
- Pricing the service incorrectly and losing in the bidding process
- Obtaining needed contractual partnerships with vendors

- The need to interface with other products required additional expertise in many different product areas without the needed expertise existing in-house

Several of the needs listed here influenced the business analysis approach. The approach had to consider current state business capability analysis with metrics and key performance indicators (KPIs), market analysis had to be conducted, and vendor assessments needed to be completed to supplement capability gaps. A business model canvas[2] was generated to assess each client type. The architecture team contributed CRM current state viewpoints for both the business architecture and technology architecture for several clients.

Multiple *solution* alternatives were provided based on different client (stakeholder group) needs. One additional alternative was added at the last minute—the cost of doing nothing. This alternative highlighted a reality to stakeholders that something had to happen quickly in this space. Gap analysis was conducted between various existing client environments based on the architectures provided and on solution alternatives to help assess impacts during transition. A SWOT (strengths, weaknesses, opportunities, and threats) analysis and transition roadmaps were included within each solution option to help in the selection of the top two solutions. A cost/benefit analysis was connected to the top two solutions.

In summary, for the CRM business case scenario, here are just a few business analysis activities and techniques that were uncovered and should be explicitly addressed by considering the core concepts:

- Interview executive sponsors to refine the CRM vision within the practice and uncover objectives specifically stating how CRM will improve the client organization's decision-making process
- Look at change from both the delivery organization's perspective and that of the client who was being served when performing activities
- Ensure assumptions are aligned and agreed upon by stakeholders for the product scope and make assumptions visible for client validation
- Identify value propositions by stakeholder that will have tangible measures
- Define current state business capability analysis with metrics and KPIs
- Perform market analysis and vendor assessments
- Develop business model canvas by client type
- Provide a *cost-of-doing-nothing* solution alternative

This is one KA as an example for uncovering business analysis activities using the BACCM. One more KA to look at that demonstrates the application of this model is Elicitation and Collaboration (E&C).

Elicitation and Collaboration Scenario

When we think of business analysis, we often start by thinking about how we will get the requirements. Who are the sources of the requirements? Will our stakeholders agree on what the problem is that we are trying to solve? Will they be cooperative? Will they *push* their own agendas? The E&C KA addresses these questions. To apply the core concepts and to illustrate this KA, we will look at a business process transformation initiative at a telephone company.

To provide some *context*, this company was going through a transformation requiring the consolidation of five billing systems into one common billing system. Even though the main billing functions were the same, there were major differences due to many years of state localized customization. The five billing systems were built on different platforms, had different localized business rules, had different interfaces to other systems, and had a multitude of reporting driven by the personal preferences of stakeholders over the years. The consolidation triggered political agendas. Stakeholders were strongly aligned to each billing system and took strong positions that their processes were better than the others. Having a process for addressing conflicts and working through the political challenges was critical. A formal procedure for decision making was created to help get to a consensus quickly. Collaboration techniques, such as facilitated workshops, were planned with the use of several decision-making techniques.

This *change* also included consolidation of manual procedures, interfaces, and reporting with underlying enterprise architectures (business, information, and technology). The current state had very dispersed systems. Mainframes were from different vendors and platforms. Years of enhancements and the lack of data architectures evolved into a multitude of *spaghetti* lines of data passing through many systems. It was difficult to know where data originated. System interfaces were in the hundreds for each location. Only a conceptual level of current-state processes could be documented. The focus was on the future state and the need for a team of subject matter experts (SMEs) from each location to dive into the details with a transition plan for the future state. The future state was developed through a series of requirement workshops bringing in empowered stakeholders to make consolidated process decisions. A process owner responsibility matrix was critical to define accountabilities.

Because of the size of the initiative and the elongated time to delivery, it was important to collaborate with many levels of stakeholders. Collaboration started with a defined steering committee to help make major decisions regarding consolidation, especially since it was a very politically hot initiative. The next level of stakeholders was made up of the operational and functional managers. They had to make sure that resources did the work, assign the needed current-state SMEs, make more detailed future-state decisions within their empowerment (process accountability), and provide assigned resources from their areas with clearly defined roles to help them be successful. This commitment from managers supported the project managers (PMs) and BAs. The lowest-level stakeholders were the actual users of the system. A formal communication plan was needed for proper communications at the right level of management, at the right level of detail, and for the right reasons.

Each stakeholder level had different *needs*. As an example, stakeholders at the executive level wanted to reduce the cost of supporting five different billing systems. Managers were concerned with the operational controls needed within each billing system. Users wanted access to calculations so they could be explained to the customer. There were many more requirements, such as solution requirements from other solution delivery resources, including how the system or solution addressed other stakeholder needs and quality attributes of the system, the need to run on a platform for improved performance, the ability to scale for a variety of volumes, and having a structure to easily customize in the future.

Each level of stakeholder had a different perspective and level of detail needed for the requirements. Elicitation doesn't happen only once. E&C occurs throughout the life of an initiative and deals with multiple types of stakeholders. So, in this case, business requirements from the executive team were elicited early during business case development to be included not only in the business case but also in the multiple project charters triggered from the business case. Stakeholder requirements were elicited during scope definition (addendum to project charter), and solution requirements were addressed during the analysis phase—at which time the stakeholder requirements were elaborated.

Value was part of the conversation during elicitation to identify the importance of the requirement. When consolidating, there is much *fluff* that goes into legacy systems. Features get added but are never removed when their usefulness goes away. They are forgotten. Stakeholders who wanted that feature are long gone. Other stakeholders may find something better or ask for add-ons. During elicitation interviews and workshops there needs to be a conversation as to: "Why is this so important to you?"; "What use does this have?"; and "How does this contribute to the final outcome?"

At the time this scenario took place, user stories were not yet utilized as a business analysis technique. We have since learned that user stories are a great way to elaborate on the value or benefit of the need. In this scenario, the focus was on writing textual requirements supporting business process models. But with the understanding that there is a need to keep the future state simple and meet a short time frame, it was necessary to prioritize and focus on the most valuable features. During E&C, less than 50% of the current-state features were carried over to the future state. Post implementation of the first release, some lower priority features slowly crept back in, but they were formally addressed in future releases.

It is difficult to conduct elicitation activities without having some solution ideas surface, especially in workshops with different telephone company stakeholders. As the facilitator, ideas were captured as *solution ideas* and retained for design consideration. But, it was still necessary to probe with questioning to uncover requirements that drove stakeholders to those solution ideas. Yet, there is no reason why these ideas couldn't be reviewed once all the requirements have been analyzed.

In summary, for the billing system scenario, here are just a few business analysis activities and techniques that were uncovered considering the core concepts:

- Because of the political nature of the initiatives, a formal decision-making process with several decision-making techniques was necessary to reach quick consensus (context).
- Requirements were needed from each level of stakeholders and from their unique perspective at different times throughout the life cycle (need).
- Value was constantly addressed through probing questions during elicitation: "Why is this so important to you?"; "What use does this have?"; and "How does this contribute to the final outcome?"

- Prioritization techniques were used to ensure the most valuable items were addressed early (value).
- Stakeholders were diverse and distributed, experts and owners needed to be clearly defined by using an accountability matrix and communications plan (stakeholders).
- Solution ideas were captured for use in solution design discussions (solutions).

This is just one more KA example for uncovering business analysis activities using the BACCM. Hopefully, these examples provide insight on their application to your real-world experiences.

AREAS OF FOCUS

As a BA, starting up any initiative, program, or project is a challenge. It can be overwhelming until you dig in and get a good understanding of the work and product scope. As a consultant, I have been exposed to hundreds of different types: different industries, different functional areas, different maturity levels in their methods, different cultures, etc. We know as we gain experience that we have to research and probe to understand all of those *differences* before deciding on our activities and how to conduct those activities.

Perspectives

The IIBA addressed these variations of activities within the *BABOK® Guide* in a section called Perspectives. Think of a perspective as a lens through which the business analysis practitioner views his or her work. One or many perspectives could apply to your assignment. *BABOK® Guide* perspectives include: Agile, Information Technology (IT), Business Architecture, Business Process Management, and Business Intelligence (BI). Previously, we addressed *agile* as an adaptive life-cycle approach example and business architecture as a strategic mindset for the BA with a possible career role as a business architect. Figure 4.1b illustrates the application of BACCM to agile. If assigned to an agile project you may look at each of the elements shown in Figure 4.1b to see how the approach might be unique or use it as a guide to learn about agile. When sitting down with the PM, you might ask, "How are changes managed in agile?" Since each of the elements drives BA activities, it is a great opportunity to leverage the elements as a tool for probing.

IT touches almost every project where there is automation, so most scenarios provided in this book have this component. For fully technology-driven solutions, Figure 4.1c assesses this IT area of focus as applied to the BACCM with a few additional suggestions. Note that for the element *Needs*, the abundance of requirements will likely be nonfunctional, but there is a danger if the change is not accessed diligently for the impact that it might have on the business environment. How many times has a business person heard, "Don't worry . . . you won't notice any difference," and the next day they can't perform any of their work because the system is holding them up?

The other two perspectives, Business Process Management and BI, will be addressed as *areas of focus*, affecting our business analysis activities. Figure 4.1d and 4.1e have been included to address

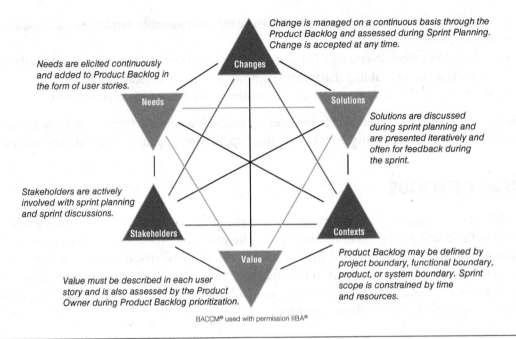

Change is managed on a continuous basis through the Product Backlog and assessed during Sprint Planning. Change is accepted at any time.

Needs are elicited continuously and added to Product Backlog in the form of user stories.

Solutions are discussed during sprint planning and are presented iteratively and often for feedback during the sprint.

Stakeholders are actively involved with sprint planning and sprint discussions.

Product Backlog may be defined by project boundary, functional boundary, product, or system boundary. Sprint scope is constrained by time and resources.

Value must be described in each user story and is also assessed by the Product Owner during Product Backlog prioritization.

BACCM® used with permission IIBA®

Figure 4.1b   Agile and BACCM

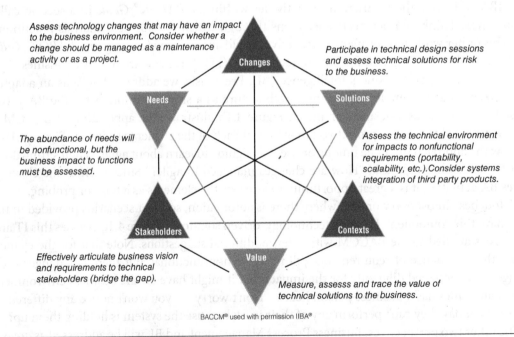

Assess technology changes that may have an impact to the business environment. Consider whether a change should be managed as a maintenance activity or as a project.

Participate in technical design sessions and assess technical solutions for risk to the business.

The abundance of needs will be nonfunctional, but the business impact to functions must be assessed.

Assess the technical environment for impacts to nonfunctional requirements (portability, scalability, etc.). Consider systems integration of third party products.

Effectively articulate business vision and requirements to technical stakeholders (bridge the gap).

Measure, assesss and trace the value of technical solutions to the business.

BACCM® used with permission IIBA®

Figure 4.1c   Information Technology (IT) and BACCM

each as they apply to the BACCM. To further define areas of focus, I want to share how this was approached in a methodology—a work breakdown structure (WBS)—used to build project plans in my past.

Routes and the WBS

When at PwC, as mentioned earlier, there existed a methodology called Summit-D. In that methodology there were *routes*—variations to the standard predictive (what we called waterfall) methodology. Those Summit-D variations included:

1. An adaptive method (in 1997 and pre-agile)
2. A business process modeling method
3. A data warehousing (which included BI) method
4. An enterprise resource packages or large package implementations method, and several more.

You could pick one or more routes based on the characteristics of your client initiative, and then download the activities into project management planning software. There were many generic roles pre-assigned to activities. The Summit-D team also had captured a history of metrics

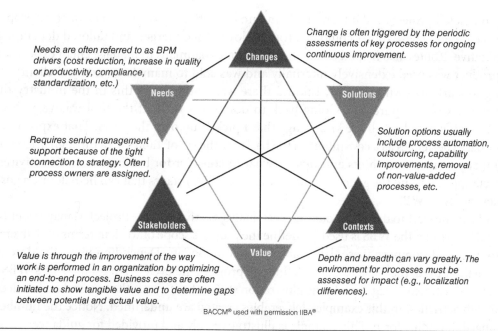

BACCM® used with permission IIBA®

Figure 4.1d   Business Process Management (BPM) and BACCM

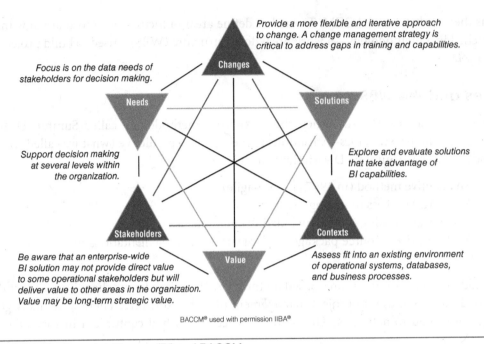

Provide a more flexible and iterative approach to change. A change management strategy is critical to address gaps in training and capabilities.

Focus is on the data needs of stakeholders for decision making.

Support decision making at several levels within the organization.

Explore and evaluate solutions that take advantage of BI capabilities.

Be aware that an enterprise-wide BI solution may not provide direct value to some operational stakeholders but will deliver value to other areas in the organization. Value may be long-term strategic value.

Assess fit into an existing environment of operational systems, databases, and business processes.

BACCM® used with permission IIBA®

Figure 4.1e   Business Intelligence (BI) and BACCM

from completed projects and integrated them into the activities to assist in estimating proposals more accurately. These routes could be brought down, then merged and tailored depending on the initiative. Routes also helped create more accurate roadmaps to manage client expectations. The product was used extensively internally and was sold to many large external clients. After leaving to start my own company, I found there was nothing like this in the industry that a small business could purchase. Going back to doing this without the tool was very difficult but still doable based on all the knowledge that I picked up over the years. That exposure, and additional experiences as a consultant, is the basis for the set of Tables 4.1a through 4.1c (shown later) that provides some hints and tips on what to consider for business analysis activities by life-cycle approach and the generic solution life cycle (SLC) stages that can help define a custom business analysis WBS.

A WBS is the start to defining your business analysis activities. The Project Management Institute (PMI) says that the WBS is used "to define the project's scope of work in terms of deliverables and to further decompose these deliverables into components. Depending upon the decomposition method used, the WBS can also define the project's life cycle."[3] An example of a WBS as a diagram is illustrated in Figure 4.2. The illustration shows the stages at the top, and each is decomposed with activities. In this example, deliverables created are underlined. Notice the numbering is arranged in outline form. This example is illustrative only and provided for guidance.

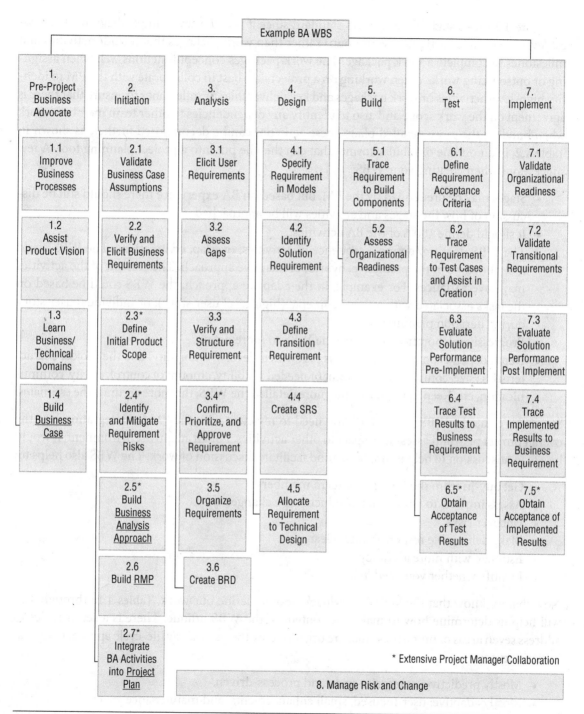

Figure 4.2 Example business analysis WBS

Figure 4.2 varies slightly from PMI's standard since it is a two-level simple diagram. The lowest level is written as activities (verb noun) rather than work packages that include activities and milestones to complete a work package. The work packages concept functions well when assigning or outsourcing work. When working on a project, it is best to collaborate with the PM to identify high-level activities or work packages and key deliverables or milestones to ensure that there is agreement on the work scope and also to identify any dependencies to other team members' work when building the more detailed plan. These activities can be decomposed further, as shown in Table 4.2, in an outline or tabular format that can then be put into a project planning tool. A few suggestions when creating your WBS:

- Stages may be predefined by the PM, but based on BA experience there should still be discussion of how the stages and activities will be approached.
- It should define 100% of the BA activities.
- The WBS does *not* define a sequence of activities, overlap, or iterations. The WBS could look the same in the predictive, hybrid, or adaptive approach. The content of the activities may have variances. For example, in the adaptive approach, the WBS could be based on the tasks associated with a theme, an epic (high-level user story), or individual user story during iteration planning.
- Progressive elaboration will drive the WBS to more detail.
- Depth depends on when the WBS is performed (level of ambiguity) and the project characteristics (size, complexity)—amount of needed visibility, amount of control, clarity, communication, etc. Keep in mind that the more detailed the WBS, the more accurate the estimates.

So, you've created a WBS, now what? You need to review it with the PM for integration into the overall project plan and assess its impact to other activities. For an adaptive environment, it would be a team discussion to help estimate size and facilitate discussion of work. The WBS also helps to:

- Get buy-in from the PM and/or team members
- Assess impacts to work when product scope changes
- Uncover risks
- Make deliverable responsibilities clear
- Estimate with more accuracy
- Identify whether you need help

Now that we know that the WBS is a valuable tool to define our work, Tables 4.1a through 4.1c will help us determine how to make the content of the WBS unique. There is a set of tables to address seven areas of uniqueness that are organized by the *most-likely* life-cycle approach for that initiative type:

- Mostly predictive: enterprise-wide and process-driven
- Mostly adaptive: user-focused, small enhancements, and maintenance
- Mostly hybrid: vendor package, data-driven, and technology-driven

Table 4.2 Example BA WBS outline

1. Pre-Project Business Advocate
   1.1. Improve Business Processes
   1.2. Assist in *Product Vision* Definition
   1.3. Learn Business and Technical Domains
   1.4. Build the *Business Case*
2. Initiation
   2.1. Validate Business Case Assumptions
   2.2. Verify and Elicit Additional Business Requirements
       2.2.1. Interview Sponsor
       2.2.2. Interview Two Impacted VPs
   2.3. *Define (or Verify) Initial Product Scope in *Project Charter*
       2.3.1. Create Context Diagram for Current State
       2.3.2. Perform Stakeholder Analysis
       2.3.3. Identify High-Level Stakeholder Requirements
       2.3.4. Create Context Diagram for Future State
   2.4. *Identify and Mitigate Requirement Risks
   2.5. *Build *Business Analysis Approach*
   2.6. Build *Requirement Management Plan*
   2.7. *Integrate BA Activities into *Project Plan*
3. Analysis
   3.1. Elicit User (Stakeholder) Requirements
       3.1.1. Conduct Requirement Workshop for Business Unit 1
       3.1.2. Conduct Requirement Workshop for Business Unit 2
       3.1.3. Conduct Requirement Workshop for Business Unit 3
   3.2. Assess Gaps Between Current and Future States
   3.3. Verify and Structure (Refine) Requirements
   3.4. *Confirm, Prioritize, and Approve Requirements
   3.5. Organize Requirements into Features, Releases, or Iterations
   3.6. Create a *Business Requirements Document* or *Request for Quote/Proposal*
4. Design (Conceptual and Technical)
   4.1. Specify Requirements in Models
       4.1.1. Develop and Validate Swim Lane
       4.1.2. Develop and Validate Conceptual Data Model
   4.2. Identify Solution Requirements (Functional and Nonfunctional)
   4.3. Define Transitional Requirements
   4.4. Create a *System Requirements Specification*
   4.5. Allocate and Validate Requirements to Technical Design
5. Build
   5.1. Trace Requirements to Build Components
   5.2. Assess Organizational Readiness
6. Test
   6.1. Define Requirement Acceptance Criteria
   6.2. Trace Requirements to Test Cases and Assist in Creation
   6.3. Evaluate Solution Performance Pre-Implementation
   6.4. Trace Test Results to Business Requirements
   6.5. *Obtain Stakeholder Acceptance of Product Test Results
7. Implement
   7.1. Validate Organizational Readiness
   7.2. Validate Transitional Requirements
   7.3. Evaluate Solution Performance Post Implementation
   7.4. Trace Implemented Results to Business Requirements
   7.5. *Obtain Stakeholder Acceptance of Implemented Product
8. Manage Risk and Change (recurring)

* Extensive Project Manager Collaboration

MOSTLY PREDICTIVE TYPES

For those initiatives that are mostly predictive, the emphasis is on having a structured top-down approach. As illustrated in Table 4.1a, we will be looking at two initiative types: enterprise-wide and process-driven.

Table 4.1a   Business analysis WBS considerations for mostly predictive life-cycle approach

SLC Stage > / Initiative Type V	Concept Definition	Requirements Analysis	Conceptual and Physical Design	Acquire or Build Solution Through Evaluate and Support Solution
Mostly Predictive				
Enterprise-wide	Leverage business architecture views to assess impact; develop cost/benefit and roadmap showing approach integration; and supplement BA plans to manage risk, change, communications, and the requirement process.	Use visual modeling and decomposition techniques to break down large processes for clarity, assign process owners, facilitate workshops across business units to reduce conflicts, re-evaluate cost/benefit for alternate solutions to get to a decision, and coordinate proof-of-concepts to address high-risk areas.	Build conceptual data model and swim lanes to identify interfaces for complex areas, communicate gap analysis (impacts) to solution users, apply change management practices, and identify requirements to transition to new solution.	Allocate requirements to solution components, assist in package configurations, identify localization differences, include end-to-end validations, support live validations, and liaison between stakeholders and QA team to facilitate validation across solution components.
Process-driven	Determine impacted organizations and assess or create *as-is* process models identifying areas of opportunity, visually show through process models various solution options considering any needs for a release structure, and identify process performance metrics.	Document stakeholder and functional requirements through use cases associated with models, elicit additional requirements from use case reviews, further decompose process models to validate assumptions and uncover additional requirements, and identify additional applicable process attributes (actors, volumes, cycle time, value-added time, non-value-added activities, etc.).	Communicate gap analysis (impacts) to solution users and apply change management practices; assist in applying use cases and process definitions to user procedures and training; leverage use cases to build test cases, storyboards, and prototype scenarios.	Coordinate to assure user or process owner continued involvement, assist in allocating use cases and processes to appropriate architectural layers and solution components, and evaluate process metrics.

Enterprise-Wide

Enterprise-Wide Defined

Enterprise-wide initiatives are always a bit more complicated, a bit more political, a bit more chaotic, and a bit more stressful! But the advantages outweigh the disadvantages because they are strategic and provide great value to the business. Ultimately, who will decide what the size or impact will be and how it will be controlled is often left to some internal governance process. But what is unique about these initiatives from a business analysis perspective? These large initiatives can:

- Cross multiple business units, cultures, and geographical areas
- Require huge resource commitments with multi-layered teams
- Affect large numbers of core business processes
- Impact many internal and external systems
- Require their own governance using steering committees and program management offices
- Affect the structure of the organization
- Require enterprise-wide architectural changes

Because of the impacts and costs, a business case and/or feasibility study is likely to be needed before any approvals to move forward, and the BA may be involved in that endeavor. Architectures, such as the business architecture, can be leveraged to conduct an impact assessment. With more governance entities involved and more need for controls, there will be more formal planning documents, even for business analysis. Business analysis-defined activities must also include other plans, such as communication plans, responsibility charts defining process owners, requirement management plans, etc.

With large enterprise-wide initiatives, there is a high probability that the solution will encompass multiple approaches, such as those defined in Tables 4.1a through c. This means that the BAs must be versatile in their approaches and in their ability to select the right techniques at the right time out of their vast tool chest for all of the various activities that will be needed. For example, with large initiatives the BA is more likely to start with executive interviews and then transition to many workshops. Or there may be ambiguity in one functional area where prototyping may be necessary.

Business Analysis Tips for Large Initiatives

A few tips when dealing with these large initiatives:

- Learn to keep thinking *just-in-time*—only go as deep as you need to at that moment in time to make the decisions that need to be made.
- Consider techniques that can decompose complex functions for clarity and for structuring product scope into releases.
- If one technique isn't working, don't be afraid to try another.

- Collaborate with program managers and PMs frequently to ensure you are kept abreast of changing assumptions.
- *Lead-up* when necessary. Have the courage to share risks with plans on how to respond to them.
- Always have a clear understanding of what the decision process is for dealing with any conflicts.
- Use work-in-progress spreadsheets to analyze information (discussed further in Chapter 8).

Finally, keep that enterprise and strategic mindset. Go beyond what you think are the boundaries so that you can uncover any additional impacts or other dependencies. In the next section, we will move toward a more tactical approach, and look at smaller efforts.

Process-Driven

Process Defined

Processes define a series of steps to transform an input into an output. Make a meal—acquire some ingredients, perform some steps, and those ingredients transform into a meal (well, if you did it right, if you followed the steps that ensure success and quality). We perform processes every day, and so does the company we work for. How consistent are we at performing these processes and how often do they change? One way to evaluate processes is through modeling. There are several types of models that can be used to reflect processes. One is the functional decomposition diagram (FDD), which shows a hierarchy of how processes are composed of other processes. The FDD helps identify which processes are in scope or out of scope, and gaps between current state and future state. Other models will be discussed in Chapter 8.

Evaluating Systems with Processes

Figure 4.3 illustrates a few business activities using the FDD. It shows that systems are composed of functions and processes. When evaluating these systems, you need to determine the domain for analysis, a.k.a. system under discussion (SUD). The SUD defines the boundaries of what will be in scope for the analysis. This can be done with any process model—but Figure 4.3 shows the FDD. What is shown in the FDD for current state is the SUD. Next, the processes are evaluated to see if they will be kept, removed, added, or changed to transition to the future state. If added or changed, those processes are targeted for specific requirements.

At lower levels, processes can be detailed with use cases. Use cases show interactions with systems and their processes and detail the many steps within a process performed by a specific user (a.k.a. actor). You can also drill down on processes using other types of models and diagrams, such as swim lanes, data flow diagrams, flow charts, etc. These will be further discussed in Chapter 8. Additional process information can also be captured in process forms such as descriptions of the process, volumes, cycle times, etc.

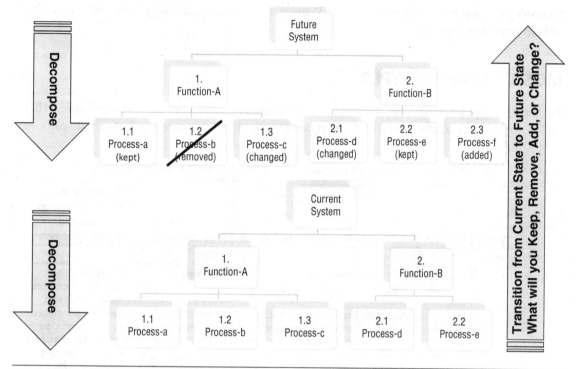

Figure 4.3 Analyzing process-focused systems

Example Process-Driven Initiatives

When working within a large enterprise, it is likely the BA will be involved in some large initiatives that are process-driven such as:

- Six Sigma initiatives work at reducing defects in manufacturing processes
- Lean initiatives examine processes to eliminate waste (non-value-added)
- Business process management focuses on improving the performance of specific processes
- Business process improvement is about redesigning processes based on finding areas of opportunity using other methods
- Business process re-engineering is a high-level strategy to improve the enterprise's work processes, improve customer service, cut the cost of operations, or other strategic objectives
- Business process outsourcing examines processes that can be contracted out to a third party

BAs also can be advisors and consultants in the area by leveraging their enterprise and strategic mindset to proactively apply the principles of many of the initiatives that were previously listed above, even at the tactical project level. Just a few words of wisdom for technology BAs: (1) don't automate a bad process, (2) not everything can be improved or provide value with technology—look at all alternatives, and (3) understand what technology solutions are available to help improve processes.

MOSTLY ADAPTIVE TYPES

For mostly adaptive approaches the emphasis is on small iterations. As illustrated in Table 4.1b, we will be looking at user-focused, small enhancements, and maintenance types of initiatives.

Table 4.1b   Business analysis WBS considerations for a mostly adaptive life-cycle approach

SLC Stage > / Initiative Type V	Concept Definition	Requirements Analysis	Conceptual and Physical Design	Acquire or Build Solution Through Evaluate and Support Solution
Mostly Adaptive				
User-focused	Conduct user experience research, understand different user classes (business vs. consumer, demographics, etc.), build primary personas, and identify design constraints and standards for user experience.	Identify user stories and usability requirements, identify areas of complexity where use cases can uncover more requirements, leverage low-fidelity usability testing (paper-based navigation) to uncover additional requirements and validate existing requirements, and coordinate more formal horizontal prototype for user experience validation.	Emphasis on designing navigation and consistent look and feel across functionality for the user, use various lightweight navigation, identify and address user skill gaps for transition to new solution, and validate site requirements have been addressed in design.	Coordinate user representation during iterative building, facilitate adherence to communicated design standards for usability, usability testing included in acceptance tests, observe users interacting with the system, bring user experience experts in for evaluations, and evaluate ongoing user feedback.
Small Enhancement and Maintenance	Ad hoc involvement, perform root cause analysis for problems and define as high-level user stories (epics), identify dependencies and alignment to strategies or other roadmaps, and rank with product owner into product backlog to schedule into iterations for active systems or group into themes (releases/projects) for less active systems.	Extract top-ranked elaborating user story during iteration planning for maintenance fixes, group into small agreed-upon iterations and identify additional requirements (business rules, nonfunctional, data, etc.) during acceptance criteria discussion, conduct storyboarding, and assist in release coordination.	Provide design constraint information from architecture teams, use lightweight models (a.k.a. model storming) in a low-fidelity form (paper or whiteboard) during iteration conversations.	Informally assist in translation of requirements, assist in demo and iterative changes, assist in testing with any external QA teams, and participate in retrospectives.

User-Focused

When we work on projects that require solutions to directly interact with users (such as portals, web apps, and mobile devices), various methods and techniques need to be considered in our business analysis approach. Figure 4.4 illustrates that we not only need to understand why the user wants to interact with the system, but also how they feel about interacting with it. On the system side, we need to focus on how we might design the system in a way to ensure that we address both empathy and needs. How do we approach it?

User-Focused Design Methods

There are many methods that address user focused designs, such as UX (user experience), user centered design (UCD), and user driven development (UDD).

UX requires effort in explicitly understanding the user and their environment, keeping them involved in the design with continuous feedback. UX is a very iterative process that emphasizes usability and making sure experts are brought in to address usability based on the specific types of users. UCD also has as heavy user involvement as UX, but it is addressed as a more interactive creation with the user and leverages user behavior data (observation, personas, web statistics, market research) as much as possible. UDD grew from lean initiatives and is already integrated with agile. UDD focuses on avoiding product waste by concentrating on the minimal viable product (MVP). The MVP centers around avoiding what most users don't want and still maximizing what we want to build to generate value to our stakeholders based on what you think, which the MVP helps validate. But it can put your reputation in jeopardy if the risk of business impact isn't managed correctly. The positives are that the MVP does give great feedback from a large group of users so you can then continue to scale up incrementally.

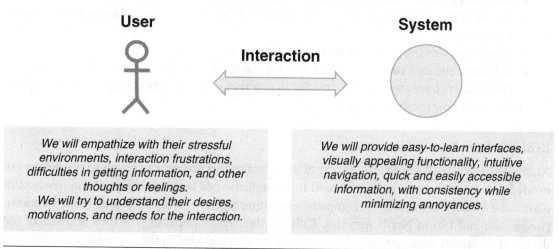

Figure 4.4   Understanding user-focused methods

Bottom line, all these methods focus on the user, and the techniques used as a BA are similar. Use of personas, observation, task analysis, and prototypes (as discussed previously) are predominately used. When creating personas, you will want to create multiple ones. For example, I was working on an electronic medical records system in which the users were doctors. You could create a persona for a "doctor", but each type of doctor requires different dialogues with the system (such as a cardiologist vs. a urologist). By limiting the persona to one version you may miss important needs, motivations, or features. But too many personas can also become confusing and hard to manage—it's a balancing act. For observations, keep in mind that there are two types. Passive observations have less impact on the user and are less likely to influence the outcomes, but active observations may be a better fit if you need to inspect the user's environment and you want the ability to ask questions as they perform their tasks. It's a trade-off and depends on the outcomes you want to achieve from the observation. Task analysis is not an observation. It is doing the research on what tasks are being performed by the user by reviewing documentation or interviewing.

User Requirement Tips

Don't forget to also utilize the all-important user interview. Below are a few tips on getting user requirements for user-focused initiatives:

- Assume you don't know anything about the user and what they do, even if you do know. Never say, "Oh, right, I already knew that." Listen and probe to understand from their perspective.
- Always ask about what they do, their tasks, and not about specific uses of software functionality. "So, tell me more about how you do that? Do you have anything that prevents you from being successful at it?"
- Ask them why what they are doing is important and what the value is to them and others.
- Ask for frustrations, pains, fears—"Why is it that the system keeps asking me for the same information!"
- When interviewing groups of users, always look for patterns.
- Ask about the user's environment, anything that hinders their tasks or adds to their stress.
- Do the users have any sense of urgency in different situations? How might that affect their tasks and how they use the system?

Example User-Focused Scenario

Another scenario to illustrate the concept of user-focused is a project that involved the delivery of newly built eLearning assets. They needed to be implemented before staffing several newly built plants at a global manufacturing company. eLearning assets were used in four main locations, two in Asia and two in North America. Cultural differences impacted the look and feel of the design and usability requirements. Therefore, a pilot was included in the approach that consisted of running the same set of requirements for one eLearning asset through the methodology used by each vendor, a different language for each, and at each location's environment. This approach uncovered several variances between the methodologies, language, and cultures, triggering the need to update and formally document the approach used at each location. Also, the use of multiple, geographically dispersed service providers introduced so many inconsistencies that a pilot was warranted.

Stakeholders varied in requirements across the locations so conflicts had to be addressed by identifying one key stakeholder decision maker. Not only would elicitation require interpreters for stakeholders, but all documentation and the eLearning assets would need to be translated into three different languages. Prototypes were conducted to test translation services to verify proper translation. Tests were added to eLearning assets to make sure that key objectives were met. Completion of assets were tracked through a newly delivered Learning Management System (LMS).

Clear priorities had to be set with various solution alternatives because of the accelerated time frames. We worked with the PMs (one per solution provider) to establish an iterative approach and had to conduct detailed tracking of assets being delivered to validate that requirements were met, especially quality attributes. This hybrid life-cycle approach helped reduce the risks and challenges with this global user-focused project.

Small Enhancements and Maintenance

Support Options

Once larger initiatives are implemented, they need to be supported. They are likely to require changes, corrections, or adding features to future enhancements. These were the types of efforts that started my career—supporting newly implemented solutions. Once solutions are implemented, owners of the business processes impacted have control of the budget for continued support. Depending on what was projected for support, there are various organizational support options. One option is to assign a full-time equivalent resource. For a technology solution, a developer might be assigned to support a set of applications within the boundaries of a particular business unit, and they may also take on the role of BA and designer. Another option is the use of an internal centralized resource pool that is tapped into when support is needed with funds then transferred. A different option might be the contracted resource from an external source. Regardless, it is unlikely that a BA will be formally assigned unless they are part of the business unit's budget. Yet, the activities still need to occur, and they should be picked up by the resource, whether internal or external, to perform the needed business analysis activities.

Risk of No BA

The risk of not having an experienced BA to monitor enhancement and maintenance requests are that changes:

- Become solution driven
- Address user "preferences" rather than requirements

- Are addressed with a silo mentality
- Do not address overall system impacts

Below is a simple example of a conversation that *should* happen with a BA or someone in that role, understanding the need to dig deeper rather than just reacting to a specific request.

User: "I need to add this license data field to my screen so it can go on my report."

BA: "Why do you want to add it?"

User: "Because it is something I need to enter."

BA: "Why do you need it entered into the system at that screen? What is the purpose?"

User: "Well, I don't have to enter it there, but I just need to make sure it eventually gets to the broker commission report."

BA: "Why is that?"

User: "Because I need to have the report sorted by state license to see which broker is licensed in which state."

BA: "I see. Why do you need a report that way? Is it a regulation?"

User: "Yes. A customer can only be assigned a broker who has a license in the same state in which the customer resides, and now that we operate in another state, we need to include it in the report."

BA: "You just gave me some great information. Now that I know how you plan to use that information, I can check with our database administrator to see if we already have that information and to see what the best solution might be for you. Entering that information into the screen you use for calculating the commissions may not be the right place and could impact other users and other systems. Also, do you know of anyone else who might be impacted by this change and the state regulation?"

MOSTLY HYBRID TYPES

For mostly hybrid types, the emphasis is on releases and prototypes or proof-of-concepts. As illustrated in Table 4.1c, we will be looking at vendor package focus, data-driven, and technology-driven types of initiatives.

Vendor Package Focus

Evaluation of commercial off-the-shelf (COTS) vendor packages has increased tremendously over the years. Many companies have determined that it just isn't worth spending the money to build the noncore or nonproprietary processes, such as human resource functions or financial functions, in-house. It is cheaper to purchase and maintain externally. I have made a career

Table 4.1c Business analysis WBS considerations for a mostly hybrid life-cycle approach

SLC Stage > / Initiative Type V	Concept Definition	Requirements Analysis	Conceptual and Physical Design	Acquire or Build Solution Through Evaluate and Support Solution
Mostly Hybrid				
Vendor Package	RFI: focus on high-level requirements; design/architectural constraints and alignment to strategy to help narrow long list; and consider solution options: single product, product with custom build, multiple products from one vendor, multiple products from multiple vendors.	Focus on stakeholder requirements/features, quality attributes, data requirements, and vendor capabilities to define weighted criteria for RFP; evaluate based on quantitative vendor responses; assess solution fit and narrow list to two solutions; re-evaluate cost/benefit for two solutions and facilitate decision; coordinate conference room pilot (product prototype) with procurement for user education or proof of concept and assist in building test scenarios.	Map requirements to product capabilities and identify unique configurations or customizations and identify additional interface or reporting requirements; communicate gap analysis (impacts) to solution users and apply change management practices; identify requirements to transition to new solution—especially population of tables and other data; assist in complying with security; and control requirement and building test scenarios.	Conduct conference room pilot and re-evaluate baseline, assist in configuring acquired product, update product documentation, facilitate integration test validation, facilitate focus group of users for validations, monitor service level agreements, provide vendor feedback on product, and continue to monitor external user group evaluations of product releases.
Data-Driven	Identify high-level business scenarios (problem, concerns, benefits gained) from stakeholders requiring information for decision making and assess or create *as-is* data models, evaluate data models to identify views needed from each viewpoint to address concerns, and leverage process models to better understand how information is used.	Identify how information will be used by stakeholders; identify information sources, quality, and forms of delivery; identify business rules: how information will be inferred, derived, be factually based, and any actions to be taken based on conditions; and define how data will be transformed (conversion, cleansing, integration, aggregation) and any associated nonfunctional requirements.	Build and run business scenarios through prototype dashboards, reports, or other BI visuals to identify missing requirements; extract data requirements from stakeholder requirements to identify initial entities; build data models to facilitate physical design; and determine if more data marts may be required to address nonfunctional requirements.	Build permission tables for access to information, test quality of sources and transformation processes, facilitate validation of outcomes with stakeholders, evaluate nonfunctional requirements to access information (e.g., performance) in live environment, and evaluate ongoing stakeholder feedback on information use for decision making.

Continued

SLC Stage > / Initiative Type V	Concept Definition	Requirements Analysis	Conceptual and Physical Design	Acquire or Build Solution Through Evaluate and Support Solution
Mostly Hybrid				
Technology-Driven (infrastructure migration example)	Leverage technology architecture to determine standards and constraints, assess connections to business architecture to assess business impacts, evaluate alignment to business strategy, and determine value proposition and costs of *doing nothing*.	Assist in inventory of components being moved and their disposition, determine transition requirements and facilitate proof-of-concepts for tools used in migration, identify nonfunctional requirements to be validated, and identify impact of data to be migrated and whether structures are changing.	Prepare for transition, compare points to ensure business continuity, and assess any security impacts.	Make sure to make connection between the technology changes and the business impacts during validation, during acceptance and regression tests validate that functions that worked before are still working, post-transition evaluation to assure stakeholders of *no impact*, and assist in retiring old platform.

of implementing vendor packages. But, the business analysis process is different than building in-house.

Solution Delivery Options

There are many solution delivery options; each may have a different approach to address the requirements management process. Figure 4.5 looks at the various options, the impact to cost, and how flexible each approach is to meeting requirements. The least flexible and cheapest is always the do-nothing option—but is it really? Sometimes we need to evaluate that option because it could be the costliest in the long run due to an increasing cost of maintenance and not having the ability to meet business needs.

An as-is buy or out-of-the-box purchase is next on the spectrum. Of course, the trade-off to cost is the lack of ability to make modifications. This solution option is ideal for *commodity* type functions, ones that are standard across the industry such as certain financial packages. The process to acquire these packages is likely to be volume based. Selections are typically based on what the technology constraints are, and comparisons are done strictly at a feature level while price negotiations are based on volume.

The tailorable buy solution is based on one package that can be tailored. There is a difference between tailoring based on changing external configurations and tailoring based on changing internal products specifically for a client, which I call *customization of a package*. The impact is great. Tailoring based on external configurations means when there is a new release of the product, the same product is released to all clients and has likely been thoroughly tested because of the

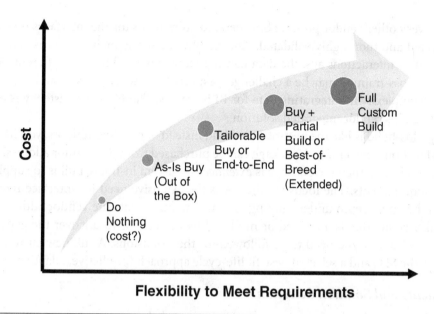

Figure 4.5   Solution delivery options

impact on such a large client base. Configuration differences will need to be tested by the client, but because of the design, is likely to have less of an impact and is easier to test. But if the purchase is a customized package, that product is only for that client. Clients have a greater responsibility for testing and it is more difficult to test since you can't *see* what was changed by the vendor. Each release of the product requires extensive regression testing to ensure the customized changes haven't *disappeared*.

End-to-end solutions are likely to have some common base requirements and features within their integrated modules with some tailorable configurations where requirements are inconsistent, possibly because of industry difference, size of company, or integration to other systems in their environment. Instead of buying products from different vendors (we will discuss that next) there is confidence that modules will work together, and we can choose whether or not to use them (plug and play). This allows for some tailoring with less risk and cost since you can negotiate price with one vendor and that one vendor is to blame if something goes wrong. But, the trade-off is that it may not address all of your requirements and the vendor, if not stable or credible, can have a business impact if some of the modules are business-critical functions.

Best-of-breed provides a better mix to address all requirements. Best-of-breed looks at selections from different vendors. Risk can be distributed for business-critical functions, but it is more likely to address more of the requirements. The downside is that when something goes wrong— there is not just one vendor to blame. The BA is likely to be the one trying to figure out where the problem resides. Another issue that may arise is incompatibility. Products have not been built to work with every other vendor product out there. Requirements for the interfaces must be clearly communicated and thoroughly validated. And finally, one of the main concerns is that the look and feel for user interactions and the data naming/storage may all be very different. As a result, training and cross-training may be a challenge—especially if the users are from the same organization. The complexity in integrating data for BI increases. Therefore, consistency is more likely to exist with a one-vendor integrated solution.

The buy-plus-build is like the best-of-breed but, instead of multiple vendors, you have a mix of vendor and in-house resources. A package can be purchased from one vendor addressing most of the requirements, and then the package is *extended* by custom in-house builds to supplement the rest of the requirements. The focus for the BA is the extensive need for interface requirements. There must be an in-depth understanding of which requirements the vendor addresses and the metadata describing the data created or modified by the vendor to uncover the gaps. Then the SLC for a new build would need to be followed for the extensions. A full new custom build will likely follow the SLC and a selected best-fit life-cycle approach (predictive, adaptive, or hybrid).

Requirements and Solution Selection

There are three main levels of requirements: business, stakeholder, and solution. Figure 4.6 illustrates each level and compares them to the different solution options. For example, when looking at a package solution you should apply the stakeholder requirements and nonfunctional requirements for evaluations of packages.

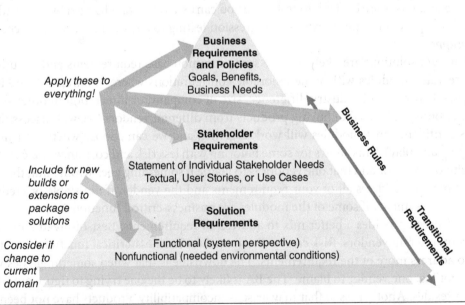

Figure 4.6   Requirement types to deliver solution options

Depending on the solution delivery method (Figure 4.5) we are looking for the *best fit* to our requirements. It is difficult to evaluate and select the best fit to a solution if we are looking at hundreds of vendor packages that might be *the one*. We need to follow a process to help us do that. Figure 4.7 provides a general flow of what the process might look like. We start with a way to narrow our search. That is where the request for information (RFI) comes into play early in the game. In the SLC it is addressed in concept definition (see first column in Tables 4.1a–c).

RFI, Request for Proposal (RFP), and the Request for Quote (RFQ)

The RFI is looking for generic product information from vendors. The main goal is elimination and exclusion—getting rid of those that don't fit right away. How do we go about the elimination? The RFI should contain those factors that are *busters*, those high-level key factors the product must have. For example, if I was looking for a financial package solution, some *busters* might be: (1) runs on a particular operating system, (2) handles a specified number of users, or (3) has federal reporting features. As you can see, there are either design constraints or some key features that the product is expected to handle, at a minimum, or they are off the list.

The result should be a more manageable list to work with. The next step takes us to more detailed requirements. If you are doing a business case, you may stop here and make some assumptions regarding the solution. If not, then you would continue to a more detailed step to evaluate solutions and will need more detailed requirements. If you are replacing one product with another, you will need to list out the features you want from the new product. If not feature based, then you will need to identify stakeholder requirements. What does the stakeholder need

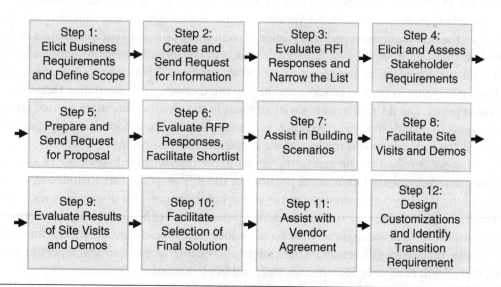

Figure 4.7   Vendor solution selection process (BA perspective)

the ability to do with the product? The RFP asks vendors for their unique solutions to address features or stakeholder requirements and quality attributes. Vendor solutions could be a specific combination of products, plug-and-play modules, or special configurations (see Figure 4.5). In the RFP, we are asking if that requirement will be met and how well it will be met. This puts you in the requirements analysis stage (see second column in Tables 4.1a–c).

An example of an RFP scoring worksheet is included in Appendix A4.1. Example features are listed for evaluation of a requirements management package. Weights can be applied to the features to determine their importance in the evaluation. Weights listed on the bottom of the worksheet show the most critical features as a higher number (5). These weights are not typically provided to the vendor to prevent influencing their responses. Vendors are expected to respond with their rating on how well they meet the requirement. Of course, we must trust but validate by using this feedback to create test scenarios later in the process. The scores are calculated by multiplying the weight with each vendor's rating to get the individual vendor's score per feature. For example, if we look at *Advanced requirements sorting and filtering*, it has the highest weight—a 5. Vendor A rated themselves at a 2—minimally fulfills. If we multiply the weight of a 5 with the 2 rating, Vendor A scores a 10. In this example, there are three vendor scores that will be compared. This technique, called feature scoring, helps to alleviate politics and favoritism by using a more quantitative method. But there is more to the evaluation of an RFP.

In addition to the requirement scoring, other factors are evaluated such as: cost/total cost of ownership, vendor credibility, financial stability, references, implementation complexity, training, and support expenses, etc. But in the business analysis, what if Vendor A met 100% of the requirements—but all of them only partially. What if Vendor B met 50% of the requirements fully—and they were all the most critical ones. Yet Vendor A scored higher. You need to look deeper into what constitutes the best fit. Sometimes it is a matter of combining different vendor packages to get you to the best solution. It requires evaluating the results in collaborative sessions with stakeholders. At the end of the evaluation, the goal is to get to two solutions. That's when negotiations happen resulting in bringing in the two vendors and having them conduct demonstrations and/or conference room pilots. The BA may need to create or assist in the creation of scenarios based on critical requirements to include in demos or conference room pilots. Once vendor demo comparisons are completed, the final selection is made, and the acquisition process begins.

BAs may get involved in the vendor agreements because of their knowledge of the vendor responses to requirements. Often, some portions of the RFP responses are included in the agreement, and the BA may be required to help in clarifying those previous discussions with the vendor. Once a solution is selected and acquired, that is not the end of business analysis activities. The product will need to be configured with possible localized special configurations (for example, state-to-state regulatory differences). There might also be interface and special reporting requirements that all will need to be identified, tested, and implemented.

An RFQ is typically used when there is little difference between vendor packages. Usually, little involvement from the BA is necessary because features included in these products are standard in the industry—such as the purchasing of virus software or word processing software. Procurement is usually involved to obtain the best volume or other discount pricing for these commodity products.

In vendor package solutions, business analysis activities address the requirements needed at the right depth, at the right time—starting with high-level requirements and constraints in the RFI, to more detailed stakeholder requirements in the RFP, to defining special configurations once the product is acquired, and finally to transition requirements. This may involve both the evaluation of packages and also comparing options that are built in-house. If that is the case, the same level of diligence should be conducted in the RFP for the in-house build or outsourced build options.

Business Analysis Considerations

Unique configurations, customizations, interfaces, or reporting requirements will need to be determined and designed into the solution (see third column in Tables 4.1a–c). Necessary changes between the old system and the new system must be communicated (change management). Identification of the transition requirements to the new solution and facilitation of the implementation must also be accomplished.

A few more hints and tips for vendor packages:

- Make sure the appropriate internal people are consulted
- Consider the enterprise strategy and operating model before selecting a solution
- Identify decision criteria for going with a commercial solution (80% match or more to fit with requirements, needed features, or other criteria)
- Determine how much customization is acceptable
- Evaluate against business and technological constraints
- Ensure that you have the capabilities to build the solution or to support a commercial solution
- Know what you might be giving up such as a competitive advantage with unique internal processes by going with a commercial package
- Verify alignment with any IT organizational strategy to help you determine whether you are looking for a *best-of-breed* addressing different features or a *suite* that provides well-integrated components
- Verify future feature scalability with added expense
- Consider the effect of doing nothing or a transitional option

Data-Driven

Data is converted to information that is useful for making millions of decisions every day. The quality of the data affects the quality of the information that is received and influences the decision making that is a result—garbage in, garbage out. When provided with data without any additional explanation—70, 55—what would you make of it? Does it provide value without further definition or understanding of the context? When provided with this data—speed limit max 70, speed limit min and trucks 55—would you feel better informed? How can the information that is provided result in knowledge that can help in making decisions? BI transforms data, enabling stakeholders to increase business value by:

- Achieving their business goals and objectives
- Improving the performance of their processes
- Optimizing their work
- Increasing sales
- Identifying process problems
- Predicting problems and forecasting changes

It is important to ask stakeholders not just what data or information they need, but what they intend to do with the information. In other words, what decisions will be made based on the information? If the plant manager says: "I would like to know how many sheet sets have been returned—listed by type of defect, by size, by color, and by thread count—each week *so that I* can help reduce the number of defects." The data or BI analyst must anticipate the functionality that needs to be built so that users can perform their work, make the decisions they need to make, and thereby satisfy business requirements. Additional considerations are: What information must be delivered? What quality should it have? Where should it come from, etc.? The BI analyst should be able to answer: "The BI system will aggregate the defect return numbers from each warehouse and classify them by manufacturing location, type of defect, and product type (sheet sets, thread count, size, and color) daily. The BI system will provide an electronic standard report with defect return information every Monday morning by 8 a.m. Eastern Standard Time."

Can you describe how information might be inferred, derived, be factually based, or its integrity ensured (definitional business rule)? Are there any other actions to be taken based on certain conditions (behavioral business rule)? The plant manager then makes a request: "Each day, send an e-mail alert to me when defects are more than 10% over the previous year's numbers." As you can see, we need a much better understanding of *how* the information is being used in order to provide value. But once we get these requirements, we must work backward to find the source of the data that is needed.

We can begin by looking at the BI outcomes on the right side of Figure 4.8—the dashboard, scorecard, queries, reports, and alerts—all these outcomes may provide the information that our stakeholders need in different forms. But if we look all the way to the left, we see that the sources of the data can come either from external or internal sources and need to be extracted, transformed, and loaded (ETL) at the arrow marked *A*. When looking at the sources of information, consideration should be given to the following types of requirements:

- Accessibility
- Availability

- Usefulness
- Trustworthiness
- Ownership (they created it for their own purpose—what might that be?)
- Volatility
- Quality standards at the source
- Cost of the data versus its value
- Contractual obligations to obtain and retain the data
- Ability to reconcile different sources

You must also assess the needs for quality once received. How current is the data being received? How long does it need to be retained? How can the data be protected? How much tolerance is there for errors?

The center of Figure 4.8 focuses on the enterprise view of data by creating a warehouse to reduce the overload to source systems, take care of redundancies and aggregation of data, and get consistent data definitions across systems. As a repository, data is never *created* at this location, only at the source. BAs involved in data warehouse types of initiatives must have a good understanding of data models. Data models are a very effective way to communicate with both the technology folks creating the databases *and* the stakeholders providing the data needs. There are various types of data models—conceptual, logical, and physical. Conceptual models are at the highest level with the least amount of detail and a clear BA responsibility. In logical models, the data requirements and business rules surface to physically build it on the appropriate platform. This mode is a grey

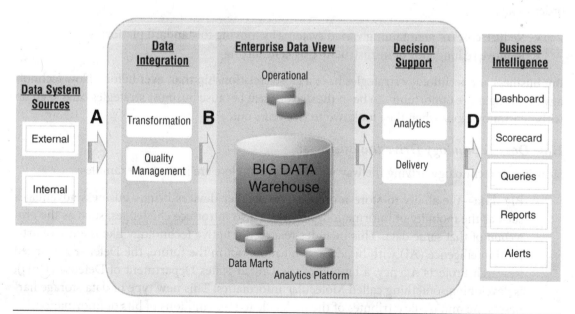

Figure 4.8   Data warehouse and BI

area of responsibility. In larger organizations it is built by a data administrator or architect—but it may also be assigned to the BA to create since it requires elicitation with stakeholders.

Even in non-data-focused projects, BAs should be reviewing requirements for data needs and creating models, even lightweight ones, for communication and validation.

Technology-Driven

What Is Technology-Driven?

Think of the phone we use. Did we ever think that there was any possibility that we could talk across land and oceans to individuals as if they were standing right next to us as we did our daily chores—100 years ago, 50 years ago, 25 years ago? How many businesses today are thinking about how to leverage social media and personal devices? We are living in a drastically changing time where technology change is exponential, and we have been lucky enough to see how technology has affected the way we communicate, learn, socialize, purchase products, etc. IIBA and The Chartered Institute for IT partnered together to address these challenges in the business analysis world: "Business analysis has certainly been affected by the influences of disruptive technologies. Developments such as Cloud computing and BYOD (bring your own device) are creating change in the way businesses manage their IT operations and both present business analysis professionals with new challenges." Disrupted technology goes beyond the definition of technology-driven. It takes technology to the level of changing the whole business, the way it operates, or the way it may compete in the market. Most businesses view technology as an enabler of business strategies in order to help:

- Reduce costs of maintaining varied systems by moving to standard platforms
- Remove redundancy of infrastructure by centralizing

But business and technology strategies have a closer relationship than ever before. Now technology is getting more opportunity to be in the driver's seat because business strategies can't keep up with new innovations when they look two to five years out.

How Does Technology Drive the Business?

How is new technology driving the way we do business? Here are just a few examples:

- **Big data**—the ability to store more data on smaller devices brings business advantages such as the mobility of information. But it can also introduce challenges, such as the *protection* of that same data. This includes related disruptive technology like the use of artificial intelligence (AI) with big data. A bit more out in the future, the Defense Advanced Research Projects Agency, a branch of the United States Department of Defense (DoD), is developing something called Molecular Informatics. This new type of data storage harnesses the minuscule attributes of the molecule to store millions of bits of information.[4]

- **Cloud computing**—the ability to have a vendor manage your infrastructure allows the flexibility and scalability needed without building an expensive organization to support it. But it can also introduce risks by putting core business processes in the control of an external entity.
- **Modernization of infrastructure**—operating systems.

The business now must be as versatile as the BA by constantly scanning what is changing in the environment and trying to keep up—possibly even getting a little ahead of it. So how does a BA prepare for this?

Driving Technology-Focused Initiatives

When there are technology-driven strategies, these strategies will then drive technology-focused initiatives. Big data strategies can trigger other technology-focused initiatives such as migrations of data to other structures and platforms for more storage capabilities and easier access. Cloud strategies can trigger application migration projects that force organizations to review all applications for six dispositions:

1. Retain the application
2. Retire the application
3. Rehost it by moving it automatically (a.k.a. lift and shift)
4. Repurchase or upgrade to new module or release
5. Re-platform the application
6. Refactor by rewriting or re-architecting it

There are other types of technology-focused initiatives driven to improve the services of the technology organization. These might include: implementing an agile approach as an enterprise initiative and service-oriented architecture (SOA).

Implementing an agile approach, an adaptive life-cycle approach that we discussed earlier, was initially driven by IT organizations, but has evolved into being more connected to business strategy in many companies, often becoming an enterprise-wide initiative. BAs need to have a good understanding of how activities must adjust to accommodate the adaptive approach as enterprise-wide (see Chapter 3).

SOA is often defined as a technical system of software design for how software communicates with one another (system services). The definition is often expanded to include the alignment to business services and processes, providing benefits of reusability and impact assessments. For system services to be reused across the company, there must be a single, centralized warehouse, or repository, so that developers will know where to look for services—and to identify who is using them and to prevent different areas of the business from building the same service in different ways or from using linkages that are incompatible. The system services must be well documented so that developers will know what they are for, how to link to them, and what the rules are for using them. Because it is an architectural strategy, SOA involves much more than merely building software. It is critical to have a centralized architecture group involved so it can consult with the different areas to choose and enable the appropriate enterprise-wide business and system services.

For SOA initiatives, the focus for the BA is to define the business services and associated processes and/or use cases. Although SOA is technology-driven, it also has a heavy process focus if driven top-down in the organization using the business and technology architectures. It is considered more of a hybrid because of the top-down approach combined with the adaptive nature of building small components. Here is an example of a use case *check credit score* that was identified as a business service and is being evaluated to see if it is a composite service of smaller ones (decomposed).

Use Case: Check Credit Score
Pre-condition: Account has been set up and fraud check conducted
Post-condition: Ready for approval
    1. Credit officer enters customer account information
    2. Credit officer submits request for credit score
    3. Credit service provider responds with credit score
    4. Credit officer validates that it is correct customer
    5. Credit officer checks corporate policy and calculations
    6. Credit officer establishes suitable credit limits
    7. Credit officers prepare for approval
Extension
    4. Returned customer information is incorrect
        4a. Credit officer calls account manager for verification
    5. Credit score not within policy and calculations
        5a. Credit officer prepares for rejection

Technology migrations to other platforms or consolidations to one platform are performed often. Table 4.1c uses a technology migration as an example for WBS considerations. When vendors aren't supporting the hardware or software anymore, businesses need to make the move, or they may get into trouble later. When data centers consolidate or move locations, technology migrations must occur. BAs must consider the quality attributes (nonfunctional requirements and service-level agreements) for these types of initiatives, not only for the target system requirements, but also the current system so a baseline is available to compare tolerance levels to the target system quality attributes. Transition requirements are also important to address with stakeholders. Remember to elicit requirements from the technology organization stakeholders for technology-focused initiatives. Even though the requirements may be more technically oriented, they will be needed to ensure a smooth transition and an outcome that will lessen the impact to the business community. This is another good reason why BAs need to have some domain knowledge with technology solutions. Another reason for the domain knowledge is to help in uncovering risks.

Risks with Implementing New Technology

Because of early exposure to technology and working in the consulting industry, technology risks are those things that, in retrospect, I would have spent much more time addressing. This is also likely true for many of the project teams that ran into trouble at the different client sites visited. The primary reason is the importance of reaction time. Earlier in this book it was stressed that the BA needed to learn to *see the smoke before the fire*. Reaction time is important when problems arise. If technology experts are not brought in early enough to resolve an issue, it may become too late for them to help or it may simply become too costly to fix.

Looking much further back in history, the DoD, after having experienced cost overruns in numerous projects involving new technologies, came up with a plan to mitigate technology risks by checking the readiness of the technology for operation. This process validates new technology from the starting point of an idea to the point where the idea is incorporated into a larger system and becomes fully operational. The frequent checks by this process allow them to see and catch problems early, allowing for increased ability to react and fix problems earlier. The technology readiness level (TRL) process is known as *The Nine Technology Readiness Levels* of the U.S. DoD.[5]

TRL 1: Basic principles observed and reported
TRL 2: Technology concept or application formulated
TRL 3: Concept or application proven through analysis and experimentation
TRL 4: Basic prototype validated in laboratory environment
TRL 5: Basic prototype validated in relevant environment
TRL 6: System or subsystem model or prototype demonstrated in relevant environment
TRL 7: System prototype demonstrated in relevant environment
TRL 8: Actual system completed and qualified for flight through test and demonstration
TRL 9: Actual system proven through successful operation

Certainly, there are many risks when new technologies are being considered on a project. Assessing the readiness or maturity of a new technology and catching issues early in the process can help the BA mitigate some of the inherent risks. Regardless of life-cycle approach, new technology and technology debt (where legacy systems or applications are not modernized and accumulate to the point of causing problems) introduces risks. We will discuss more about risks in Chapter 5.

Various areas of focus have been discussed thus far. For additional information, summarized by life-cycle approach, refer to consolidated matrix Tables 4.1a through 4.1c, which is also included in the expanded table within Appendix A4.2. These tables serve as a useful guide for defining a unique business analysis WBS.

INDUSTRY SPECIFIC FOCUS

One last area of focus is industry. Industries have their own unique characteristics such as their culture, external influences, organizational structures, risk tolerance, etc. Having a better understanding of industry-specific factors is another way the BA can adapt their approach.

Government

For government entities, their customers are their constituents. Taxpayers want to know where their money goes. Visibility and documentation are important. As a result, strict policies and regulations are defined for procurement. Vendor relationships are controlled, and the bidding process is managed through structured fair practice guidelines and ethically guided procedures.

Due to these factors, business analysis in government is more likely to have very strict audit requirements. Business rules analysis may be extensive because of the many policies and regulations that drive government processes. BAs must be aware of the procedures and ensure they are being followed. In addition, within governmental entities there is often less acceptance and tolerance of risk. Life cycles are much more structured and less adaptive. Change happens slowly because of the hierarchical approval processes. A predictive or hybrid approach is a better fit for this environment.

Nonprofits

The biggest challenges surrounding nonprofit entities are funding and resource turnover, causing requirements to change often. Other challenges are the opposite of the government challenges. Nonprofits tend to lack structure such as not having a strategic plan or implementing project management or portfolio management (mostly because of the attempt to keep administrative costs low).

In this type of environment, the BA must be more willing to accept change—change of stakeholders, change of direction, or a lack of funds triggering changes in scope. Without the supporting structure and with the constant changes, these challenges warrant the use of a more adaptive life-cycle approach.

Manufacturing

The manufacturing industry is converting raw materials to finished products and can be very process heavy (production routing, material costing, warehouse management, etc.). Quality initiatives are always in place, whether Six Sigma, lean, or compliance with the International Organization for Standardization (ISO). This industry has implemented many different enterprise resource planning suites of products, such as SAP and ORACLE, and is moving to the next generation—Cloud ERP.

The use of process models in large enterprise-wide initiatives is commonplace, in addition to the use of methodologies to improve processes. Use cases are likely to be the tool of choice for capturing more detailed process information because it can be easily translated into job procedures, training, etc. Implementation of large vendor packages (enterprise-wide) requires intensive gap analysis. A hybrid life-cycle approach would likely be the best fit.

Within the manufacturing category there are some special considerations for certain manufacturing types. The technology industry, such as those that design and build electronics and communication networks, move quickly with new products, but tend to be more of a hybrid with some adaptive teams working within it. Hybrid is recommended overall because of the need for a product-release structure and the live validations with the public. There still needs to be innovation internally requiring a much more adaptive approach. Technology companies tolerate more risks and tend to be less regulated than most other industries.

Another subcategory of manufacturing is the pharmaceutical industry. They tend to be more regulated, particularly when it comes to clinical trials. The regulations in this area are strict and can be very large and complex as well. At the same time, there are phases, such as the discovery phase, where things are more unstructured and would take on a more adaptive approach. For pharma, it is beneficial to have a good understanding of how a product gets to market. Knowledge of the details of the product life cycle and the service life cycle are helpful. Pharma stakeholders will likely be scientists, and that requires having the ability to communicate in their domain of expertise to get a better understanding of their needs. For the BA in this environment, it is important to gain more domain knowledge—intimate knowledge of policies or regulations—and develop very good data analysis skills.

Services

Service companies may include entertainment, hospitality, utilities, transportation, trades, consulting, education, and finance. The finance industry is a volatile one. Stock brokerage firms feature *low latency transactions* as a competitive advantage in trading and push forward for faster transactions. Banking is concerned with the security of their customers' financial assets in an online world. Credit card companies are on the attack by using personal mobile devices to curtail lost or stolen accounts. Technology has not only made it better, but it has also made the environment fearful of cyber attacks. BAs will always need to keep focused on security requirements and how they are changing. Business rule engines are being implemented to enable ease of maintaining the constantly changing policies and operational decisions by providing the ability to manage the rules (define, classify, connect to processes and data) externally from software, bringing the need to uncover these rules during analysis. Also, the importance of connecting information between the various products and services across the silos within finance organizations triggers the need for business architecture. Finance organizations, because of their volatility, are more likely hybrid and adaptive with their initiatives.

In healthcare, consider the stakeholders you will be working with. In pharma it will likely be scientists, but in healthcare, it will likely be doctors. Again, it is important to have the ability to communicate in their medical domain of expertise. In healthcare, observation techniques are critical because of the environment constraints and safety concerns. As with pharma, domain knowledge, intimate knowledge of policies or regulations, and data analysis are more important than most other industries.

Industry Domain Knowledge

There are a variety of industries in which a BA may have a role and we have touched on several in this section. The different areas of focus for industries can impact the knowledge we need and how we approach business analysis. In addition to the information provided in this chapter, there are many ways for the BA to get information and gain understanding about different industries. Below are just a few ways to acquire that knowledge:

- Become a member of professional organizations developed around industries
- Peruse the different industry websites
- Look at standardized conceptual models in that industry[6]
- Ask for a business model or use the questions in the business model canvas to learn more about the industry
- Find those who have knowledge about the industry and plan an informal *over lunch* conversation

There is one last area to address in this chapter—how the organizational assets of the enterprise might affect our approach. Regardless of my employer, large organization or small, there has always been a repository of information that was thought to be valuable for the future (assets). For projects, what is to be retained in these repositories was decided at the discretion of the PM. But often, there was a more overarching strategy to have some consistency across projects for reuse and for integration into architectures. Part of the business analysis activity planning should include activities for retention and reuse. Which of the outcomes from our activities do we need to transfer into a repository? What state does it need to be in? Does it have to follow any standards? Who will maintain it? Who is the owner and who is accountable for it?

When it comes to these repositories, every organization is unique as to who contributes to it, how it is managed, and how it is used. In Chapter 8, we will discuss work products that the BA needs to retain for themselves as a transition to deliverables, as an audit trail for themselves, and for future knowledge retention.

In conclusion, we have looked at the different characteristics of a project or initiative and its environment to develop the best business analysis approach. In the next chapter, we will look at how we may need to adjust our approach based on the identified risks.

SUMMARY

- The business analysis approach taken can be dependent upon whether the assignment requires a predictive life-cycle approach, an adaptive life-cycle approach, or a hybrid of the two.
- Determine the level of commitment of the stakeholders, the benefits to both the business and the delivery organization, the schedule, the scope, the performance level of the team, and the risks.
- Analysis of the current situation is critical in determining which functionality should be incorporated in the solution based on the reason for the change and value derived and measured.
- Determine the level of metrics used to measure whether or not the needs are being met and determine the associated risks involved.
- The E&C KA is an important part of the process and is meant to be iterative, regardless of approach.
- BAs must manage the politics of bringing disparate groups of stakeholders together.
- The WBS does not define the sequence of activities, overlaps, or iterations and depends on the project characteristics.
- Evaluation of vendor packages typically includes an RFI and an RFP to determine the best fit to requirements.
- In process-driven initiatives, current system processes within the scope of analysis require assessment as to which processes need to be kept, removed, added, or changed to define the future solution scope.
- In data-driven initiatives, analysis of data is required to determine the value of the information derived, along with its quality, reliability, volatility, accessibility, cost of the data relative to its value, as well as contractual or legal requirements for data retention, protection, and disposal.
- User-driven initiatives require the need to understand how and why specific users interact with a system and may vary among user categories. Both passive and active observations of the various tasks that a user performs in their environment can aid in determining how the new system can make them more successful while reducing frustration and resistance to the new system.
- Enterprise-wide initiatives are costly, complex, and can be very political since they may cross different functional business units, geography, and cultures. These initiatives require a large number of resources, multi-level teams, impact a broad spectrum of systems and core business processes, are highly visible, and require enterprise-wide governance.
- Maintenance and enhancement to existing systems may be performed by internal or external staff. However, it is still important to ensure that features and functionality are actual requirements of the business, identify impacts to other systems, and that they are solution driven.

- Technology-driven strategies can drive technology-focused initiatives such as big-data migration or cloud-application migration. Other technology-focused initiatives might include SOA.
- There are solutions that require a hybrid approach based on a global implementation, cross cultural requirements, and varying user implementations.
- There are several ways to obtain industry domain knowledge such as reviewing standard conceptual models in the industry or using the business model canvas questions to probe for understanding.

QUESTIONS

1. What are the core concepts that every BA should be aware of when assessing their work?

   _____

   _____

   _____

2. (a) Why should the BA create a WBS? (b) Who do you review it with and why? (c) Would you create a WBS for an adaptive life-cycle approach?

   _____

   _____

   _____

   _____

   _____

3. For process-driven initiatives, name three unique business analysis activities.

   _____

   _____

   _____

4. For data-driven initiatives, name three unique business analysis activities.

   _____

   _____

   _____

5. For user-focused initiatives, name three unique business analysis activities.

_____

_____

_____

6. Locate a specific example of an industry provided in this chapter and do some domain knowledge research using the business model canvas. What characteristics might influence your business analysis approach and how?

_____

_____

_____

_____

NOTES

1. International Institute of Business Analysis. (2015). *A Guide to the Business Analysis Body of Knowledge (BABOK® Guide) v3*. Toronto, Ontario, Canada: IIBA.
2. A business model visualizes how an enterprise or organization may create, deliver, and capture value. A business model canvas is a visual showing nine basic blocks that cover four main areas: customers, offer, infrastructure, and financial viability (Osterwalder and Pineur 2010).
3. Project Management Institute. (2006). *Practice Standard for Work Breakdown Structures— Second Edition*. Newtown Square, PA: Project Management Institute, Inc.
4. Ghose, Tia. (April 5, 2017). "Computers of the Future May Be Minuscule Molecular Machines." LIVESCIENCE. www.livescience.com.
5. Developed by NASA researcher initially in 1974 then formally defined and adopted in the 1990s. www.nasa.gov/topics/aeronautics/features/trl_demystified.html.
6. Example conceptual models include: APQC for manufacturing and operations (https://www.apqc.org/pcf-process-classification-framework); ACORD for insurance industry (https://www.acord.org/standards-architecture/reference-architecture); and eTOM for telecom industry (https://www.tmforum.org/business-process-framework/).

5

STEP FOUR—ADJUST BASED ON RISKS

"As the chefs, we as business analysts (BAs) should have the confidence to adapt and make changes, to make substitutions if needed, and know what we have available to us to make it work. We may have even predicted this and have a backup plan. Our advanced preparation in anticipating change gives us the courage to make the needed adjustments without a fear of failure because we are ready to improvise. We are willing to take on the risks for the rewards."—Chapter One

RISK OVERVIEW

BAs need to use their experience to predict potential risk on a project. All projects have some inherent risks—even if they are small ones. Imagine you are hired right out of college at a large telecommunications company and assigned to the IT department responsible for customer billing. The main coding expert for billing adjustments suffers a heart attack and is not available to make the necessary changes to the billing program. Although new to the company and relatively inexperienced, management asks for your assistance after noticing that you had taken a course in college relating to the necessary programming language. Management asks that you make this "small change" to a monster program, which will affect a small group of customers. Excited about this small but important first assignment, you jump in with both feet. You work hard and quite independently to make the coding change. You rely on a helpful peer to show you how to test and load the program to production. You pat yourself on the back for meeting the strict deadline. Unfortunately, you failed to see the *big bend* in the road up ahead for which you and management were unprepared.

Months after your changes were put into production, you learn that an external auditor discovered the rounding calculation for call minutes had been changed by your program. It affected all calls billed to all customers, which was not the intended result. Further, the change calculated the minutes incorrectly (in the customer's favor) costing the company approximately a million dollars, money that they would not be able to recoup. Unfortunately, this is a true story and it was my own introduction to working in IT—and learning to understand risk. Although my career survived, this is just one example of how hard it can be to see the danger ahead. From this experience some valuable lessons were learned:

1. Become much more educated on business analysis techniques by understanding the current environment and the business impacts of the changes being made—thinking through requirements *before* coding.
2. Walk through the code with someone, even though they do not know the language, in order to confirm your own interpretation.
3. Discuss with your manager the risks of not having a subject matter expert to interpret the business rules, how the time pressure will affect quality, and how ambiguity will affect the interpretation of the business rules. Yes, just a *little* change can have a big business impact.

We know that risks are uncertain events that are identified as a possibility of occurring. We may need to change something to decrease the likelihood of the event happening or change something to minimize the potential impact (positive or negative) if it were to take place. Figure 5.1 breaks down the steps of a generic risk management process:

- *Step 1*: **Identify**
  - Tap into experience and history
  - Look at previous risks in similar situations
  - Review project and business analysis deliverables
  - Discuss stakeholder concerns
  - Determine impacts to business, customer, and operations

- *Step 2*: **Analyze**
  - Assign a numerical probability
  - Assign a numerical value to the impact
  - Multiply probability by impact to obtain a score
  - Prioritize the risks by score

- *Step 3*: **Respond**
  - Risk owners and assigned responsibilities
  - Results of analyses
  - Planned responses to identified risks
  - Specific actions to implement the chosen response strategy
  - Budget and times for responses
  - Contingency plans and fallback plans
    - **Risk Responses**
      - Avoid—eliminate the cause
      - Transfer—shift the risk to a third party

- Share—split the ownership of the risk with a third party
- Mitigate—reduce the probability or adverse consequences
- Accept—live with it
- Provide contingencies or reserves—have a backup to reduce the impact

- *Step 4*: **Control**
  - Did the response do what was expected?

- *Step 5*: **Communicate**
  - Every team member is responsible for communicating risks
  - Make risks transparent
  - If potential severity is high, push for action

Now imagine your manager approaches you with a strategy for the upcoming year to outsource some core business processes from the company to a vendor located in Asia. Can you identify some risks? Consider that some vendors in Asia have been known to sell intellectual property to competitors. Enforcement for intellectual property infringement has historically not been enforced as stringently in certain Asian countries. Starting with identifying requirements, we have identified one risk—that intellectual property might fall in the hands of competitors. The next

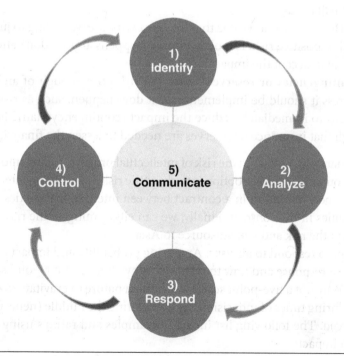

Figure 5.1   Risk management process

step is to analyze the risk, probability of occurrence, and impact of occurrence to the business or project. We know from our peers in the industry that the probability of loss is high, and 90% of our peers have taken actions to protect their assets. On a scale of 1 to 4 for probability, we give it a 4 if we don't take any action. The impact of the occurrence depends on the core functions being outsourced. We could decide to assess the impact based on each core function. We have five high-level functions and decide that two have the highest potential for financial impact—a 3 out of 4 on the probability scale. Severity scores are calculated (probability x impact) and the risks with the highest overall score should be responded to in some way to the identified risk. If a risk is positive, the probability and impact is enhanced (increased). If the risk is negative, the severity is reduced based on our responses.

Responses can be posed as questions within the six general response strategies as previously shown in Step 3 of the risk process:

- **Avoid the risk**—could the risk be eliminated or avoided such as by not taking any action?
- **Transfer the risk**—could another party assume the risk such as including it in a contractual agreement with a vendor?
- **Share the risk**—could we allocate a portion of the risk ownership to someone else?
- **Mitigate (negative) or enhance (positive) the risk**—could some actions be taken to change the probability such as implementing additional controls to reduce the chances that the risk will occur?
- **Accept the risk**—we acknowledge that the risk exists; are we willing to just wait for the risk to happen? For positive risk, is it okay if it just happens and we don't attempt to pursue it? Are we willing to accept the impact?
- **Provide contingencies or reserves**—does the risk pose enough of an impact that some plan to address it should be implemented if it does happen, such as risk alerts or triggers to take actions to immediately reduce the impact (contingency plan)? Is the financial risk great enough that insurance or reserves are needed to lessen the financial impact?

In the previous scenario, we can avoid the risk of intellectual property falling into the hands of competitors by not outsourcing. Another option is to share the risk by including international clauses (a negotiated, agreed-upon resolution in a contract between international parties that addresses law conflicts) and penalties in the contract. Finally, we can either mitigate the risk by selecting a U.S. vendor or just accept the risk and still outsource to Asia.

We may not want to respond to all risks. Analyzing probability and impact can help determine which risks require a response and how to respond. Why choose a four-point scale to rate probability and impact? Why not a five-point scale? It is human nature to gravitate toward the center (or neutral response) during times of indecision. By eliminating the middle (neutral) option, decision making can be forced. The following list includes examples and ratings using a four-point scale for probability and impact:

Probability
4—Very likely
3—More likely than unlikely
2—More unlikely than likely
1—Very unlikely

Impact
4—Extreme impact (can't function)
3—High impact (costly business/enterprise impact)
2—Moderate impact (costly to stakeholder)
1—Low impact (just monitor)

If a risk has a probability of 2 and an impact of 4, a simple risk score of 8 (2×4) can be calculated. Table 5.1 provides an example of assessing the risk scores for response. The example shows a visual classification of risk scores to determine which to: respond to, monitor, or accept. For example, scores in the upper right-hand quadrant are the highest (9–16) and require a response.

Table 5.1 Risk score example

Probability						Severity Score	
	4	4	8	12	16	9–16	Respond
	3	3	6	9	12	6–8	Monitor
	2	2	4	6	8	1–4	Accept
	1	1	2	3	4		
	0	1	2	3	4		

Impact

RISKS AND BUSINESS ANALYSIS

There are two main categories of risks that BAs must address. The first category is associated with the ability to perform business analysis activities and will be referred to as *business analysis risks*. These risks are under the control of the BA but still need collaboration with the project manager (PM). These risks can be addressed by adapting to an alternate approach, using different techniques, or using more formal documentation. These risks can be classified as the ability to successfully:

- **Perform business analysis work**—risks that will affect the business analysis work breakdown structure (WBS) activities, our own work, and what might hinder us from being successful, such as *lack of domain expertise*.
- **Manage product scope**—those risks that might affect the scope boundaries that we are responsible for as BAs, such as *hidden scope expansion* (*scope creep*).

- **Implement business requirements**—those risks that may impact the success of implementing the high-level requirements including goals, objectives, vision statements, and benefits, such as *misalignment with strategy.*
- **Implement stakeholder requirements**—those risks that may impact the success of implementing mid-level requirements from the perspective of each stakeholder, which could affect their ability to use the solution.
- **Implement solution requirements**—those risks that may impact the success of implementing the most effective and *implementable* requirements such as functional, nonfunctional (a.k.a. quality attributes and design constraints), and transitional requirements.
- **Implement business rules**—those risks that may impact the success of implementing both behavioral and definitional business rules that can affect the quality of processes, policies, regulations, and the integrity of information.

As illustrated in Table 5.2, some of these risks may be a higher risk in some approaches versus others. Because these types of risks are more general and business analysis work related, they warrant a discussion with the PM *before* probabilities and impacts are assessed and analyzed. This becomes what is commonly known as the *business analysis risk management plan.* Most risks that are listed in the example may be addressed within the approach regardless of probability or impact. Keep in mind that the earlier you can determine how the response to these risks might change your plan, the more accurate your estimate will be for the project.

Table 5.2   Business analysis risks by life-cycle approach

Affects the ability to...	Business Analysis Risks	Life-cycle Approach with Highest Risk	Reason for Occurrence	Recommended Approach Adjustments
Perform BA Work	Lack of domain expertise (BA)	Predictive, in-house build	Learning time, access to domain information	Move to a more hybrid approach with more iterative learning for areas lacking expertise Collaborate with PM to bring in external experts (increases cost)
	Key stakeholder unavailability	Hybrid, in-house build	Schedule conflicts, priority conflicts	Include stakeholder activities and dependencies in project plans to communicate need for each release Collaborate with each stakeholder regarding involvement during stakeholder analysis Evaluate backup stakeholders in stakeholder analysis and include in responsibility/ accountability matrix Schedule around busy times Ask for PM and sponsor assistance

Continued

Affects the ability to...	Business Analysis Risks	Life-cycle Approach with Highest Risk	Reason for Occurrence	Recommended Approach Adjustments
Perform BA Work (*continued*)	Stakeholder turnover	Predictive, enterprise-wide	Organizational instability	Review previous completed stakeholder analysis to assess impact
				Use change control process if objectives or requirements change
				Be proactive; mitigate the risk if you are aware of turnover
				Assist with the transition
	Inability to get to solution agreement	Predictive	Different political agendas	Sheer size of solution and number of stakeholders impact this, so include agreement on how the decision will be made
				Bring stakeholders together in a facilitated workshop and walk through interests; apply win/win negotiation tactics
				Identify champion/key decision makers during stakeholder analysis
	Not getting what you need	Predictive	Too busy; doesn't have information; not the right person	Be prepared
				Communicate roles/responsibilities and decision/approval process
				Manage expectations with turnaround time
				Communicate impacts of missed dates or reduced quality
				Assess if different resource is needed
	Requirements continue to be too large	Adaptive	If at bottom of product backlog, it is fine to be at high level; if near the top and ready for iteration, more discussions needed—the *right* size is much more important in adaptive	Try some hybrid techniques; e.g., creating a use case to help break it down (user story splitting techniques)
				Discuss splitting stories with product owner as they are groomed up to the top of the product backlog in preparation of next iteration
				Draw out an informal process flow with the product owner
				Continue with story point rounds to uncover assumptions and continue splitting
Manage Product Scope	Hidden scope expansion (scope creep)	Predictive	Lack of scope visibility, communication, and validation	Use more modeling to show boundaries (more visual validation techniques)
				Include a list of exclusions based on ongoing conversations
				When conducting elicitation activities, continually communicate scope boundaries

Continued

Affects the ability to...	Business Analysis Risks	Life-cycle Approach with Highest Risk	Reason for Occurrence	Recommended Approach Adjustments
Manage Product Scope (*continued*)	Constantly changing requirements	Predictive	Could be driven by external policies or regulations, unknown requirements become known with progressive elaboration	Determine root cause—*why* the changes Can they be packaged into a future release (move toward a hybrid approach)? Do the changing requirements fall within one functional area? If so, can that function be prototyped?
	Misalignment with strategy or architecture	Adaptive	Lack of access to information, lack of communication, no one on team responsible to make connection	Address during each iteration planning session, not just once during product backlog build Roadmaps should include alignment approach Change approach and include an additional iteration just to address architecture Bring in an architectural advisor during iteration planning
	Gaps in requirements	Predictive	Not identifying most impacted stakeholders and not having the time to hear from those most impacted	Specify requirements through use of modeling techniques Be better prepared for understanding scope with a scope model (as-is and to-be) to trigger probing questions Use a variety/combination of elicitation techniques to uncover gaps (such as interview, observation, and then prototype)
	Vendor misinterpreting requirements	Hybrid—vendor package	Lack of domain knowledge, requirements are ambiguous	Put more context around requirements Use more visuals and tables Have consistent terminology and structure for requirements, make more effective Avoid strictly textual requirements—use cases textually but also with models
	Gold plating—adding functionality not requested	Adaptive	Can impact adaptive timebox more than most; it could happen with any team member: *would it be nice to just change this or add that*	Teams should self monitor and ensure scope boundaries are discussed in iteration planning and conversations

The second category of risks is very specific to the elicited requirements. Each stated require-ment is reviewed for possible risks. But don't try to uncover risks for every single requirement; it is a one-to-many relationship. We will refer to these as *specific requirement risks*. BAs should ask themselves; "Is it even worth it for us to list the risks for this specific requirement?" If it is a user story that is ranked at the bottom of the product backlog, it may be unnecessary, a waste of time. In a predictive approach, risks can be associated with the requirement attributes of priority and impact or identified separately as its own requirement attribute—risks. These specific require-ment risks would need to be coordinated with the PM since they have an overall effect (both positive and negative) on the project's scope, time, budget, quality, procurement, communication, stakeholders, and dependencies with other projects. Responding to risks carries an associated cost, so trade-offs may be required. When reviewing requirements for specific requirement risks, what should we be looking for? As with the characteristics of effective requirements, you need to ask what is the feasibility of the requirement based on the following trade-offs and tolerances:

- **Cost**—can this requirement be implemented within the current project budget?
- **Schedule**—can we implement this requirement within the *two-month constraint* imposed on it? Is it feasible with the significant business impact that it has?
- **Scope and change**—is there a likelihood that the scope for this requirement will change?
- **Legal**—is there potential for violating a law, regulation, or policy by implementing the requirement?
- **Environmental**—could the user environment be impacted by the implementation of the requirement or could there be external impacts to the public?
- **Technology**—will this requirement still work within the current standard operating environment?
- **Resources**—do we have existing capabilities to implement the requirement? Are we sure the vendor can handle our localized configurations? Another vendor's client has the same configuration needs; could we just reuse them (example of positive risk, an opportunity to save money)?
- **Benefit or value**—will stakeholders get what they expect from this requirement?
- **Dependencies**—if this requirement gets implemented, will it impact other requirements or projects?

Some of the specific requirement risks will likely get integrated into the overall project risk man-agement plan owned by the PM, but they can, in turn, assign responsibility for monitoring certain risks to the BA. An example template used in project management is shown in the last few pages of the Business Case Template Appendix A2.2.

RISKS AND LIFE-CYCLE APPROACHES

In Chapter 3 we referred to Table 3.1, a comparison of the life-cycle approaches. Risk was one of the variables that was addressed, showing that risks are handled differently by life-cycle approach. Looking at it simplistically, Figure 5.2 illustrates that the more risk or complexity, the more need for control, and the predictive approach provides the most controls.

Predictive Life-Cycle Risk Management

With the predictive life-cycle approach, risks are addressed very formally with risk management plans owned by the PM, with a big picture perspective over the longer cycle. Business analysis risks and specific requirement risks may be integrated into project risk management plans at the PM's discretion, but the BA should still retain his or her own plans to track the effectiveness of approach changes. Detailed planning, especially with the use of a WBS, allows for integrating responses into the approach. Progressive elaboration will likely uncover more risks as each stage of the life cycle completes and the baselines are re-evaluated. During the change control process, change requests should be evaluated for risks.

Hybrid Life-Cycle Approach Risk Management

Risk is formally addressed like the predictive approach but has a *fail-fast* philosophy like the adaptive approach by introducing prototypes and the evolutionary approach with a roadmap of releases. In the hybrid approach, risks are also formal, but it likewise adapts the fail-fast philosophy by moving risk up front. Risks are also associated directly with use cases that are assigned to releases and iterations.

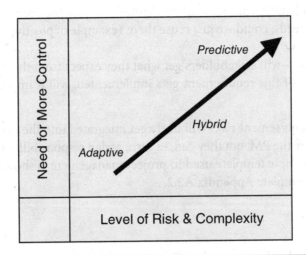

Figure 5.2   Risk versus control and life-cycle approaches

"RUP [rational unified process] takes a quite general approach to risk-based planning. It basically guides a practitioner to identify risks, identify strategies for mitigation, include risks when prioritizing use cases, and document these risks as goals for assessing the iteration. It provides few specifics on how to actually do this"[1] (Aked 2003).

Adaptive Life-Cycle Approach Risk Management

In the adaptive approach, risk management lacks any formality. Informal conversations with the product owner during product backlog grooming can uncover high-risk requirements that can be moved up the backlog to address risks in earlier iterations to fail fast. But most of the risk conversation would be with team members during the iteration. For example, experts such as architects might be brought into iteration planning meetings to discuss technology risks. Specific requirement risks can also be addressed in iteration acceptance criteria discussions. Because of the informality, teams need to be encouraged to communicate risks immediately during Scrum *stand-ups* (daily brief team meetings) and still manage them in a lightweight way. I have seen teams manage risks by posting them on their kanban boards as color coded cards (kanban is a visual board of cards showing user stories and task status). The adaptive philosophy helps to address risks early and frequently throughout the iterations.

POTENTIAL RISK BY INITIATIVE TYPE

Tables 4.1a–c referred to the following initiative types:

- Enterprise-wide
- Process-driven
- User-focused
- Small enhancement and maintenance
- Vendor package
- Data-driven
- Technology-driven

There are some risks that are associated with each of these types and their characteristics, which are discussed in more detail in this chapter.

Vendor Package Risks

Missing Requirements

The number one risk for vendor packages is missing requirements, which is why a BA should be involved with large package purchases. Stakeholders may only see things from their own perspective and not understand how everything interconnects. As a result, they may jump to make a purchase after seeing a product without performing due diligence. Missing requirements can be found in certain functional areas that did not get covered because a certain stakeholder was not considered but should have been, or the details within a more complex functional area were not uncovered because the time wasn't spent to uncover them. The risk is high with such a purchase because the company enters into a contract and the money is spent before it is apparent that the product will not work for them.

When there isn't an existing system, you need to rely on the people who are performing the processes to tell you their function and which process they want to *keep, remove, add,* or *change.* In addition, existing documentation such as user procedures or training documents can be reviewed. System analysis activities are critical, including understanding of all manual processes. When there is an existing system, reliance on those who support the systems will be necessary to learn additional details of a functional area. Often the technology group will know more about the business domain because of their knowledge of the internal workings—knowledge of how things work. It is helpful to review existing documentation if available. This can be used to reverse engineer what exists today and how the functions and features will change in the future.

Not Addressing the Nonfunctional Requirements

Nonfunctional requirements characterize the expected system behavior. Quality attribute and design constraints define nonfunctional requirements. Design constraints ensure that the vendor package can run in the environment, such as the operating systems or hardware platforms. Quality attributes describe specific properties in three environments: operational, deployment, and development. Table 5.3 provides a quality attribute checklist for those environments needed to evaluate vendor packages.[2]

Table 5.3   Quality attributes list

Classification	Attribute	Classification	Attribute	Classification	Attribute
Operational	Data integrity	Deployment	Auditability	Development	Customizability
	Performance		Availability		Efficiency
	Reliability		Data retention		Escrow
	Robustness		Flexibility		(a.k.a. Code protection)
	(a.k.a. Fault tolerance)		Interoperability		Maintainability
	Security		(a.k.a. Compatibility)		Reusability
	Usability		Portability		Testability
	(+ Accessibility)		Recoverability		
			(+ Disaster recovery)		
			Scalability		
			Safety factor		

Evaluating Unproven Vendor Packages

An organization's tolerance for risk varies greatly. My dad always told me not to buy the newest car model because it had too many undiscovered kinks that hadn't been worked out yet. However, many in today's world view this very differently. They want the latest technology and are willing to spend the extra money and aggravation for the new or extra features, in addition to allowing for the opportunity to integrate with the need for future iterations (tailoring at the vendor's expense!).

Clients and companies also have a wide range of risk tolerance. Surprisingly, some of these clients exist in very conservative industries. For example, when customer relationship management wasn't even a term yet, a bank wanted to be the first to apply this new concept. But it required building a data warehouse (also a new concept at the time) with new technology that would support the huge volumes of data. Again, they were the first to try this new technology, but felt the risk was worth it to push them ahead of other banks. To manage the risk, a very comprehensive risk management plan was created that included bringing in consultants at key review points, many iterations of proof-of-concepts, pilots, and several contingency plans.

Process-Driven Risks

Silo Thinking

Silo thinking is a failure to recognize other processes that are affected by an implemented change. Processes have many inputs and outputs, but it isn't the direct connection to another process that is usually the challenge, it is the multiple processes or systems downstream. Imagine a change made to a process that also changed a data field in one category of outputs—a simple change. But that simple change flowed through three different systems before it crashed a week later. It may take days of root cause analysis to determine which change initially caused the crash. This is where having the system and enterprise mindset helps. The larger and more complex the process-driven initiative, the more modeling tools necessary to help expand thinking and help identify areas requiring more thorough integration testing.

Process Failures

Will the process live up to the expectations of its stakeholders? If it is important to know the quality of a process, then it needs to be measured. Developing appropriate metrics is critical. There is a method that has been around for a long time and was originally developed by the U.S. government—failure modes and effects analysis (FMEA). Process-related FMEA is a method that allows early anticipation of process failures so that they can be corrected with less impact. *Failure modes* refer to the different ways a process can fail and *effects* are those harmful occurrences resulting from the failure. Like the risk management scoring referred to earlier, failures are prioritized based on the seriousness of the consequences, how often the failures happen, and how easy it is to identify the failure.

Use cases are a description of a process. The exceptions to the use cases are the things that might happen—the *what-ifs*. So, if I were to *buy a book of stamps* from the ATM, what might happen? Those are just a few potential failure modes in FMEA:

- Book of stamps does not dispense
- ATM user does not take the book of stamps
- Got more books of stamps than requested

FMEA goes beyond the identification of the failure and the system response. FMEA also has you examine the effect of the failure with severity ratings, the potential causes with an occurrence rating, any alerts, controls, or other mechanisms (beep if ATM user does not take the book of stamps). It merges the process information with risk management.[3]

Transition Failures

How will transition work? Push a button and it switches from the old system to the new system? As a team lead for the conversion team, the team was responsible for converting the current billing system to a new billing system developed by another external team located many states away. Our team worked virtually but very closely with the development team working to identify transition needs. As the conversion team, we kept pace with the development team by creating our own process models and conversion applications. The conversion applications converted hundreds of data bases, loaded just as many reference tables, built a multitude of transition reports, and ran the system in parallel for several weeks. But what really made this a successful transition was the risk management plan. Putting in place multiple checkpoints and contingency plans for a smooth transition.

Contingency plans are critical for transitions. First, there must be recognition of a problem; hence the need to monitor the transition closely. But once a problem is known, how quickly can it be fixed before impacting business continuity? Is there a work-around? Is there a backup plan? What is the cost/benefit of each alternative? If the contingency plan gets implemented, for how long? How do we recover? Risks should be addressed within any transition plan, the event identified that will trigger contingency plans, and the answers included to all those questions. Critical processes should be identified and an impact analysis of the process should be conducted ahead of time as part of the planning. The BA should work with the business manager and the PM to ensure that the plan addresses the transition requirements and the risks associated with those requirements.

Change Management

Changes in processes will likely change the way people do their work or interact with a system. People don't like change. You will need to become a change agent (see Chapter 2) and be able to communicate the benefits of change.

Data-Driven Risks

Data Quality

Data quality is our perception of how well the data will serve its intended purpose, such as the need to create a dashboard for management. But that perception of quality is always overestimated (yes, I agree with that statement). Bad quality can lead to bad decisions. It is extremely difficult to determine the quality when you are bringing in data from multiple operational sources and attempting to integrate the data. In addition to all the variety of data that exists, data's *life* is becoming shorter and shorter because change and opportunities for decision makers are happening faster and faster. To move forward, you may need to have someone to talk to whoever has accountability for that data—which is difficult to do. Start assessing quality risks. What is the likelihood of these risks? Here is a list of some quality risks to look for:

- Inconsistencies in data definitions across sources
- Duplication (same data created at multiple sources)
- Outdated information (data decay)
- Lack of adherence to standards (cross company standards don't exist)
- Unintentionally altered data
- Fields not used as intended

The use of unstructured data (pictures, videos, voice, text messaging, e-mails) has grown exponentially over the last few years and will continue to grow since there are many more opportunities to capture the data with new technology. There are even more challenges with the quality of unstructured data. To help you address some of the quality risks you may encounter, the following list contains some tips:

- Ask for metadata—information about the data
- Identify data owners
- List standards that were applied or should be applied to the data
- Understand how the data was used or how it was processed at the source
- Map out data name alias
- Ask about how current the data needs to be

Protecting Privacy

With data being spread across the world through social media, the European Union took on the challenge of the risk of protecting individual privacy by implementing the General Data Protection Regulation (GDPR) in 2018. The GDPR forces businesses to be more transparent when data breaches have been identified. As a BA, you need to be plugged into the stakeholders in your organization who have responsibility for implementing these types of policies—you have to *stay in the loop.*

User-Focused Risks

Users are a subset of stakeholders. Specific user-focused methods have been developed to mitigate risks associated with users—for example, user-centered design (UCD), user-driven development (UDD), user experience (UX), and lean UX.

User Behavior Variations

UCD addresses risk areas in which the dialogue with users is very important and may vary. An example is an electronic medical records (EMR) system. Different doctor practices or specialties have different dialogues with the solutions. This requires different user behavior data to be used for design decisions (observation, personas, interaction stats, etc.).

UDD also addresses risk areas in which the user needs a more iterative approach for acceptance. The focus is on rolling out core functionality first, known as the minimal viable product (MVP). This is what you want to try out with the users first, then build on later.

User Skill Set Variations

UX addresses risk areas around usability of the product. Often, experts are brought in who have the experience needed for specific types of users. Usability experts often look for: how consistent the interaction is, how much freedom the user must have to be successful, the user's awareness of a system's status, how well the system connects with the user's real world, the use of help tools, the efficiency of navigation, and the use of visuals.

As a trainer conducting an onsite business analysis class at an automotive company, my room assignment was across from the usability lab. The lab took up most of the building's floor, and for its time, it was state-of-the-art. It included two-way mirrors, room cameras to record user behavior, desktop cameras capturing eye movements, and utility desktop applications capturing keyboard and mouse movements. The company made a huge investment on usability and planned on developing strict internal standards for business users. Their approach to addressing many of the usability risks was to have a team of experts work on developing internal standards for business users.

Business-to-business (B2B) users have different skill sets and experiences than business-to-consumer (B2C) users. B2B skill levels are more consistent based on job standards, so usability standards can be very advantageous. This is also why B2B users are more likely to accept complexity. B2C users have varying skill levels. If the solution is too complex, there may be a risk of losing existing B2C customers. All these user-focused methods can be incorporated into other methodologies, both predictive and adaptive, to address user risks.[4]

Enterprise-Wide Focus

Miscommunication of Requirements

Because of the large teams involved in enterprise-wide initiatives, you often need to communicate requirements to vendors, consultants, or other third parties. The sheer diversity of stakeholders can cause miscommunications and interpretation differences. To prevent these issues from occurring, consider:

- A consistent use of terms and structure
- Use of visuals and matrices
- Adding additional context
- Clarification through more decomposition

Getting to an Agreement

If the culture is a consensus-driven culture, then add lots of contingency time to get stakeholders to an agreed-upon decision.

To get buy-in and agreement across multiple political entities requires:

- A strong facilitator and negotiator
- Agreement on a decision-making process *before* the need for decisions
- Courage (see Chapter 1) to address issues with executives

Lack of an Enterprise Architecture

Implementing large initiatives without a business, information, or technology architecture is like building something in the dark. It probably can be done, but it won't be easy. Things often missed in this type of environment may include:

- Interfaces
- Impacts across the enterprise
- Ability to know if strategies were implemented and show evidence of progress
- Knowing if we are investing in the right things
- How changes in certain processes impact the technology and vice versa

Technology-Driven Risks

Review Quality Attributes

The best way to look at technology risks is to review the different quality attributes. Table 5.3 provides a list of attributes that are classified as operational, deployment, and development. An operational quality attribute is performance. If we are conducting a technology migration, there might be risks associated with the performance measures between the current system baseline and the target system. Are there any unknowns that we would need to respond to? If the risk is that the technology in the target system has not proven its performance with the number of transactions that runs through our current system, then we may need to do some special operational testing for that requirement. Each quality attribute should be evaluated for technology risks.

Hitting Capacity

Who hasn't seen this risk occur? Capacity as it relates to technology is the maximum input or output that the infrastructure can handle. Technology has its limits. But, how we design capacity and how we effectively use the capacity across the infrastructure are two different things. We can design a system with three servers, which we know will handle the input and output volume. But what ends up being the problem is the storage. Hitting the capacity of technology is the pain that we try to prevent by going to Cloud solutions or other more flexible, scalable solutions because we often lack the crystal ball that can help us determine where we will be in six months, one year, or beyond. When identifying volumes, a BA should always be asking the questions: What will the volume look like in six months? Do we have any information on the trends or patterns of the volumes in the past that can help us make predictions for the future? Has anything changed that will affect the volumes?

Data Loss

Recovering from a data loss can be stressful and devastating to a business if data cannot be recovered. The cause could be a problem with the physical device, power failures, the network being down, the logic storing the data, inability to access the data, corruption of the data, user error (unintentional delete), computer viruses, accidents, etc. Each of these could have different responses. But as a BA we need to identify maintenance, backup, and recovery requirements that should be validated.

Security Vulnerabilities

This is more important in some industries than others, but security vulnerabilities can be caused by broken software, lack of controls, flaws in the hardware, old inadequate systems, or even human error. The *actors* who will leverage the vulnerabilities could be internal (employees) or external (criminals). The affect could be financial, disruptive, reputation impacting, and in extreme cases, could even affect employee or customer safety. Therefore, most organizations have a security entity that specifically addresses these risks. The BA, being responsible for eliciting security requirements, should work closely with these groups to understand the policies and regulations to help in identifying security risks through requirement reviews.

PEOPLE RISKS

There are several risks that a BA will run into regarding people. Foremost is the risk that there is a gap between the competency of those with whom we are interacting and our own capabilities to perform our role compared to the competencies and capabilities that are necessary for the initiative. This is not specific to business analysis, but part of sourcing any initiative. Specific to business analysis, the lack of domain knowledge affects the BA the most. If we are unable to gain the understanding of the current and future state, we are in trouble right from the start. Our lack of domain knowledge makes it difficult for us to probe and ask the right questions, but if the stakeholders also lack that critical domain knowledge, there is no one to answer those questions. When planning business analysis activities, we must make sure we specifically address these knowledge gaps.

Education, knowledge transfer, bringing in other resources to address competency gaps, extra time, or money may be needed to respond to people risks. Additionally, the overall approach may need to be adjusted. These plan changes need to be worked out with the PM. For example, the BA might collaborate with the PM to include a vertical prototype (see Figures 3.7 and 3.8) in the overall approach for a specific functional area in which knowledge is lacking. A vertical prototype is an approach that takes a specific area into which the team will dive in deeper and completely develop the solution just for that specific area in order to visually flesh out that part of the solution before building out the rest.

Other more common people risks include challenges with stakeholders. We may miss identifying a stakeholder, thereby missing those requirements, or the stakeholder may be resistant to the goals of the initiative, or there may be lack of consensus among stakeholders. In addition, stakeholders may be unavailable when needed, lack accountability, or are not empowered to provide the information and decisions necessary. Spending the time to perform stakeholder analysis, implement an involvement plan, and communicate clear responsibilities can mitigate many of these risks.

Certainly, some of the challenges with stakeholders can negatively impact a project. Unavailability of key resources can be devastating. Resources often change in the middle of an initiative. You may think you have finished documenting the requirements, then find that the key stakeholders have changed, and they want to review the requirements. They may disagree about which requirements are a priority. They may change the scope.

Could we have predicted this turn of events? Some risks are unknown and not visible. That is why methodologies and other processes are tools to help us address these changes. For example, most methodologies have a change control process in place. The aforementioned situation could have been handled within such a process.

BUSINESS AND ORGANIZATIONAL RISKS

To address business risks, you may need to put on your *strategy hat*. How connected are we to the strategy to show value to the organization? What is the likelihood that the strategy may change? Will the external business environment change (economic environment, a looming acquisition or merger, introduction and passing of laws and regulations, new competitors, etc.)? Will the changes in the environment force our sponsors to make changes to the business strategy? Although these are risks that we cannot control, we must still act. The probability of the business environment changing may need to be addressed within the approach. One example is a vendor who wants to introduce a product for EMR before the law is passed by Congress to allow it. The vendor designed the software and made it very easy to change, so even if the law passed as it was written, what are the risks that the law might change again with a new administration? If so, they made the software easier to change by allowing that flexibility with the design.

Most risks are undesirable, particularly if you take a risk that is illegal or unethical such as taking a bribe to select a specific vendor. However, the acceptance of certain risks might be more strategic because there is an expectation to get a return on investment by taking on certain risks. These are risks that are pursued, yet managed, because of potential payoff.[5]

RISK CULTURE

There are traits of strong risk cultures that support quick responses to risk and may share some common traits, which include:

1. Acknowledging the risk
2. Encouraging transparency
3. Ensuring respect for the risk
4. Building up the culture to effectively deal with the risk
5. Finding consensus on the risk culture
6. Sustaining vigilance[6]

There are a few team dynamics that are detrimental to managing risk and should not be promoted as part of the culture. These include: groupthink, normalization of deviance, confirmation bias, and escalating commitment. Groupthink applies when support is obtained from the group and those not in line with that support suppress their objections or get rejected from the group if they voice their objections. Groupthink is more likely to happen when the team has a manager who is overbearing. Normalization of deviance is when we continually observe or have been advised of warning signs and just tolerate them (fire alarm going off and no one reacts because they become immune to it going off). So, the team falls into following along and agreeing—"everything will be ok, it is just a minor alarm." Confirmation bias is when we believe information that supports our position and we reject information that contradicts our position. We escalate commitment to a failure, such as a project, by throwing more resources and money at it hoping that it will make it better (Kaplan and Mikes 2012).

> "Obviously, a shortage of risk consciousness will lead to trouble. But it is all too easy to assume that a thorough set of risk-related processes and oversight structures is sufficient to avert a crisis. Companies cannot assume that a healthy risk culture will be a natural result. Rather, leadership teams must tackle risk culture just as thoroughly as any business problem, demanding evidence about the underlying attitudes that pervade day-to-day risk decisions" (Krivkovich and Levy 2005).

SUMMARY

- All initiatives have risks. Risks are uncertain events that have the possibility of occurring and identifying the impact on the initiative if they occur.
- There are various methods of dealing with risk; it can be avoided, transferred, shared, mitigated, or enhanced—or it can be accepted.
- There are business analysis risks that can impact the performance of business analysis work, product scope, and the implementation of requirements (business, stakeholder, solution, and business rules).
- Requirements should be reviewed for risks to resources, cost, schedule, scope, legal, environmental, technology, vendor, benefits, and dependencies.
- In a predictive life-cycle approach, risk management is owned by the PM, the BA provides input to the PM based on the risks associated with the requirements. In a hybrid life-cycle approach, risk may be formally managed but may incorporate a fail-fast approach. In an adaptive life-cycle approach, the fail-fast concept provides a framework for identifying risks quickly and addressing them in early iterations.
- Requirements traceability is a critical function of process-driven systems to manage change and risk when a change is made at a high level and can affect other processes and systems downstream.
- Quality can only be achieved if it can be measured. The key is to identify impacts and risks early in the process when the impact can be minimized and contingency plans made.
- During the transition to a new system, critical processes should be identified with contingency plans in place to mitigate any impact on the business. Change management should take place in parallel to ready the *people side* of the transition to ensure a smooth transition.
- Data quality should serve the purpose of providing the information that is needed to make business decisions. Often there is duplicate data, inconsistencies in data definition, outdated data, or data that doesn't adhere to standards. Data privacy and cybersecurity are becoming more critical.
- There are multiple methods for capturing user interactions with a system. These methods have been created to mitigate risk associated with users and can be incorporated into predictive, adaptive, or hybrid methodologies to identify and reduce user risks.
- Enterprise-wide implementations require an increased level of communication including vendors, consultants, and third parties perhaps on a worldwide basis. This has its own special challenges and risks, including culture, language, and geographical dispersion.
- The BA needs to have courage, be a good negotiator and facilitator, as well as get agreement and buy-in on the decision-making process—sometimes even before decisions are needed.
- Availability of subject matter experts, stakeholders, decision makers, and users can be a risk if unavailable or if they lack the breadth of understanding of the current state and future state of the solution. These risks need to be identified and communicated to the PM.

- Other risks may include a changing business or regulatory environment, new technology or competitive pressures, acquisitions, mergers, and corporate cultures—all of these need to be identified and communicated so that contingency plans can be put in place.

QUESTIONS

1. For each situation, identify three risks (this may require you to do some research online) and determine how you might adjust your business analysis approach to respond to those risks.

   a. You are working for a bank and you are implementing a Cloud solution package for your HR benefits organization. It is the first time a Cloud solution will be used for your company.

   _____

   _____

   _____

   b. You are working for a training company that currently does all instructor-led workshops and will be implementing the first all eLearning program to sell as a solution for their clients.

   _____

   _____

   _____

2. For the following risk scenario, identify why you would want to respond to the risk and name three different strategies to respond to the risk.

   Sally is planning to parachute jump out of a plane for her 40th birthday. There is a risk that her parachute may not open properly.

   Why respond: _____

   _____

   Three risk strategies:

   1. _____

   2. _____

   3. _____

3. Name three key considerations for identifying risks specifically associated with a requirement?

   Three key considerations:

   1. _____

   2. _____

   3. _____

4. In an adaptive life-cycle approach, which user stories are likely to not be addressed for risk?

   _____

   _____

   _____

5. For the following two scenarios, identify the risk(s) and provide a response to the risk(s).

   *a) When wrapping up the interviews, you realized that 80% of stakeholders were consistent with their needs, but 20% were conflicting. You are pressured to move forward, but you **do not** feel confident that this should be passed on to design this way.*

   Risk: _____

   Response: _____

   _____

   Lessons learned: _____

   _____

   b) The PM is asking if the estimate for implementing the new system will be impacted based on the requirements you have gathered. You believe the estimate will be impacted, so you set up a meeting to go over the information captured so far. It looks like 60% of the requirements are identified as highly volatile requirements and about 20% are highly complex with a large business impact.

   Risk: _____

   Response: _____

   _____

NOTES

1. Aked, Mark. (November 2003). *Risk Reduction with the RUP phase plan.* IBM. https://www .ibm.com/developerworks/rational/library/1826.html.

2. Gottensdiener, Ellen. (2005). *The Software Requirements Memory Jogger,* pp. 329–334. Goal QPC.

3. Tague, Nancy R. (2005). The Quality Toolbox, Second Edition. American Society for Quality. Quality Press.

4. Courage, Catherine and Kathy Baxter. (2005). *Understanding Your Users: A Practical Guide to User Requirements Methods, Tools and Techniques.* San Francisco, CA: Morgan Kaufmann.

5. Kaplan, Robert S. and Anette Mikes. (June 2012). "Managing Risks: A New Framework." *Harvard Business Review* Article. https://hbr.org/2012/06/managing-risks-a-new-framework.

6. Krivkovich, Alexis and Cindy Levy. (May 2015). "Managing the people side of risk." Mckinsey & Company Article. https://www.mckinsey.com/business-functions/risk/our -insights/managing-the-people-side-of-risk.

6

STEP FIVE—ALWAYS FOCUS ON VALUE

"To be a master chef is to go beyond the doors of the restaurant. It is about looking at food trends and new opportunities; constantly reviewing our menus, cooking processes, and techniques for potential improvements; evaluating the customer's response to changes in our menu items; and making the needed adjustments to provide more value to not only the restaurant patrons, but to the restaurant owner as well."—Chapter One

WHAT IS VALUE

How does each stakeholder see value? Businesses typically look at value in terms of finances, such as return on investment (ROI), net present value (NPV) and internal rate of return (IRR). These are further described in the Business Case Template Appendix A2.2 and later in this chapter. But each industry may have a different view, as might each organization or stakeholder. In addition to financial terms, value could be described in terms of:

- **Employee performance**—time-to-hire, reduction of churn rate, satisfaction index, etc.
- **Operational performance**—reduction of waste, capacity utilization, time-to-market, etc.
- **Market related**—brand equity, market share, market growth rate, etc.
- **Customer value**—retention, satisfaction, value over lifetime, profitability of each, etc.
- **Sustainability of environment**—carbon footprint, energy consumption, waste reduction, etc.
- **Servicing the poor**—financial independence, sustainable work, etc.
- **Quality related**—reduction of defects

Value is subjective, based on the priority and trade-offs of many elements—*not* just *one*. As strategic business analysts (BAs), we need to especially understand the business trade-offs. Are we, as a company, willing to pay more to get better quality? Are we willing to risk environmental concerns to get a better ROI? Value should also be viewed holistically across the enterprise. An increase in value for one stakeholder group might decrease the value for another. For example, if we implement a change for sales that increases their sales by 20% but we don't make any changes to production to handle the increase, then the impact would be negative for production since they can't keep up with the sales. Do we address both? Do we worry about sales first, then another release for production? Do we implement production changes first in preparation? Ultimately, we should be looking at the value to the customer. They will be impacted if we don't balance both. If we don't put that enterprise thinking hat on, we might help one group and hinder another without considering the overall impact.

If quality is also a component of value, then what is quality as it relates to what we do as tactical (project-related) BAs? Quality from a BA perspective is how well our requirements are defined, traced, and accepted throughout the life cycle.

BE A VALUE MANAGER

The Role

BAs should put on the value manager *hat* to look out for the value that a solution will bring to their stakeholders (solution value) *and* for the value that the business analysis activities (BA work value) provide to the process, which ultimately provides the solution. When in the role of a value manager, you should always:

- Help stakeholders and team players figure out what is valuable to them and how to accomplish it while determining which of your own activities and techniques performed are more valuable than others (apply lean thinking, eliminate wasteful activities)
- Connect value to requirements and recommended solution alternatives
- Look backward to ensure alignment with the original expectations of value (traceability)
- Look out into the future to determine if value is sustainable and contributes to an overall goal (solution evaluation)
- Monitor value and address gaps between expectations and what is being delivered (manage stakeholder expectations)

Create a Value Story

The solution value and the business analysis work value each have their own value story, but they also need to connect. Both of those value stories should be elaborated into an informal or formal requirements management plan (RMP). Or you can think of it as the *value stream* business analysis approach.

Take the chef/cook example that was brought up in the first chapter of the book. What is the outcome that the customer values (quality, needs, and timeliness) and how does it tie to the value defined by internal stakeholders (make a profit)? Can we understand the value perceived for each stakeholder? Can we balance them to meet all our stakeholder expectations? By looking at the value of the steps in our approach (BA work value), we should ask ourselves, did we connect the steps to the stakeholder's perceived value and eventually to the solution value? The chef had an old-world pasta recipe he wanted to try for his Italian food lovers. He had the process down and knew that the type of flour for the pasta was a special whole wheat flour, the pasta cooking time was critical, and the cheese had to be a sheep's milk parmesan that had aged for seven years. All of these ingredients had *business rules* associated with them—standards to ensure the quality of the dish. He also added a special ingredient with the cream sauce—truffles. Since the ingredients are twice the price of his other dishes, he raised the price. It now costs more and takes more time to make, but what a great dish! If the chef messed up, will the customer let the chef know? Is there a process for feedback to ensure the customers are still getting their perceived value for the dish? Will they just not order the dish, or not come back? How can the chef know how to change the dish before it becomes a larger problem? How flexible is the chef to change in the moment (customer has allergies to truffles)? What could the chef do to adjust the process to validate assumptions of value? Does the restaurant owner perceive value if now there is much less profit on this dish?

A friend had a recent bad experience at a restaurant. She received a steak that was gray and had an odor. She did not eat it and told the waiter who promptly got a new meal for her. She saw the waiter throw out the dish and wondered if the waiter told anyone. The next day, she decided to call back to make sure the manager was aware of it. Turns out, he was not. He mentioned that all returned dishes were supposed to go into a separate section of the refrigerator and the manager was to examine any returned meal from that previous day for lessons learned with the kitchen staff. That did not happen. The waiter did not want to get the chef in trouble, so the dish got thrown out and the manager never knew it happened. So, that nicely defined process was not being executed. Should she expect the situation to be corrected and give the restaurant another try?

Managing expectations of our stakeholders is part of the value manager's job. Figure 6.1 shows the importance of stakeholder involvement. The gap between expectations and what the team is building as a solution just gets bigger and bigger as you progress through the solution life cycle (SLC) if it is not addressed. In an adaptive life-cycle approach, the user story owner should be committed during the life of the iteration. For predictive and hybrid life-cycle approaches, there is a more formal need to address stakeholder involvement. Stakeholder involvement communications should include:

- Whether the involvement is a requirement or optional
- Degree of involvement and frequency
- Discussion of any involvement concerns (such as scheduling conflicts, need for a backup, etc.)
- How they are to participate
- Preferred elicitation method if they are a source of requirements (optional)
- Their communication preference (optional)

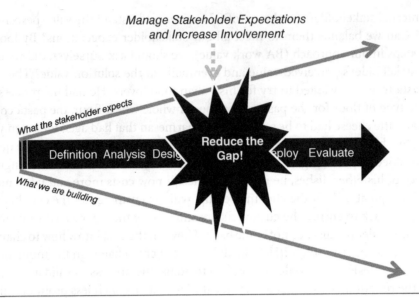

Figure 6.1 Manage stakeholder expectations

To summarize stakeholder expectations, there is a *customer bill of rights* that I adapted from a requirements book by Wiegers and Beatty[1] that is a valuable perspective from a stakeholder's viewpoint. "I, the customer, expect you, the BA, to:

1. Speak my language,
2. Learn about my business and objectives,
3. Record requirements in the right form to communicate to the technical folks,
4. Educate me on requirement practices and deliverables,
5. Understand that requirements may change,
6. Appreciate and respect the time I am investing,
7. Provide alternative solutions and make suggestions (advise me),
8. Guide me through the detailed characteristics to make the product easy to use,
9. Communicate ways or alternatives for accelerating development, and
10. Deliver a system that meets my functional needs and quality expectations."

Look at number 10. How exactly do we do that?

MOVE FROM INTANGIBLE TO TANGIBLE

"Anything can be measured. If a thing can be observed in any way at all, it lends itself to some type of measurement method. No matter how *fuzzy* the measurement is, it's still a measurement if it tells you more than you knew before. And those very things most likely to be immeasurable are, virtually always, solved by relatively simple measurement methods"[2] (Hubbard 2010).

Start with Value Propositions

Defining value propositions for stakeholder groups helps to distinguish the different perceptions of value. Value propositions can be used as part of stakeholder analysis or formally included in business cases to uncover benefits and to make benefits more tangible. There is no set template for writing a value proposition but always make sure that you clearly identify the stakeholder receiving the value and that you talk their language, specifically convey the value and show why this recommendation is the right choice to make. Here are three examples of convincing value propositions from different perspectives for the same initiative:

- **Example One**—Based on information gathered from benchmarking results, the value of allowing the ATM customer to purchase stamps as a convenience and for a small fee by offering the stamps at ATMs could represent a minimal amount in profits (10% profit margin) but may influence customers to use our ATM services with this added convenience. A survey conducted in 20XX showed 5% of customers specifically asked for this feature.
- **Example Two**—The teller could direct customers to the new *purchase stamps* feature and as a result would reduce the need for customers to go into the bank for the same service or having the teller worry about keeping a supply of stamps. This could represent additional reduction of teller time allocated to this function with a potential savings of over $900 per bank per year.
- **Example Three**—Bank executives could improve the third-party relationship with postal service by providing these stamps at ATMs. Allowing our bank to sell custom stamps will further establish our brand. Since the custom stamps are a new offering from the postal service, we are willing to pilot this new product with the postal service within the next year.

Value propositions are just a start to becoming tangible. How can we make them more tangible? We started with the idea that generated the need to justify it and get approval—a business case. We identified our stakeholders and then we wrote our value propositions as shown in the examples.

You could put some more measures in the value statement. But that is still not enough if we don't have a method to measure and the metrics needed in order to measure. That takes it all the way to tangible—something we can measure with a way to do it. As long as the value is clearly stated, you can ask the question, "How can we measure this?" In example one it looks like the move to tangible might be easier than the rest since some quantifiable analysis or measures have already been done. You add some further analysis to determine the formula for the measures defined in the value proposition—10% profit and how the reduction in teller time was calculated. Then determine how some of these measures (which ones?) could be captured for future monitoring with associated metrics (% of instances when books were bought when other transactions were performed, cost of books, cost of maintenance impact, etc.). And finally, make the determination of the method to measure—where and how in the process. This is where a process model can be very helpful in making that determination (data capture points).

Business Requirements Example

Business requirements are the high-level requirements, regardless of life-cycle approach, that provide the business perspective on an idea or change—what it is and why we want to do it. These requirements are often at such a high level that it would be difficult to know whether we have accomplished them or not. A concept called *SMART*—translates to specific, measurable, achievable, relevant, and time-framed—can help address that problem (other versions of SMART replace *relevant* with *realistic* and *achievable* with *acceptable*). SMART is based on a management by objective theory that is over 60 years old and aligns goals within an organization.[3] Since business requirements also include business objectives, this theory is commonly used to help in measuring business requirements and adding robustness to the requirement while making it more tangible.

The following scenario illustrates the SMART concept by considering a statement made by the vice president who oversees procurement, "In the next three years, we must reduce the number of our direct suppliers, deflect supplier risks to fewer and larger suppliers, and automate standard interfaces to these larger suppliers, which will eventually reduce our vendor management and procurement costs."

- **Specific**—this is where scope and boundaries need to be considered. I might ask whether we are addressing a specific set of suppliers; for example, only those suppliers that are providing us with raw materials. What risks do we want deflected and which suppliers do we consider to be large?
- **Measurable**—this is where you need to know whether you have met the expectations of the requirements. Is there an expectation as to how much they want to reduce costs? Is there a specific number of suppliers they want to reduce to (quantity or percentage)? How will that reduce costs? Are there any quality expectations?
- **Achievable**—do we have the capabilities to accomplish this need? Are there dependencies to other business requirements or other external dependencies for us to accomplish it? Are there any risks? Maybe before this consolidation can happen, we need another technology organizational initiative to obtain business intelligence data for these suppliers that we don't have today to test the feasibility. It may be necessary to break this requirement down into multiple business requirements depending on the scope of what can be accomplished and when it can be accomplished.
- **Relevant**—does the objective describe why it should be done and what the impact would be? Yes—reduce cost, which needs to be measurable. But is this aligned with another overarching strategy? Does it describe the value or how it supports an enterprise vision?

- **Time-framed**—it does specify three years. But that is a long time to check whether it has been accomplished. Can we wait that long? What happens after it is implemented? Will this be done in phases to verify the value earlier? Are there any measures that could be checked at deployment and can continue to be monitored?

The value in defining SMART concepts is the clarity it provides in communicating what the solution must achieve to establish a basis for justification, to help make decisions, to uncover assumptions that may need to be documented, and to manage stakeholder expectations. Regardless of approach, SMART business requirements are a necessity whether they are described in a business case, project charter, business use case, or an epic within a product backlog.

In predictive life-cycle approaches with larger initiatives, a business case to justify the initiative is required to make sure we are investing in the right things. Although we won't go into building the business case in this book, we will address those components that may require our versatility. For the adaptive life-cycle approach, Leffingwell suggests the use of a lightweight business case template for business epics that estimates the investment and applies a weighted rating and a simple roadmap.[4]

As mentioned earlier, business requirements should be SMART regardless of approach. Value propositions can be informally addressed as part of personas or user stories in the more adaptive approaches but would need to be formally documented as part of the business case in predictive life-cycle approaches. The business case is needed for large initiatives in order to demonstrate: (1) strategic alignment, (2) a sense of initial scope, (3) the trade-offs of cost versus benefits versus risk, and (4) how benefits (value) will be monitored to realization. In Chapter 3, we discussed the business case when referring to the predictive life-cycle approach in the concept definition stage.

Business requirements, which include benefits, must go beyond SMART within the business case. In order to manage value expectations with the stakeholders, all stakeholders should participate in defining the benefits and how they will be tracked. In the value manager role, it is important to facilitate the process and identify the benefits measures, the owner, the target, when the benefits will be realized, the cost/savings, and how it will be formally tracked through the life-cycle approach. Any changes should be assessed to see if they will increase or decrease the overall benefits.

MOVE FROM POTENTIAL VALUE TO REAL VALUE

The potential value of solutions was considered when we justified the initiative at the program level. But we have another chance to look at potential value since it becomes more real during the progression in predictive and hybrid life-cycle approaches once the stakeholder requirements have been identified for build versus buy decisions and again after solution requirements have been identified for design options. As in the business case, you may perform many analysis techniques to assess value: estimates, cost/benefit analysis, risk analysis, financial analysis, etc. We hope that benefits exceed the cost, especially as we progress and we have a more detailed view of what the solutions might look like. In the business case we made many assumptions, but at this point, those assumptions become validated: (1) some have changed, (2) some have become *true* and turned into more detailed requirements, and (3) some have remained since they apply to future SLC stages.

Assumptions that were made early in the business case for the predictive approach or even during business epic conversations for the adaptive approach are likely to evolve as we learn more (progressive elaboration). When looking at potential value again as it becomes more real (at SLC stages or during backlog grooming), we need to address previous assumptions and manage stakeholder expectations if original assumptions have changed (revisit Figure 6.1).

Value Versatility at the Enterprise Level

Strategy to Balanced Scorecard

Consulting firms had a big boost in the 1990s (I was in the midst of it) when large companies were going through some major changes and they were having difficulty making sure their strategies were being implemented. Program/project management and other governance processes took off and put money in consultant's pockets. Not to say it wasn't deserved, but it was apparent that companies had some pains that became opportunities for them and others. In 1996, the balanced scorecard was introduced by Kaplan and Norton[5] in a book that was based on a study conducted in 1990 by the Nolan Norton Institute—the research arm of the consulting firm KPMG. The balanced scorecard was used for measuring and managing operational perspectives that are aligned to the business's vision and overall strategy—a management system. The focus in measurement had always been on short-term financials, but the study found that a balance was needed for organizations to "stand the test of time."

The balanced scorecard is organized into four perspectives: financial, customer, internal business processes (also other versions identify this balance as employees), and innovation and learning (a.k.a. learning and growth). These perspectives can also be used to help facilitate the definition of business objectives. For example, an objective for a financial perspective may be to increase sales of a newly designed drill by 10% within a certain time, but an objective from the customer perspective might be to earn a satisfaction rating for that drill of 90% or better while increasing the sales. An internal business perspective might be to increase production of that drill also by 10% to ensure that it keeps up with the sales, and the learning perspective may be to increase the capabilities of the sales staff in understanding the new features of the product. Like the value propositions discussed earlier, you are looking at different perspectives.

Figure 6.2 illustrates an example balanced scorecard using the training company scenario that was first illustrated as a business model canvas in Figure 2.2. The vision of "creating supplemental eLearning modules for our courses that can be used to enhance our customer's learning outside of the workshop" is looked at from the four perspectives. Each perspective looks at: (1) what actions

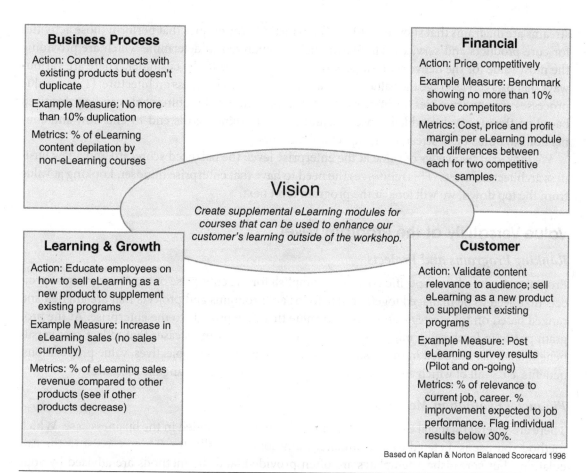

Business Process

Action: Content connects with existing products but doesn't duplicate

Example Measure: No more than 10% duplication

Metrics: % of eLearning content depilation by non-eLearning courses

Financial

Action: Price competitively

Example Measure: Benchmark showing no more than 10% above competitors

Metrics: Cost, price and profit margin per eLearning module and differences between each for two competitive samples.

Vision

Create supplemental eLearning modules for courses that can be used to enhance our customer's learning outside of the workshop.

Learning & Growth

Action: Educate employees on how to sell eLearning as a new product to supplement existing programs

Example Measure: Increase in eLearning sales (no sales currently)

Metrics: % of eLearning sales revenue compared to other products (see if other products decrease)

Customer

Action: Validate content relevance to audience; sell eLearning as a new product to supplement existing programs

Example Measure: Post eLearning survey results (Pilot and on-going)

Metrics: % of relevance to current job, career. % improvement expected to job performance. Flag individual results below 30%.

Based on Kaplan & Norton Balanced Scorecard 1996

Figure 6.2   Example balanced scorecard: training company

need to be taken, (2) the measure for the action, and (3) the metrics needed to measure it. This is when we know that we have implemented a balanced strategy. As a BA, we would take this down to the tactical level to determine how these can be measured—which processes are impacted, do we have new data requirements, do we have new functional requirements, and do we have new business rules? The balanced scorecard is the bridge to make that strategy operational. These are used in place of or in compliment to the SMART business requirements. Because it is at the enterprise strategic level, if it does exist and was created to ensure strategy implementation, then it should be applied regardless of life-cycle approach.

Value Views in the Business Architecture

In Chapter 2, we addressed the business architecture. There are several assets of the business architecture that can show value. One example at the enterprise level is a value stream. Value streams are diagrams that show end-to-end activities and the entities that perform those activities for core products and services. These activities are analyzed to determine which are providing the most value for the delivery of the product and our service to the customer. There are various ways that BAs can leverage the value stream assets located in a business architecture: (1) low-value processes are opportunities for improvement or elimination, (2) requirements can be prioritized based on the most value-added processes, and (3) understanding the end-to-end flow and connections to other value streams for impact assessments.

We looked at two views of value at the enterprise level: the balanced scorecard and a few business architecture assets. This reinforces the need to have that enterprise mindset. Looking at value from the top down, we will look at the program level next.

Value Versatility at the Program Level

Ranking Programs and Projects

Programs can be a list of specific goals to accomplish for the enterprise or may be a group of projects that need to be managed together. Portfolios are programs and projects that are aligned and ranked based on the strategic and financial value that they provide to the enterprise. At the program portfolio level, value might be shown by comparing business cases that reflect cost versus benefit analysis. Included in the business case may be measurable objectives, value propositions, benefits, etc.—all of which are used to provide both tangible and intangible measures.

Financial Evaluation Methods

There are several financial evaluation methods that may be included in the business case. Which method you use is dictated by your financial advisors. Typically, the BA may assist in the calculations, but spreadsheet templates are often provided, and the methods are advised by your financial groups:

1. Initial cost method (= initial investment)
   - Initial price is the sole decision criterion to choose between two or more investment alternatives
   - Ignores potential for variations in the future cash inflows for each of the alternatives

2. Payback period (= initial investment/annual savings)
   - Length of time needed to recoup initial investment through cash flows generated from investment
   - Does not account for cash flows after payback period, so not a good measure of profitability
   - Does not consider the time value of money

3. ROI (= annual net benefits/initial investment)
   - Reduces uncertainty about cost and benefits and can prevent wasteful spending

- Helps uncover stakeholder expectations
- Develops priorities for investment management
- Focuses on expected outcomes and benefits realization
- Builds management support for capturing data
- Uses credible sources when estimating value
- Avoids applying to strategic initiatives
- Considers hurdle rates (used to budget capital expenditures)

4. NPV (= sum of annual discounted inflows minus initial investment—a.k.a. discounted cash flows)
   - A dollar earned today is more valuable than a dollar earned in one year
   - Future revenue streams are discounted to reflect today's values so that they can be compared to today's expenditures
   - Discount rate is based on the marginal cost of capital

5. IRR (= the rate at which NPV equals zero)
   - Finds the average ROI earned through life of investment
   - Determines the discount rate that equates the present value of future cash flows to the cost of the investment
   - Considers time value of money

A program charter is created to commit the resources and funding to move forward on the program. The program charter will generate individual project charters, a road map of business-level epics depending on the life-cycle approaches used. Figure 6.3 shows how an adaptive life-cycle approach can provide ROI at each iteration, whereas the predictive life-cycle approach won't show ROI until after its implementation for the full product launch, which can be many months out (Leffingwell 2011).

Regardless of approach, value can be tracked many ways at the tactical level—for example, by aligning and tracing requirements such as stakeholder requirements to solution requirements.

Showing Value at the Requirements Level (Within Projects or Iterations)

Elaboration from Business to Stakeholder to Solution Requirements

Value can be shown by aligning requirements through their three levels: (1) business requirements, (2) stakeholder requirements, and (3) solution requirements:

Business requirement: *BIZ12—Allow non-commercial members access to our online Health Fit system, expand features for public use, and expand market exposure by at least 10% within one year after implementation.*

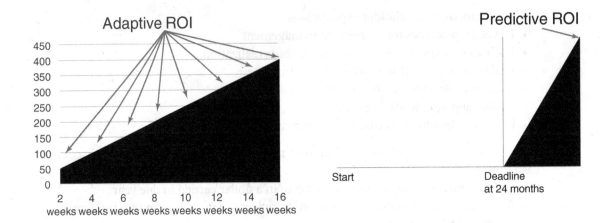

"Sooner we deliver value to our customer the sooner they will pay us for it."

- Dean Leffingwell

Figure 6.3   Adaptive versus predictive ROI

Business requirements are often stated in terms of: increase, reduce, improve, satisfy, comply, etc. They are from a business perspective. In the predictive approach you would give them a unique identifier for traceability. In an adaptive approach, there is little need for formal traceability because: (1) there is a lot of collaboration, (2) there is a very short time-box for the iteration, and (3) someone on the team (the BA) should have their enterprise and strategic mindset to ensure there is discussion around it. There may be a need when: (a) policies or regulations drive traceability for audit purposes and (b) there is a business-level epic (high-level user story similar to a business requirement) that the product owner wants to track across multiple iterations. But they can only be implementable if stakeholders' requirements (user stories) define what they *need the ability to do* to help accomplish that business requirement:

Predictive stakeholder requirement: *SR88—Public member needs the ability to track and display their health statistics* (traced to BIZ10).

Adaptive stakeholder requirement: *As a public member I want to track and see my own health statistics so that I can check my progress weekly.*

These statements coming from stakeholders can be at various levels, whether they are written in textual form within deliverables for the predictive approach or structured as user stories and put in a product backlog for an adaptive approach. If we were to buy a vendor package, we may stop here, at the stakeholder requirements (black box—we don't care what happens inside). But if we are to build it, we need to go deeper and define the solution requirements (white box—we care how the stakeholder requirements get accomplished). The stakeholder requirement is not effective enough to build from, so we need to understand what is expected from the solution to support the stakeholder requirement. There may be many solution requirements associated with one stakeholder requirement. One functional and one nonfunctional example is shown:

> Predictive functional requirement: *FR290—Health Fit system shall display the weight in pounds for the last 12 months when the public member selects the weight statistics option* (traced to SR88).

> Predictive nonfunctional requirement: *NFR123—Health Fit system must utilize the enterprise security system to prevent unauthorized access to client medical information.*

In the adaptive example, the solution requirements would be defined in the acceptance criteria when elaborating on the user story during iteration conversation.

Adaptive acceptance criteria (functional and nonfunctional):

a. Weight is displayed for last 12 months on a graph.
b. Weight loss/gain is calculated and shown separately providing motivational messages.
c. Blood pressures are displayed as a list for each instance taken in the last month.
d. Health coach comments are displayed.

In a hybrid life-cycle approach, use cases are likely to be used. Use cases show both the stakeholder and the functional requirements. Also use cases can start at a high-level goal, *UC21 Manage Health Statistics*, and can also be broken down into *UC21.1 Obtain Weight Statistics, UC21.2 Obtain Blood Pressure Statistics*, etc. Within each, the interaction between the actor (public member) and the system (Health Fit) would be defined as sequential steps (see use case example and template Appendix A3.1). The steps that describe the system response are the functional requirements.

Requirement Verification

Verification means that we are checking our requirements and designs against some standards of quality. By adhering to quality standards, we can then provide the solution value that stakeholders expect. Is the requirement well written? Is it easily understood? Does it reflect reality? Can it be used?

- Example characteristics of effective requirements (predictive):
  - Is the requirement *bounded* by a condition or capability?
  - If we get our questions answered for the ambiguous words, is it *unambiguous, concise,* and *understandable* (business terms, no reference to technology) enough to pass to someone who will design and build the solutions?
  - Is it *testable* so we can validate that it was fulfilled?
  - Is the requirement *feasible*—can it realistically be accomplished?
  - Is it *unique, consistent,* and *prioritized* across the full set of requirements?
  - Are there attributes that can help *organize, package,* or *document* the requirement?

- Is the requirement *independent* of technical solutions?
- Is it *complete* and at the appropriate level to guide us in future work?

- Example characteristics of effective user stories using the acronym INVEST[6]—independent, negotiable, valuable, estimable, small, and testable (adaptive):
  - Can dependencies to other user stories or projects be removed so that the user story is *independent*?
  - Can we continue to *negotiate* trade-offs?
  - Can business benefits be clearly understood to convey how *valuable* the user story is?
  - Is it possible to understand the user story's scope well enough to *estimate* the work?
  - Is the user story *small* enough that it can be accomplished within an iteration?
  - Is the user story *testable* so we can determine that it is acceptable and complete?

- Example characteristics of a quality use case (hybrid):
  - Systems mid-level use case is unique with one primary actor and their goal
  - Pre-conditions and post-conditions define the boundaries
  - Basic path (a.k.a. normal path or main success scenario) ends with a successful delivery and the steps show the interaction between the primary actor and the system progressing toward the goal
  - Extensions define additional scenarios that may be exceptions or alternate paths
  - Descriptions of design elements are avoided

Requirement Validation

Validation is the process of evaluating the solution at certain points in the life cycle to determine whether or not it satisfied the requirements. There are several ways to conduct validation. Figure 6.4 illustrates validation for both predictive and hybrid life-cycle approaches using: reviews, prototypes, test phases, and live validations (pilots, releases, parallel adoption).

Reviews are conducted throughout the life cycle to validate that the requirement is being addressed. It is much less expensive to review a design document and find a missing requirement than to wait until a test is conducted of an already built solution. Conducting requirement reviews by testers could reveal defects early. Prototypes are common for hybrid life cycles and give stakeholders an early opportunity to validate for themselves whether some of their requirements are being met. Each test phase, as described in the SLC in Chapter 3, has a purpose. Determining what tests are needed depends on whether there is a need to know the internal workings. Figure 6.5 illustrates the difference between white box testing, black box testing, and grey box testing. Unit tests validate the integrity and quality of what is built and requires a good understanding of the internals—white box testing. Component and integration testing validates interoperability, which requires understanding of how information is being passed and the interfaces that convert that information—grey box testing. System testing validates nonfunctional requirements and

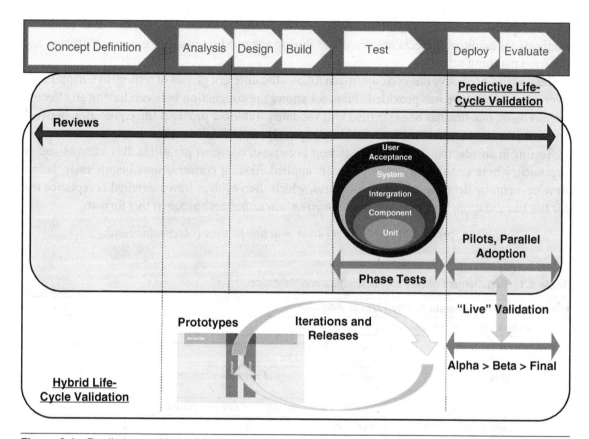

Figure 6.4   Predictive and hybrid life-cycle validations

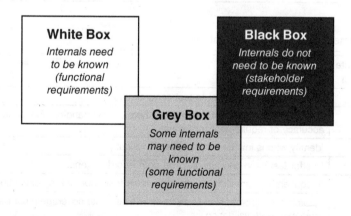

Figure 6.5   Do you need to know internal workings?

user acceptance validates stakeholder requirements—black box testing. Reviews and validation methods for adaptive projects are discussed during the product backlog grooming process and iteration planning activities.

Testing in a predictive life-cycle approach follows the different phases of testing. In Chapter 3, an overview of each type was provided. Table 6.1 shows the connection between having an effective requirement, one that has been verified and validated. Table 6.2 provides the connection between a few requirement attributes (discussed in Chapter 2) and validation.

Testing in an adaptive approach is different because of the short iterations. It is a *test-as-you-go approach*, where test-driven development is applied. Testing conversations begins early, before development, by defining acceptance criteria, which then evolves into a detailed acceptance test for use in validation. This example uses the *given/when/then* technique in this format:

given (pre-condition) / when (actor + action) / then (observable result)

Table 6.1   Requirement quality characteristics and validation

Verification of Requirement Quality	Use in Validation
Bounded by a condition or capability	Use to create test cases.
Unambiguous, concise, and understandable	May result in different outcomes based on assumptions. Consistent outcomes needed for validation.
Testable/Verifiable	Must know the criteria of outcome acceptance eliminating opinions or preferences.
Feasible	Consider if it can be tested; if not, is it feasible?
Unique, consistent, and prioritized	Prioritization helps to identify testing priorities.
Organized, packaged, and documented	Helps to organize test cases for validation.

Table 6.2   Requirement attributes and validation

Requirement Attribute (about requirements)	Use in Validation
Unique identifier	Use to trace requirement to test components.
Status	State of the requirement. Identifies if there are outstanding questions or issues. Impacts accuracy of requirement for testing.
Source and owner	Identify who is involved in test results validation.
Priority and urgency	Use for test case prioritization and go/no-go decisions.
Stability or volatility	If requirements are likely to change, adjust test approach by expecting changes.
Complexity	Impacts test approach and use to determine if test coverage must be increased with more extensive validation.
Release or iteration	Impacts test plan and approach.
Supporting material	Helps in test case development (sample screens, reports, etc.).

The acceptance test using the *given/when/then* format for acceptance criteria *A* (weight is displayed for last 12 months on a graph) would look like this:

> Given *public member is on results page* when *the weight statistics option is selected*, then *the weight will be displayed in pounds on a list ordered in ascending order by date for up to the previous 12 months.*

Another approach for the adaptive acceptance test is using the *specification by example* technique, also for acceptance criteria *A*:

> *2017 12/30 140 lbs.*
> *2017 12/15 135 lbs.*
> *2017 11/30 137 lbs.*
> *2017 10/15 132 lbs.*

The hybrid approach also has a smooth transition for test validation. Figure 6.6 illustrates a use case and how it might transition to a test case. The pre-condition can establish the initial state and the post-condition can describe the expected result (call-outs show an additional example from the ATM scenario). The steps can show the test interaction. The use case will also drive

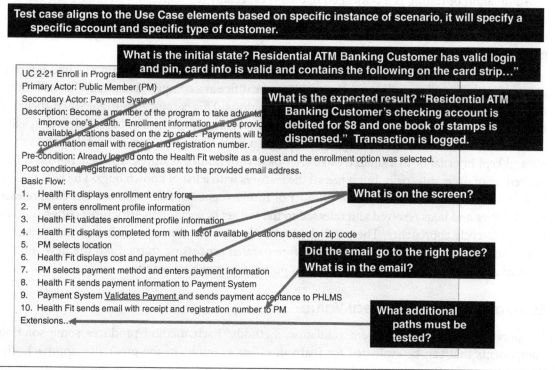

Figure 6.6 Use case validation

additional questions from testers about the data requirements and other requirements that do not get documented within the use case. Those requirements need to be provided elsewhere. That is why in a hybrid life-cycle approach, traceability is important to trace use cases to other supporting requirements in addition to test cases.

Decision tables are used in both predictive and adaptive approaches to clearly display business rules. An example would be the acceptance criteria for *B*—Weight loss/gain is calculated and shown separately with motivational messages (see Table 6.3). By putting the acceptance test in a table, many questions may surface. Are there many different motivational messages depending on the variance from the goal (2%, 4%, 8%, etc.)? What might the messages specifically say for each? Can the list of messages be put into another table? Can we assume no messages exist if they are not moving toward the goal?

Table 6.3   Decision table

Goal is a Loss	Yes	No
Less than 2% of goal	Message 1	Message 2
Goal is a Gain		
More than 2% of goal	Message 3	Message 4

Automation of testing is a critical component, especially for regression testing. Unit, component, and some integration testing will happen within the iteration. More extensive integration testing, system testing, and full project user acceptance testing is likely to happen outside the iteration or may require a separate iteration.

Live validation includes pilots, releases, and parallel adoption. Pilots are run in a live environment but with a smaller implementation, such as one office at a company location. This still allows corrections to occur before rolling out to other locations. This is most important when there are high risks associated with the implementation or if there is a very large user base. Releases in a live environment are structured as an alpha, a beta, and a final. The alpha release is likely to be unstable and kept internal or to a small trusted user base with limited features. The beta release is to a limited set of users externally, but it has all the features with a list of known bugs. The beta release is often used to demonstrate the new product or future versions of the product. The final release has all issues and bugs resolved and released to the full set of users. This structure is often used in hybrid life-cycle approaches. The parallel adoption is planned during transition with transition requirements identified, built, and tested before parallel processing starts. Both the new and old systems run together and there are validation points that compare results.

Evaluate Solution for Real Value

We previously discussed different validation methods. Each method produces some solution components that can be evaluated for real value. For example, in the predictive approach, the different test phase results could be evaluated; in the hybrid approach, the outcomes from the different prototypes or releases could be evaluated; and in an adaptive approach, the result of each iteration could be evaluated; and for all three, it could be different releases of the deployed solution. To evaluate solution performance, measures would need to be identified, analyzed, assessed, and actions recommended in order to increase its value:

> *Scenario: The solution that was implemented was to reduce the time it took to fulfill an average-size purchase order by 20%. The previous system baseline for an average-size purchase order took three days from order to fulfillment. A vendor package was selected to automate parts of the process. In the pilot test the new solution took two days. The three-month assessment shows the new solution is now taking two and a half days. Do we need to take any actions? What if during the assessment you determined there was some redundancy that could be eliminated with a simple change?*

The BA, having assessed the performance of a solution, is in the best position to provide advice on taking any actions to change the solution. It may require some root cause analysis and a formal recommendation. The change could entail lean principles of reducing waste, Six Sigma principles of reducing defects, business process improvement principles of reducing complexity or redundancy, improving organizational capabilities, or making organizational changes.

Recommendations may also result in the replacement of a solution because it no longer provides value to the enterprise (limited life) or because other replacements would provide more value. An issue that I have personally seen with many clients is the inability to *let go*. There could be many hidden reasons for this such as the amount of investment that was made is hard to recover from (sunk cost), the psychological resistance to change, the *it's my baby* scenario—where they were the original implementers, or they have a political reason (such as a vendor relationship) that they don't want to sever.

Moving from potential value to real value is the role of the BA as the value manager. This can be done by:

- Having the enterprise mindset leveraging the balanced scorecard and business architecture
- Being involved in business case creation and portfolio management
- Addressing requirement level value through traceability and requirement validation
- Evaluating the solution at multiple opportunities pre- and post-implementation

SHOWING YOUR OWN VALUE

> *"The worth, importance, or usefulness of something to a stakeholder in a context"* (IIBA).

Value is a Business Analysis Core Concept Model (BACCM™) core concept (Figure 4.1a). The BA is expected to *conduct performance analysis to ensure that business analysis activities continue to produce sufficient value for the stakeholders.*

Our Opportunity Story

For those in any consulting field, you may have experienced that managers will continually reinforce the pursuit of opportunities to improve internal processes or improve the client's condition. The more opportunities presented to the client, the more likely you would become an advisor rather than a worker, and the more valuable you would be in your role as a consultant. Regardless of the role at the time, the work performed for your client, or the contractual arrangement, you have been told to always look for those things that could be changed for the better to ease the client's pain and improve the situation they are in.

As a coach to many new BAs, keeping a notebook to log daily activities for at least a year provides a chance to reflect and look for areas that could have been presented differently, approached differently, or ideas that should be presented to management—an individual retrospective. In my experiences, I have found that opportunities often exist beyond the boundaries of the project. Stakeholders will often discuss problems that are out-of-scope. These discussions should not be readily dismissed. BAs must be the advocate for the business and they must show value by being an advisor. The behavior of watching for, documenting, and presenting opportunities plays a big role in advancement.

There are traditional opportunities that continually surface such as reduction of labor and material, avoidance of regulatory or legal risks, expanding product markets, improving product quality, and improving the efficiency of processes. There are needs that may be anticipated such as exploring changes in social behaviors, globalization challenges, and economic conditions. There are also opportunities that you may create based on innovative strategies in technology, processes, architectures, etc. (examples: Cloud, business architecture link to technical architecture).

At a more tactical level, we should look for opportunities in our everyday business analysis activities:

- Current stakeholders and project activities
- Deliverable and organizational asset reviews
- Solution evaluations
- Customer assistance requests
- Customer feedback
- Past pains
- Lean and Six Sigma or other major initiatives
- Benchmarking activities

Keeping a log of these opportunities, where they came from, and documenting a quick feasibility assessment is something that you will continue to do for a lifetime.

Support the Business Advocate and User

Consider this extract from Cooke's book, *The Power of the Agile Business Analyst*:

". . . the inclusion of an Agile business analyst on the Agile team means the business user has someone to pair with, giving the business user all of the knowledge sharing and quality control benefits that pairing provides to the Agile developers . . . It is important to remember that business users generally have primary operational roles that will likely have been put on hold (or reduced) in order for them to be available to work with the Agile team during the project timeline. Once the solution is implemented, these business users will most likely need to return to their primary roles on a full-time basis, which substantially limits their ability to provide the ongoing support needed to ensure the delivered solution is successfully integrated into business operations. Where a business user may have limited post-implementation availability, the primary role of the Agile business analyst can be expanded to deliver any ongoing support needed . . . "[7]

Being an advocate not only means to listen, but it means stepping in to help and ensure stakeholder concerns are being addressed in their absence. It also means assisting stakeholders in making the best decisions possible based on your analysis. For example, to fully support the business, you many need to consider more than one option for a solution and when you do, then consider different solution evaluation techniques to help others decide on the solution that brings them and the enterprise the most value, using techniques such as SWOT (strengths, weaknesses, opportunities, and threats) analysis or feature scoring (see Appendix B8.1).

When recommending a found opportunity or solution to a problem you must consider how formal the recommendation must be. Determine if there is any governance protocol. For example, I have had to present my recommendations in a specific format and, being a vendor, had to follow a specific hierarchy protocol through the organization. But regardless of formality or protocol, make sure to clearly convey your findings based on your audiences' language. Always describe how the opportunity was uncovered and illustrate the opportunity using diagrams. Know what your audience and those impacted are getting out of the opportunity, each should have a value proposition.

Value is subjective, but it can also be measured to ensure that we have provided value to our stakeholders from the solution we have deployed.

SUMMARY

- Value can be described in terms of financials, employee performance, operational performance, market-related, customer value, sustainability of environment, servicing the poor, and quality-related. As BAs, we need to understand the trade-offs between them.
- BAs should always wear the value manager *hat*. Managing expectations of our stakeholders is part of the value manager's role.
- Solution value and the business analysis work value both interconnect. The business analysis approach can affect the solution value that is provided to stakeholders.

- Value propositions help to define the different stakeholder's perception of value.
- The value of defining SMART business requirements is the clarity it provides in communicating what the solution must achieve to establish a basis for justification, to help make decisions, to uncover assumptions that may need to be documented, and to manage stakeholder expectations.
- At the enterprise level, both the balanced scorecard and several assets within the business architecture can show value.
- At the program level, the business case shows value through several different financial evaluation methods.
- At the requirements level, value can be shown by aligning requirements (business to stakeholder to solution), verifying requirements, and validating requirements.
- BA's behavior of watching for, documenting, and presenting opportunities plays a big role in career advancement.

QUESTIONS

1. What is the difference between solution value and business analysis work value?

   _____

   _____

   _____

2. In the following scenario, what are some value challenges that should be considered? How might you determine which is more important to address if all of them cannot be accomplished?

   The company's "Green" team wants environmental waste reduced by 20% by reducing the use of a particular material—QBGOOD—and replacing it with a better environmental material—QBOK. Marketing wants to do a holiday promotion of a new product by reducing the price by 35% for a two-week period. Evaluation of customer feedback says that customers love the QBGOOD material and are willing to pay more for the product to get that feature. The CEO wants to increase profits the next quarter by 20% and is hoping the new product will help reach that target.

   _____

   _____

   _____

   _____

3. Write a value proposition for the following scenario:

   You were mapping the features of a financial software package to the stakeholder needs. You noticed that 30% of the features were unmatched and most affected the procurement area. These features could be fully addressed by interfacing to a procurement software package that you knew about from your previous employer. After a brief discussion with the boss, you think it could reduce the time to procure equipment by 10%.

   Value proposition: _____

   _____

   _____

   _____

4. Based on your answer to #3, what would be some measures that you would want to make more tangible?

   Answer: _____

   _____

   _____

   _____

   In the role of value manager, what can you do to ensure potential value becomes real value?

   Answer: _____

   _____

   _____

   _____

NOTES

1. Wiegers, Karl and Joy Beatty. (2013). *Software Requirements 3rd Edition*. Microsoft Press. pp. 31–34.
2. Hubbard, Douglas W. (2010). *How to Measure Anything: Finding the Value of Intangibles in Business, Second Edition*. Hoboken, NJ: John Wiley & Sons.
3. Drucker, Peter. (Original Print 1954). *The Practice of Management*. New York, NY: Harper Collins eBooks.

4. Leffingwell, Dean. (2011). *Agile Software Requirements: Lean Requirements Practices for Teams, Programs, and the Enterprise.* p. 465. New York, NY: Addison-Wesley.

5. Kaplan, Robert S. and David P. Norton. (1996). *The Balanced Scorecard: Translating Strategy into Action.* Boston, MA: Harvard Business School Press.

6. Wake, Bill. (August 17, 2003). "INVEST in Good Stories, and SMART Tasks." XP123 Article. https://xp123.com/articles/invest-in-good-stories-and-smart-tasks/.

7. Cooke, Jamie Lynn. (2013). *The Power of the Agile Business Analyst—30 Surprising Ways a Business Analyst Can Add Value to Your Agile Development Team.* Cambridgeshire, UK: IT Governance Publishing.

7

STEP SIX—BRIDGE THE CAPABILITY GAP

"A true master chef networks with other chefs to share ideas, pursues new certifications and award opportunities, and writes and shares recipes with the community."—Chapter One

Accomplishing successful outcomes for initiatives by gaining acceptance of those outcomes from stakeholders is critical. Stakeholders must trust that expectations will be met and that it is worth the organizational investments being made. Trust is built through repeatable success. An important component to achieving repeatable success is to improve the capabilities of business analysts (BAs) and the organizations that support them. Improvements cannot be accomplished unless you have a good understanding of where you are today (a reality check) and have established a baseline.

Assuming that your proficiency is beyond the basics but that you're not yet considered a master, opportunity exists to bridge the capability gap between your competencies that exist today and those that will help you to your goal of mastery. As a BA in a more advanced position, you may also be asked to assist in improving the capabilities of your organization.

ASSESSMENTS

Assessments help establish a competency baseline and identify where you want to go by defining your targets. The assessments included in Appendices C7.1, C7.2, and C7.3 provide you and your organization with a starting point. There are many ways to *slice and dice* and vary the competencies depending on the scope of the defined role. The Project Management Institute (PMI) business analysis guide provides the following competency classifications: analytical skills, expert judgment, communication skills, personal skills, leadership skills, and tool knowledge. The International Institute of Business Analysis (IIBA®) Body of Knowledge classifies competencies as: analytical thinking and problem solving, behavioral characteristics, business knowledge, communication skills, interaction skills, tools, and technology.

Competencies and Capabilities

Competency assessments, like the ones in Appendix C, look at the skills that one has, the knowledge gained, and specific behaviors or attitudes. It provides you with the ability to rate yourself and/or have others rate you. With the results, you can determine the gaps and identify areas where training or other improvement programs can help fill them. Even though you are being provided with a couple of types in Appendix C, there are many more available to choose from. Regardless, to truly evaluate how well you have mastered business analysis, you need to go beyond assessments. They don't evaluate how well you make everything work together or demonstrate that you know when to apply the right competency at the right time and in the right situation—thereby, the purpose of this book.

Competencies Are Transferable to Other Roles

Yes! Many of the *soft skills* competencies (such as leadership) and techniques like negotiation can be easily applied to many other roles. These soft skills and techniques can be used in positions like project manager (PM), change agent, or business architect. We will cover techniques and variations as to how they might be applied differently—by role—in Chapter 8. (There are some competencies that are less likely to be transferable, like those that center around business analysis functions.)

Proficiencies

To get the whole picture, we need to look at proficiencies. When you are evaluated on the job, you are being graded on your proficiency. Your performance is being measured against a specific standard, which may be set by certification requirements or may vary by organization. For higher levels of proficiencies, certifications can also determine how capable you are in assessing more difficult and complex situations using standard exams. When applying to take a certification exam, you will likely be required to provide evidence of your experience in applying some of the knowledge areas being tested. Figure 7.1 provides an example of BA proficiency levels used in a large company. Notice that the levels evaluated were for the combination of training, certifications (which were both internal and external), and experiences advancing to projects of increasing complexity. In the example, the company was strictly working with the predictive life-cycle approaches.

There are very clear distinctions between the levels shown in Figure 7.1. The diagram is supported with a capability assessment tied to the organization's strategies. This method has been used for many years. It is similar to a framework that was used at a company where I was employed. They had a direct link to their global business strategy, and the capability framework provided the list of capabilities that were needed by consultants in order to support organizational goals. These capabilities were organized into a foundational level (further defined into three additional levels)

Figure 7.1 Example BA proficiency path

and a mastery level (also defined into another three levels). For example, each capability-assessment statement varied slightly at each level of competency to assess the capability at that level. At level 1, if assessing process capabilities, the statement would ask how aware you were of process modeling practices and whether you took the initiative to ask for help in applying the concepts. At level 2, the statement asked if you could recognize a simple process and then document it. At level 3, the statement assumed you moved to more of an advisory role where you not only recognized processes but made suggestions to improve them. At level 4, the assumption was that you had the capability to redesign end-to-end processes. The progression from level to level was evident. Also assessed was whether certifications or certificates in that organizational capability were obtained—and whether they were also demonstrated through experiences on different levels of project complexity. As this example may lead you to believe, the more formalized the organization's support of the role, the more formal the assessment process and ability to move into higher career levels within the organization.

The very top level of Figure 7.1 is mastery. You have reached a state where it is gratifying to share knowledge, advise, mentor, and coach others (and it is also a place for your own continued learning process). However, mastery is almost always examining current reality to see if there is a way to improve and learn from it.

Individual Assessment

The individual assessment focuses on the individual competency goal needs for the BA, which can be adjusted to match the vision of the BA role and career levels within their organization. The organizational assessment focuses on organizational capabilities and considers organizational goals for processes and technology which can also be adjusted to match the organizational vision. Both require some orientation regarding the role and terminology used.

For the individual, the assessment evaluates current state possessed competencies to determine knowledge or performance of business analysis functions and techniques. These competencies (see Table 7.1) determine performance of the function or technique at a tactical capability level (current and near-term future projects) and at the strategic capability level (overall career growth). Whatever proficiency standard is defined as your goal, the assessment of competencies, organizational capabilities, and applying knowledge from this book can advance you toward your

Table 7.1   Example individual assessment (© 2018 E.C. Schmidt)

| Name: _____ | Completion date: _____ | Revisions: _____ |
| Manager: _____ | Review date: _____ | |

Ratings: 0 = No exposure   1 = Awareness and some knowledge   2 = Some training or coaching
3 = Knowledgeable and   4 = Knowledgeable with   5 = Considered expert and
some practice   extensive experience   shares knowledge

Current rating is based on your exposure and experience today
Tactical capability target is where you think you should be specific to current or upcoming initiatives and varies based on organizational goals
Strategic capability target is where you think you should be specific to individual career goals
Review notes should provide actions to address any gaps or changes based on manager review

Competency	Current Rating	Tactical Capability Target	Strategic Capability Target	Review Notes
Example 1: Understands overall guiding principles, strategies, policies, and regulations to assess impact on business analysis approach	2	2	4	Opportunity in next year as team lead on larger project
Example 2: Assesses needs of audiences for work products to match the correct tool, level of detail, language, etc.	3	3	3	No change needed, but opportunities exist to assist in presentations

goal. For more business analysis breadth and depth, there are more extensive competency assessments, descriptions of proficiency levels, and certifications available by several organizations.[1]

Organizational Assessment

For BAs to be successful in their roles, they need to be in or to establish the right environment. The organizational assessment addresses the *right environment* by defining and promoting the role, providing resource support, and supplying guidance through training, coaching, and knowledge sharing. Additionally, in order to formalize the BA role within an organization, this supporting environment must exist; thus, the organization assessment also includes an evaluation of the organization's ability to support business analysis. Organizational assessments look at three points in time: today, short-term periods of one to two years out, and long-term periods of three to five years out (see Table 7.2).

Most business analysis training focuses on BA competencies with a defined role and the capabilities associated with performing that role. This assumes the organization will support this role with:

- Standardization of some deliverables
- Recommendations of techniques that work within the organization's culture
- Processes that manage expectations around deliverable handoffs

Table 7.2   Example organizational assessment (© 2018 E.C. Schmidt)

This tool assesses the organization's ability to support business analysis activities for successful outcomes through its people, processes, and technology. This assessment provides the opportunity to identify where gaps exist with organizational support. Two examples are provided below.

0 = No capability
1 = Capability isolated and based on individual performance
2 = Capability isolated and based on team performance
3 = Capability repeated across organization
4 = Capability is measured and continuously improved
5 = Capability is optimized; considered best practice in industry

	Today	Tactical Target	Strategic Target	Review Notes
Support Individual Business Analyst Competencies and Capabilities				
EXAMPLE 1: Collaboration with human resources defines a career path for BA positions	*1*	*3*	*3*	*Job position career paths are very long term—perhaps 5 years out. Focus will be on individual performance rewards as part of annual management objectives.*
EXAMPLE 2: Formal BA job descriptions exist for each level	2	3	4	*Job descriptions are by business unit today, but consideration is to have consistency across the enterprise and have some measurements. A focus group of BAs will be launched to address this and several other gaps.*

- Flexibility depending on the type of project and project risks
- Tools for collaborative sharing and archiving
- Measures for quality expectation and tolerance levels
- Procedures for managing change, risk, prioritization, approvals, and escalation

ORGANIZATIONAL MATURITY IMPACT

An organization's commitment and maturity can profoundly impact the ultimate success of a BA. An organization's buy-in and commitment to spend up-front time on analysis—with the understanding that it will reduce future maintenance and rework—greatly supports the effectiveness of the individual BA.

BA Role *Expansion*

The organization's maturity may influence the BA's capability to perform their work, or it may require the BA to pick up the roles that are not clearly defined (but activities must still be performed). For example, if the organization lacks project management consistency in processes, the BA may need project management competencies to have the capability to perform that work when the role is required to produce a successful outcome for stakeholders. How many of you have performed in more than one role?

Often the BA is the best person for a variety of roles because of their business domain knowledge, as well as skills with stakeholders, but the acceptance and performance of the role is likely to be informal (as the organization may not recognize the effort that is required). Organizations that do not put in the resources needed to support the role will find BAs doing a lot of *churning* or spending time and effort without results (and the individual is likely to be blamed). This is especially true on larger and more complex projects in the predictive life-cycle approach. In smaller iterations, as in the adaptive approach, there is an expectation that a team member will perform multiple roles, which works well in that intended environment. However, for predictive and hybrid life-cycle approaches, more clarity in roles is critical. Maturity of the organization and clarity of roles within the processes that are shown in Figure 7.2 can influence the breadth and depth of the BA's responsibilities, and his or her need to have different competencies.

What can be done as an organization? The following list provides a few top suggestions for organizations that are at the lower levels of maturity in these processes:

- Involve the BA in up-front estimating and business case creation
- Allow for more time—more planning for business analysis activities
- Invest time in communication and clarify methods and roles across the organization
- Cross train resources that fill multiple roles (PM, BA, solution architect) and increase awareness of the various roles—giving them the knowledge and resources to be successful in each

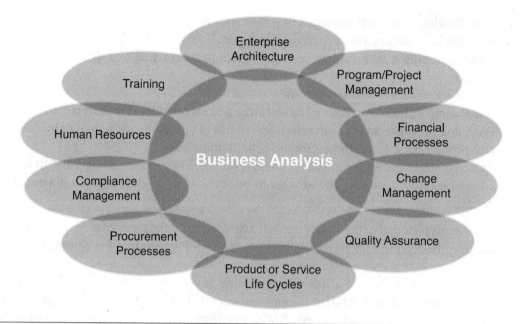

Figure 7.2 Organization interactions

- Track unplanned rework—know what it is costing you
- Allow time for learning and absorption of new knowledge and ideas

Business Analysis Competency Center

Organizations may develop a Business Analysis Competency Center (BACC) or a Business Analysis Center of Excellence (BACE) to provide support to business analysis activities, which will quickly increase the organization's success in business analysis capabilities. The BACC improves business value and project success by:

- Implementing and managing consistent best practices for BA processes, artifacts, techniques, and tools
- Providing internal consulting and coaching to support project teams and working to make sure the uniqueness of project characteristics is considered when best practices are implemented
- Maintaining a repository of templates and reusable business analysis artifacts
- Including quality checklists and procedures (reviewing, tracing, value mapping)
- Continually improving organizational and individual capabilities by implementing and monitoring programs
- Acquiring qualified resources to conduct business analysis activities

- Coordinating other methodologies or governance processes
- Defining business analysis critical success factors
- Communicating a clear understanding of goals to be reached and defined measures of success
- Aligning activities to business drivers
- Addressing organizational reporting structure and stakeholder influence risks
- Providing the organization with resources capable of communicating in both business and technical terms, with an understanding of both domains
- Proactively addressing the impact of change, the need to monitor change, and to leverage champion teams that have found ways to be successful by adopting recommended best practices

Many of the items included in the organizational assessment are the types of activities commonly integrated into these *centers* for providing best practices and governance for an organization or enterprise.

Another approach in place of a BACC is providing governance through an already existing program management office (PMO) at the enterprise level. The PMO may already have funding and resources to improve project success. BACC functions can be structured within the PMO, promoting business analysis competencies with existing resources in the short term, and then establishing a pool of business analysis consultants. Ultimately, competencies for business analysis must be addressed across the organization to support the implementation of needed activities.

Program and Project Management

The BA is also impacted by the organization's maturity in the implementation of other consistent processes, as illustrated in Figure 7.2. Program or project management at the organizational level can drive consistency for the governance of projects. Project management governance, often performed through a PMO, may dictate the methodology and approaches for business analysis by providing organizational assets (templates, examples, best practices) and reuse of current state models and business rules. By having a consistent methodology, there is also clarity around roles and how deliverables interact with each other, especially between the BA and PM as illustrated by showing each of those processes and deliverables (see Figure 7.3). All team members working on predictive life-cycle projects should have knowledge of the project management processes.

In a predictive life-cycle approach, processes for project approvals, change control, traceability, and baseline approvals are likely to be predefined. Also, project deliverables may include components that are the responsibility of the BA. The project charter, a project management deliverable, includes a scope definition statement that is the responsibility of the BA, as illustrated in Figure 7.3. There may also be standardized project management tools. The BA will need to review the governance processes, policies, and standards to ensure compliance, but must also have the courage to negotiate and influence when there is a need for exceptions.

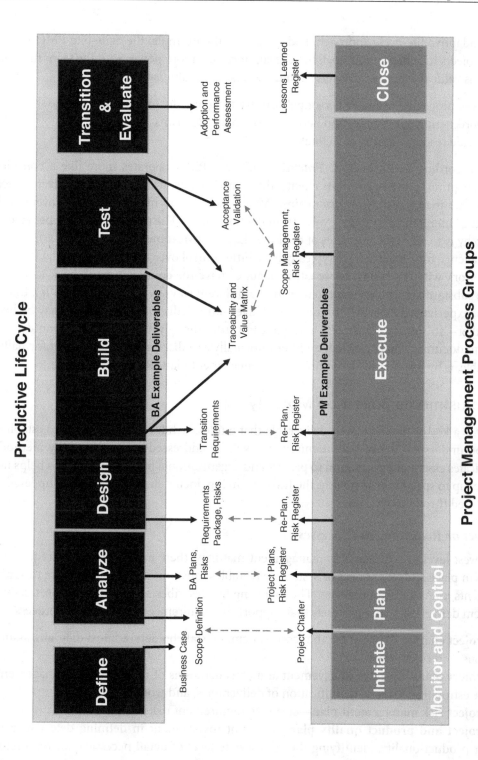

Figure 7.3 Business analysis and project management interactions

For an adaptive life-cycle approach, taking agile as the example, the agile-like PMO will still support projects to achieve their goal, but the support puts more power with the team members. The PMO is value driven, as all PMOs should be. It is also multidisciplinary:

- Developing standards and personnel with training, mentoring, and knowledge sharing
- Coordinating communication between multiple agile teams
- Provide resources, such as facilitators

However, according to PMI's *Agile Practice Guide*, the PMO operates more like a consulting business, adapting to the needs of its clients, the project teams. It is relationship driven by team requests rather than top-down relationships.[2] Meadows and Wright agree with this overall principle, stating "hierarchical systems evolve from the bottom up. The purpose of the upper layers of the hierarchy is to serve the purposes of the lower layers"[3] (Meadows and Wright 2008).

The challenge for BAs is that we typically have little control over the structure of the PMO and how they work with the teams, so we either adapt or have the courage to push back with information to substantiate why we want to do things a different way (by showing trade-offs). In these situations, experience helps, but so does knowledge—knowledge of why one way may be better than another—so we can collaborate and work toward a thoughtful and agreed-upon decision. One way to document that knowledge, either informally as a discussion document or formally as a deliverable, is by formulating a requirements management plan (RMP).

RMP Adjustments Based on Maturity

The RMP is a key business analysis deliverable that guides each level of maturity and establishes a common understanding of how requirements will be addressed using an orderly method. It communicates essential information to project and organizational participants. It also helps newcomers get up to speed. Consequently, the RMP is a living document that needs to be updated and supplemented throughout its life.

No Project or Requirement Processes

At the lowest level of requirements management maturity, there are no project or requirement processes in place and key project or system deliverables must initially be put in place to support requirements management processes. The following list describes some sample project deliverables, system deliverables, and products that support the requirements management process:

- **Project charter**—containing the scope statement, stakeholders, context diagram, assumptions, and constraints
- **Project plan**—up-front involvement and considerations of requirements management in the estimating process, identification of deliverables, and work effort
- **Project risk management plan**—ensuring requirement risks are addressed
- **Project and product quality plan**—up-front involvement in defining defect measures for product quality, identifying the appropriate level of detail necessary for requirement

management documentation, and ensuring plans for traceability of requirements to design/development solutions

- **Product backlog**—a repository of requirements written in the form of user stories at various levels of detail and used for continuous ranking, modifying, elaborating, and selecting user stories to be implemented in an adaptive manner
- **Test plan**—determination of what are acceptable deliverables as input to the testing process and traceability from the requirement to the test case

If the BA cannot influence these processes, then an RMP will need to be expanded to include many of these deliverable components. At this level of maturity, introducing just a few key requirement deliverables can begin the process of change. This may impact the business organization, so building buy-in early is critical for acceptance to future changes.

Some Project or Requirement Processes

At the next level of maturity, there are some project or requirement processes in place, but limited requirement deliverables (project level). The approach would be to conduct a quick gap assessment to determine how to best integrate the requirement management processes into existing processes. Here are some sample contents of an RMP at the project level:

1. **Requirements management roadmap**—a graphic showing the touchpoints with key deliverables in the project plan
2. **Purpose by type of project**—you may have more than one template depending on the project and processes used
3. **Project context**—relevant project content to help in orientation (from project charter)
4. **Requirements approach** to:
   a. *Elicitation*: techniques to gather requirements that are relevant for this type of project (facilitated workshop, interviews, document review with subject matter expert follow up, etc.)
   b. *Documentation*: which levels of requirements are necessary to document for this project (business, user, and solution), requirement attributes to be captured (prioritization, business impact, volatility, etc.), how requirements will be organized, and where they will be documented
   c. *Validation*: validation methods to be used and who will perform the validation
   d. *Traceability*: the level of traceability required for this project and who performs the traceability checks
   e. *Change control*: how changes to requirements will be managed
5. **Appendix** may include:
   a. Requirement management deliverable templates
   b. Real examples of each type of requirement to be captured
   c. A glossary of business terms commonly used in the requirements

Again, iterations of deliverable additions and flexibility by type of project are key to change acceptance.

Both Project and Requirement Consistent Processes

If there are both project and requirement management processes in place with consistency in deliverables, then a quick assessment will help determine the extent of effort in building the RMP. At this level of maturity, you must get ready for standardization at the organizational level. Sample content for the RMP at this organizational level of maturity is as follows:

1. **Key requirement management principles for the organization**—provides strategic guidance as to the value of requirements management within the organization
2. **Requirements management roadmap**—similar graphic as at the project level but shows touch points with organizational standardized processes
3. **Project type decision tree**—provides guidance by project type illustrating which templates, techniques, and tools are relevant
4. **Decision trees for requirement documentation and management reporting**—determines requirement level, depth of detail, and which attributes to capture
5. **Checklists for requirement quality**—checklists may address how requirements should be structured, the use of certain terminology, and checklists for requirement reviews
6. **Technique suggestions**—depending on project characteristics
7. **Tools and tool features recommendations**—what to use for documentation, collaboration, archiving, and traceability
8. **Procedures**—for managing change, mitigating risk, and managing requirement conflicts
9. **Location and access**—how to get to requirement management deliverables templates and examples
10. **Additional considerations**:
    a. Communicating requirements in a distributed team environment
    b. Applying requirements management in an iterative, Rational Unified Process, or agile environment
    c. Communicating requirements to vendors or to offshore resources
    d. Integrating requirements management processes when external processes are used (such as a vendor's process)
11. **Appendix**
    a. List of techniques
    b. Tools
    c. Location and access to deliverable templates and examples

Having an organization that can support the BA role and the requirements management process will greatly improve project success.

We need to consider organizational uniqueness, yet at the same time be consistent and repeatable in our efforts. What?! Yes, it can be quite a balancing act. Think of it as *practice what we preach.* Even if you are helping to improve an organization's business analysis capabilities, it is a change. It is an opportunity. It is a project. That opportunity still needs funding. Essentially, you need to conduct business analysis *on* business analysis! Who are the stakeholders? What are their needs? Etc. The assessments are gap analysis tools.

To illustrate further, let us look at an example from my own experiences. A food producer was initially looking for someone to provide training, but the role grew into much more than that. The reason? I took the opportunity to understand their business strategy, especially their vision. They had several very large initiatives coming up and they needed to get BAs on board quickly. They wanted to establish a clear BA role to support those initiatives.

In this situation, the organizational assessment proved to be helpful. The first assessment was to look at how the organization currently supported business analysis through its processes. (Keep in mind that this can be done regardless of BA role formality as a specific job description.) The organization can still support business analysis by ensuring the processes are there and that the role can be picked up by any job title if they need to perform business analysis activities. The individual assessment guided the organization's expectations for the role. Much of the focus in the process section of the organizational assessment is making sure that business analysis is integrated in. Does the organization account for business analysis activities when estimating projects? How does the organization make sure that someone on the team is picking up that role? Are there organizational procedures to communicate the things that might influence business analysis activities, such as priority, risks, constraints, standards, change control procedures, escalation procedures, etc.?

CLOSE CAPABILITY GAPS

Any gaps between the current state and future state in individual competencies and organizational capabilities can hinder the performance of the organization. There is a tendency to try to resolve gaps—what Peter Senge calls "creative tension."[4] To close the gap you can pursue training, self-learning, or coaching. Options for an individual usually include standard public training courses that are offered by educational institutions or training companies for business analysis. When a team needs to be trained, there are more options, but they can be costly: a standard course or a tailored course could be brought onsite to the team (tailored is likely to be more expensive). Nonetheless, don't be afraid to get creative. Here are a few ideas to support and promote self-learning:

- Give teams opportunities to share experiences
- Make rooms available for informal knowledge meetings
- Create a team library and obtain access to online resources
- Plan webinars and special learning events
- Pay for memberships to organizations that promote the role

Coaching is conducted post training or can replace training for more advanced individual competencies, groups, or teams—and is best conducted during project assignments so the coach can help throughout a real-life experience. Later in the chapter we will cover how to be an effective coach.

Change takes time, and every organization's starting point is different. If the organization is at a lower level of capability maturity today, change will require iterative rollouts of deliverables, processes, techniques, and tools in order to move the organization up and to help promote business analysis.

LEVERAGE INTELLECTUAL ASSETS

We looked at how the organization can promote business analysis, but we should also address how you can promote business analysis as you continue to advance in the role.

Share Knowledge

Why? Why take the time to share information with others? If we keep the information to ourselves, it gives us some power, right? Here are some reasons (whether or not it is done with good intentions) as to why people share knowledge:

- Influences others to do something or provide something in exchange, part of a negotiation or bartering
- Increases credibility around expertise
- Validates views and expands on knowledge
- Builds confidence through validation
- Cultivates trust when sharing; this works both ways
- Expands knowledge resource network (see next section)

Another perspective of sharing knowledge:

> *"Sharing knowledge is not about giving people something or getting something from them. That is only valid for information sharing. Sharing knowledge occurs when people are genuinely interested in helping one another develop new capacities for action; it is about creating learning processes" (Senge 2006).*

Expand the People Knowledge Network

Sharing knowledge is valuable, but knowing what other human resources can contribute in different situations is just as valuable. Often the teams we work on are temporary, so we must make an effort to stay connected. Think about this scenario: a project applying the predictive life-cycle approach just finished and a lessons-learned session is being conducted. This project was your first data-driven project and the data architect was a master who had spent time helping you with some conceptual models. Knowing it was likely the last time the team would be together before everyone was distributed onto new projects, you took some time after the lessons-learned session to thank the data architect and to ask if you could stay connected. You also offered to share some books you had recently picked up.

A few months later, the data architect e-mailed you to say the books were helpful on a recent project and thanked you. She asked if you would be interested in a new project coming up at the enterprise level? A few months after that, you are on that new project and the PM comes to you for some advice about finding an external expert to come in to address some performance issues occurring with various systems across the enterprise (with all the different integrated products, it is difficult to find the root cause). The PM knew you had worked on a special technical team in the past dealing with vendor service level agreements. The PM asks if you know anyone who can help.

The opportunities for networking are endless. One of my managers at the consulting firm used to say: "You don't need to know everything, you just need to know who knows." This also goes back to Chapter 1—you also must *cultivate* relationships and build trust.

Be a Mentor

"No one learns as much about a subject as one who is forced to teach it."[5] Mentoring is not something that we take on and start doing at a specific point or moment. Instead, we find that we mentor others every day—our partners, children, peers, and even our bosses (which happens more often than you may think). But these instances are informal. The more interactions we have, the more we learn about how to approach the process of transferring knowledge in a better way, and we also develop an interest in helping others (which, for most people, feels pretty good!). Part of mentoring is coaching, but it can be difficult to distinguish between the two. For mentoring, you need the expertise and you are sharing knowledge. In coaching, you do not have to be an expert (since the goal is to motivate and encourage others to accomplish their goals) and coaching can be beneficial for everyone involved.

BAs perform in a coaching role more often than you might imagine, but sometimes coaching is not enough. Let me give you an example: if you want to lose weight, you might ask a sibling who had accomplished their own weight loss goal to coach you and help keep you motivated to achieve yours. But what if you have their support and are still struggling? Maybe it is time to seek the help of experts (like a weight loss clinic or your physician) so that you can explore other options or possible causes for your weight loss plateau or lack of success. Perhaps there is a health issue that is prohibiting you from achieving your goal, in which case, your coach may not be qualified enough to assist.

Table 7.3 provides some hints and tips for both the mentor and mentee. But I would like to provide a bit more structure around the role of mentor. Here are a few steps to consider (is there some similarity to business analysis?):

1. Interview the mentee to determine their vision and goals.
2. Probe to understand their education and experience.
3. Have them take an assessment and discuss the gaps.
4. Prioritize gaps based on targets.
5. Define agreed-upon measurable objectives to address gaps.
   For example: *Create a minimum of three Level 2 "as-is" process models of a domain you want to know more about by January 31, and review with at least two individuals with written feedback.*

6. Define an approach to reach objectives, include a schedule, and allow time for practice and real-life opportunities.
7. Structure each meeting with an agenda.

   For example: *Review practices and real-life outcomes, share challenges and lessons learned, present next objective and topics, review next session preparation and assignments, review and refine learning objectives, and confirm schedule.*
8. Build individual growth plan, include area for status (see Appendix C7.4 for template).
9. Closure—summarize accomplishments, establish a continuation of a self-learning plan.
10. Follow up as part of networking, share something interesting!

Team mentoring requires a few adjustments. First, there are more stakeholders. Figure 7.4 illustrates an example context diagram showing stakeholders for a BA team mentoring and coaching program. Second, each learner has individual needs that still need to be addressed. So, the particular engagement reflected in Figure 7.4 required an individual growth plan and a separate team growth plan. Two of the learners had project issues and needed to be coached in real time during those engagements.

Table 7.3 Mentoring hints

Mentor	Mentee
Stick to business-related issues	Don't expect a personal therapist
Guide and advice	Be strong, make your own decisions
Don't get upset if advice is not taken	Consider advice, ask for alternatives
Provide opportunities to practice	Practice
It is ok to make mistakes—learn from them together	It is ok to make mistakes—learn from them together
Work through scenarios first	Provide some of your own scenarios to work through before the real thing
Let mentors first assess themselves	Be ready with how you feel a practice session went
Try to break up information into chunks	Share your learning style
Remember, goals are for the mentee	Make your goals well known
Encourage	It is ok to be unsure—but try
Keep conversations private, ask to share any information	
If you don't know, say so, but work together to find a resource	

BOTH Mentor and Mentee
Respect differences
Share experiences
Be respectful of time
Keep it professional

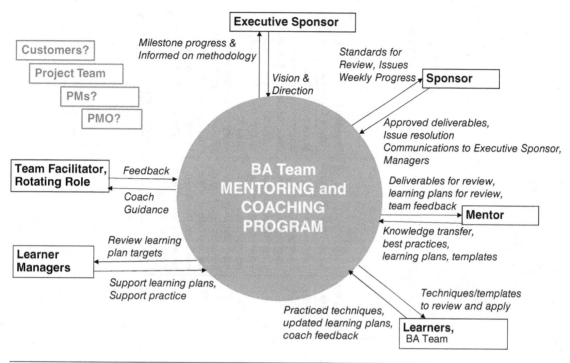

Figure 7.4   Example mentoring context diagram

Coaching real-time engagements can be a challenge, but well worth it. There are two types of coaching during these engagements. One is the *audit* method, which is more reactive (quality control) based on the project schedule for the team you are coaching where deliverables could be provided to you (the coach) to review before any other formal reviews are conducted. Another type is the *proactive* method, which is based on ensuring that the team is doing the right things before the deliverable is created (quality assurance). Which one you use depends on the team's experience, confidence, and the project constraints.

Your Own Development

There are huge benefits to mentoring and coaching, but you cannot fully depend on them. They are not a replacement for your own efforts; you must take accountability for your own development. Most of the knowledge you acquire is through self-learning and knowledge sharing. The individual growth plan can be used for mentoring, but it is also a valuable plan for self-learning. Table 7.4 is an excerpt from the plan with an example. Combined with the assessment, it can provide the actions needed to address the gaps and is a valuable discussion tool with your manager. Once a certification is obtained, most programs require re-certification. Those programs define several expected learning methods to be used: training, attending meetings or seminars, special events, webinars, reading books on relevant topics, mentoring, knowledge discussion with team members, etc.

Table 7.4 Example BA individual growth plan

Competency and Goal/Value (Improvements identified in self-assessments, from team learning plans, input from coach, input from manager, or other areas of interest)	Short-Term Objective	Target Date	Complete Date	Long-Term Objective	Lessons Learned and Future Considerations
Business modeling as identified in the team learning plan. Will be performing process modeling of current processes on project starting in two weeks. Manager also sees me as becoming an expert in this area to help other teams and BAs.	Create one swim lane model using notations and techniques learned during coaching session and have it reviewed by a peer within one week of project start. In that same week, do a second one and have that reviewed by the coach. Also validate by the process owner.	4/14/20xx	6/30/20xx	Gain enough experience and confidence so I can coach others on our team within one year. Also gain enough experience so I can estimate how long it takes me to create a model so that it can be estimated within a 20% accuracy goal.	Make sure to label diagrams with *as-is* or *to-be*. Make sure to add a legend to each diagram so process owners don't need to be educated every time. Allow some flexibility on notation as to not bog down discussions. Remember to focus on the *happy path* first before digging into exceptions (slows process down).

A FEW CHALLENGES

Finding the Time to Learn

This is one place a coach can help. Coaches are great at helping, prioritizing, focusing, and keeping their team motivated. Find a learning group (like a book club) where you commit to attending a meeting in advance (we don't usually miss those, right?) When pursuing their project management certification, a group of very busy consultants would have pizza brought in for lunch twice a week and study together. A few months (and maybe a few extra pounds) later, they all got their certifications and learned a lot from the process! This was structured and planned learning through a learning group, but was not sanctioned by the organization. This is often called a *community of practice*, which is a group with common goals that simply want to share information, while at the same time bettering themselves and the organization. This group may or may not be sanctioned or funded in some way by the organization. In contrast, there is also learning that isn't planned—and that can happen by just being an inquisitive person. Often inquisitive learning on the job is about asking questions like, "Hey Joe, how did you fix that problem yesterday?" or "Sue, could I help you with the use cases you are creating? I would like to learn more about them!"

Finally, you may have to ask for the learning time, so plan to negotiate. It may look something like this: "Jack, this next project that is awaiting approval will be a vendor package and we will likely have to put a request for proposal together. I have never put one together before—is it ok if I take a few days to learn more about it? The result will eventually be a template that we can all use, and it will speed up the project once it is approved. What are your thoughts?"

Knowledge Transfer

Knowledge transfer, as it relates to business analysis, is: (1) the process of passing not only information, but how information is applied and used during the performance of one's job; (2) domain knowledge that is gained by working with the business and technology; (3) passing knowledge of role responsibilities to someone else (new internal resource or external resource). Problems that are associated with knowledge transfer that frequently occur may include:

- Different experiences and backgrounds of individuals promotes miscommunications
- Lack of motivation or incentives
- Threats of job loss (knowledge is protection, lack of trust)
- Lack of capabilities to receive the knowledge
- Not knowing when the knowledge transfer is *done*
- Those transferring the knowledge have their own opinions and biases
- Not enough time allocated for knowledge transfer (e.g., contracted resources leaving at a specific date)

- Resource is remote
- Incomplete knowledge transfer (such as developer to developer) affecting the requirement management process

There is a risk that with employee turnover, loss of valuable knowledge can disable the operation of an initiative and the entire operation of a business; the knowledge transfer process can mitigate the risk. Loss of knowledge risks need to be addressed early and often, especially for key knowledge workers. Here are just a few example situations where knowledge transfer had to be formally addressed between resources: (1) a financial institution outsourcing the support of all their non-core processes to a vendor with resources in India, (2) a manufacturing company acquired two other smaller companies and the support of the technology was going to be centralized, (3) a telecom company provided a retirement incentive that impacted a large number of their knowledge workers.

A few hints and tips if you are transferring the knowledge:

- 5Ws + H = *who* from and to, *what* is being transferred, *why* is it important, *where* will it take place, *when* do you know you are done, and *how* will it happen and how long should it take
- Walk through initiative processes and completed deliverables
- Conduct proper introductions to a network of people and stakeholders
- Identify ways to test the knowledge (e.g., have them write a use case to test their knowledge of a process)—ask a series of situational questions
- Work together for a few days (active observation)
- Provide a list of backup support resources

As BAs we are likely to be in a position several times in our career to either conduct a knowledge transfer ourselves or to manage a larger knowledge transfer process for our organization.

Person Is Not *Coachable*

Are there people that are hard or impossible to coach? It does happen. There are people that may have been told they *must* have a coach or mentor (which may turn them off to the idea). So, if you get assigned to someone like this person, what can you do? You can try influence techniques, which often work, but if not, there is some root cause analysis that you must perform to help uncover why your mentee may be reluctant to work with you. The *Five Whys* that all BAs know can help you get to the root cause in this situation. Could it be a lack of confidence? Too much confidence? They don't see the benefit? There may be a point when you both realize that this pairing will not work. Talk through it and discuss alternatives. You don't want to waste time for either of you.

No Opportunities to Gain Experience

It is surprising how many times a new BA has the belief that they can't get a certification because they believe they don't have the necessary experience. Don't be afraid to go over your own learning plan with your manager to see how your organization can help you meet your goals. When mentoring I found that after about an hour of a little probing, listing, more probing, then evaluating the list, they realize that they possess much more experience than they had previously imagined. Those small projects—projects we pop in and out of and even those that we want to forget (because maybe they didn't go so well)—that's all experience that was built up and placed into a brain repository somewhere. We just need to take the time to recall it.

Other opportunities to gain experiences and to learn don't have to be through our *day job*. You could seek opportunities to continue your education by working for a nonprofit as a volunteer or by helping a colleague write a book. Keep in mind that after getting most certifications, you are required to maintain them with continual learning and work experience within the discipline—this was always a great motivator for me to look for those additional opportunities to grow my skill set.

SUMMARY

- Have a good understanding of your competency baseline (current state) and consider evaluating targets to determine gaps in competencies.
- The organization should provide the environment to support the BA role.
- An organization's commitment to allow up-front time for analysis activities, estimating, business case creation, and learning can greatly support the effectiveness of the BA.
- Lack of consistency for various organizational processes may require BAs to pick up roles that are not clearly defined.
- A BACC provides support to business analysis activities, improves business value, and facilitates project success.
- Project management governance, and other governance entities, may predefine a methodology and approaches for business analysis by providing organizational assets to use.
- The RMP is a key deliverable that guides common understanding as to how requirements will be addressed and can be adjusted based on the organization's maturity.
- To close competency gaps and improve proficiencies: share knowledge, expand your network, and develop others through mentoring and coaching.

QUESTIONS

1. What is the impact to your business analysis approach if your organization does not have any consist project management processes in place if they use predominately predictive life-cycle approaches?

_____

_____

_____

_____

2. As a volunteer business analysis mentor, you are to meet your BA mentee for the first time in a few days. What should you do to prepare?

_____

_____

_____

_____

3. What types of competencies are likely to be transferable to other roles?

_____

_____

_____

_____

4. Name five benefits of having a BACC established at your company.

_____

_____

_____

_____

5. What is the difference between mentoring and coaching?

_____

_____

_____

_____

NOTES

1. A few certifications for business analysis: IIBA Entry Certificate in Business Analysis (ECBA™), IIBA Certification of Competency in Business Analysis (CCBA®), IIBA Certified Business Analysis Professional (CBAP®), IQBBA Certified Foundation Level Business Analyst (CFLBA), IREB® Certified Professional for Requirements Engineering (CPRE), PMI Professional in Business Analysis (PMI-PBA)® Certification, BCS International Diploma in Business Analysis.
2. Project Management Institute. (2017). _Agile Practice Guide._ Newtown Square, PA: Project Management Institute.
3. Meadows, Donella H. and Diana Wright. (2008). _Thinking in Systems: A Primer._ Sustainability Institute.
4. Senge, Peter. (1990, 2006). _The Fifth Discipline: The Art and Practice of the Learning Organization._ New York, NY: Currency Doubleday.
5. Drucker, Peter F. (1993). _The Practice of Management._ New York, NY: HarperBusiness.

6. What is the difference between mentoring and coaching?

NOTES

1. Certifications for business analysts: IIBA Entry-level Certificate in Business Analysis (ECBA), IIBA Certification of Competency in Business Analysis (CCBA), IIBA Certified Business Analysis Professional (CBAP), IIBA Certified Foundation Level Business Analysis (AAC/ME/RFB), Certified Professional for Requirements Engineering (CPRE/RE), Professional in Business Analysis (PBA), Certified BCS International Diploma in Business Analysis.

2. Project Management Institute (2013). Agile Practice Guide. Newtown Square, PA: Project Management Institute.

3. Maister, Donald H. and David Mailer (2005). The Trusted Advisor. A Primer. South: Wiley Interscience.

4. Senge Peter (1990, 2006). The Fifth Discipline: the Art and Practice of the Learning Organization. New York, NY: Currency Doubleday.

5. Drucker Peter F. (1997). The Practice of Management. New York, NY: Harper Business.

8

STEP SEVEN—BUILD UP THE TOOL CHEST

"Finally, in order to be that master chef, the chef must mentor others in their mastery by ensuring that they at least know the basic techniques of food preparation and that they can grow to be creative and innovative in combining different techniques and even creating techniques of their own—all in an effort to keep their knowledge fresh and to be innovative in their passion."—Chapter One

TECHNIQUES

Techniques Overview

The objective of this section is *not* to review every technique—rather, the objective is to show the versatility that a business analyst (BA) has in the application of many different techniques. There isn't just one way to perform a task. For example, if we want to elicit requirements, we may want to use a combination of techniques depending on the situation. Examine this scenario:

> *We just had a turnover of stakeholders and many of those who knew the current and future needs are now gone. The newly assigned replacements are not subject matter experts. Is there a combination of elicitation techniques that can help when lacking business domain expertise?*

For instance, consider a standard elicitation technique like interviewing—this technique alone will probably not help in the scenario. But, if we combine it with benchmarking, document analysis, observation for the current state understanding, and maybe even include modeling, use cases, and vertical prototyping for future state understanding, we will get a pretty good start on the requirements for the functional areas that lack the needed expertise. These additional techniques require additional effort and more than likely an iterative approach in order to address the lack of business domain expertise.

Techniques such as conducting prototypes can also be applied to other types of tasks, such as design validation. While benchmarking is not known as an elicitation technique, it doesn't mean you can't use it to get current state information (for example, of a package that might be implemented by a vendor's customer conducting a similar process). Each initiative can have many different scenarios of which you could apply different sets of techniques.

The International Institute of Business Analysis (IIBA®) has identified at least 50 techniques that are used not only across Knowledge Areas, but also across disciplines. Many of the same techniques are used for project management, quality management, or general management activities (although they may have slightly different names). While some might be classified more for an adaptive life-cycle approach such as Kano analysis in this scenario, it doesn't restrict you from using the technique in a predictive or hybrid life-cycle approach. Appendix B.2 not only provides a glossary of techniques, but also includes any known alias and how each is most often used. What is *not* included in this glossary are the interpersonal techniques such as active listening, questioning, conflict management, facilitation, networking, etc. Although these are very important, we will not cover these since they are less likely to vary depending on the specific characteristics of an initiative or life-cycle approach.

Techniques Across Life Cycles and Areas of Focus

Although many bodies of knowledge and methodology experts might suggest certain techniques align with certain approaches, the recommendation here is to try to keep an open mind regarding this sort of mapping. If you re-examine the differences between the life cycles (Table 3.1), it can give insight into the way the technique might be applied differently. Techniques suggested for predictive life cycles such as modeling, can easily be used in an adaptive life-cycle approach when presented in a different way. Also, the needs of the initiative may require that the outcomes from techniques show information in a particular way to help in understanding the information and help make decision making easier.

There are several modeling techniques. In this section we will focus on process and data modeling. Our goal is to give you a few examples of how models may be presented differently, especially by life-cycle approach. Models may vary by notation, the type of information presented, or the depth of the information. For any model when there isn't a standard, at minimum, you should make a few things very clear on the model itself: (1) have a legend that interprets the symbols (or provide a link to a tutorial or guide to interpret the symbols), (2) identify the type of model in order to promote a common language, and (3) always label models that are works-in-progress and whether they reflect the current or future state.

Process models in a traditional predictive life-cycle approach typically use Business Process Model and Notation (BPMN) while adaptive and most hybrid life-cycle approaches use Unified Modeling Language (UML®), but it may also be dictated by the tool being used or the type of initiative the models are for. Figure 8.1 provides an example of each notation for comparison. Both

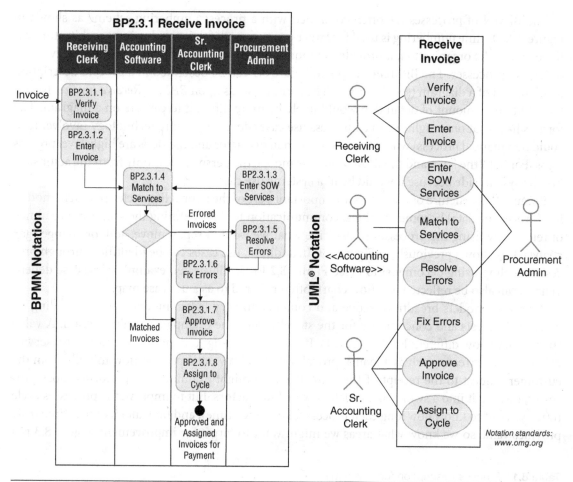

Figure 8.1   Comparing BPMN to UML notation

BPMN and UML are managed by the Object Management Group (OMG®).[1] BPMN tends to be more acceptable across the organization because of its use in enterprise initiatives, while UML is more limited to software engineering disciplines and was specifically developed for object-oriented design—but has been expanding because of its use in various life-cycle tools.

If you were to bring in models from the enterprise architecture, you may be likely to run across the ArchiMate® notation managed by The Open Group.[2] Data models also have their own unique and varied notations, including UML. Conceptual data models built by BAs are likely to use the Martin or Chen notations. UML will likely be used when building class models (data plus behaviors, object-oriented). There are many more notations that we don't list here, but it should be clear that BAs need the ability to adapt between them when working with different tools and approaches if there isn't an apparent standard.

The BPMN of processes are often combined with a process numbering scheme as shown in Figure 8.1. Outline numbering is used for larger projects, and if there is a business architecture defined within the organization, it provides a unique identifier for traceability and can signify depth or level of processes. The BPMN example in Figure 8.1 can be described in a process description form instead of a diagram (see Table 8.1). The form expands upon *BP2.3.1 Receive Invoice*. Notice the additional amount of detail that would likely be more difficult to capture on a diagram. The form is like what one might see in a business use case (does not require technology involvement, could be a manual process) where there is more than one actor and the steps are high-level process steps. For both the form and the BPMN process model, the perspective is only from the actor side, not the system side because it would be in a system's use case.

Because the structure of releases is an important part of the hybrid life-cycle approach, modeling (process or data) becomes a critical communication tool for defining the scope and roadmap of releases by using the processes to describe what we would keep, remove, add, or change (gap analysis), as shown previously in Figure 4.3. In addition, use cases can be identified through process modeling using decomposition (see Figure 8.2 for an illustrated example). Use case dependencies can also be reflected in a flow chart, often referred to as a use case map.

A process model's breadth of scope and content can vary (a.k.a. model view) depending on what the interests and concerns are for the stakeholder. One example is a value stream. A value stream may show different levels of details. If we were looking to improve an end-to-end service delivery value stream, such as a loan approval, we may draw out a process flow initially from the customer request to the receipt of the loan. Then we might examine who performs those processes, turning it into a swim lane, which now includes actors. But to improve the processes cycle time, we want to know how long each process takes (clock time), and how much of that time truly provides value so we know what areas we might want to target for improvement. Figure 8.3 is a

Table 8.1 Process description form with metrics

Description and Goal	Receive invoice
Process Identifier	BP2.3.1
Actors (participants in the process)	Receiving clerk, account sr. clerk, procurement admin., accounting software package
Steps	(1) Verify invoice, (2) Enter invoice, (3) Enter SOW service, (4) Match to services, (5) Resolve errors, (6) Fix errors, (7) Approve invoice, (8) Assign to cycle
Exceptions	Resolution of error conditions: no SOW services found for vendor, no SOW services match for vendor, invoice beyond service dates
Triggers	Invoice received
Timing	10 minutes without exceptions Each exception + 10 to 15 minutes each
Metrics	30 invoices per day, 6–8 per day with exceptions

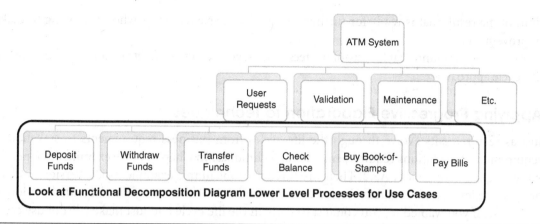

Figure 8.2   Use process models to identify use cases

Loan Approval: From Request to Signed Loan Contract

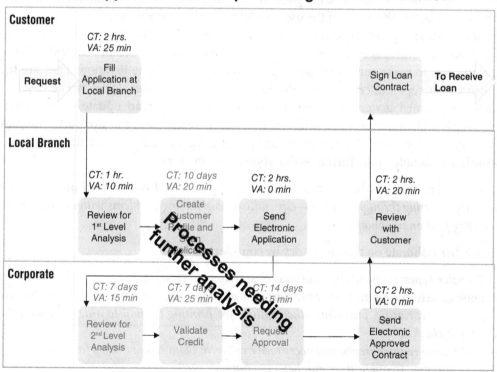

CT = Cycle Time   VA = Value Add Time

Figure 8.3   Value stream draft for stakeholder review

draft of the result that is ready for further analysis by the stakeholders who are looking to make improvements.

Again, keep in mind that for any of the techniques, you can create *light* versions for the adaptive life-cycle approach.

Applying Progressive Elaboration to Techniques

Just as requirements evolve through the life cycles from business requirements to stakeholder requirements to solutions requirements, so do techniques. In Chapter 3, we examined the personas examples in Appendix A3.2. There are three versions in this example: Brief: Version 1, Elaborated: Version 2, and Detailed: Version 3. In Appendix A3.1 there is a *fully elaborated* version of a use case. If you wanted to, you could start early in the life cycle and just make a list of use cases with the primary actor, their goal, and a brief description, like in the Personas Brief: Version 1. You could use this use case list to do a quick inventory of which use cases are in scope. As in the personas, you could also have an Elaborated: Version 2 of the use case that could include the basic flow steps (happy path). Once there is a good understanding of the main path, you dive into more detail for the Detailed: Version 3 of the use case by adding the extensions.

User stories also progressively elaborate as they progress up the ranking in the product backlog. They start out as a business epic, organized into more user story epics, and then split up more (if they are too big) to make sure they can be accomplished within one iteration. They are further elaborated with acceptance criteria and additional requirements. User stories can be split by roles (personas), performed as steps (use case), or even CRUD (create, read, update, delete) functions. During iteration planning sessions when user stories are estimated, the work and assumptions around scope are discussed. These discussions can also further elaborate on the user story. The following is an example of the further elaboration of a user story:

> *As a traveler, I would like to print a boarding pass so that I can proceed quickly to the next step—getting through security—especially if I am having problems with displaying the boarding pass on my phone.*

We can further elaborate on this user story by considering:

- *Traveler types*: *frequent flier, business class, economy class, etc.*
- *Look at alternate paths or scenarios*: *seat already assigned/not assigned, printing for the first time/reprinting, providing other options for printing (e-mail to a device), pre-checked/ not pre-checked*
- *Additional requirements and acceptance criteria*: *Data requirements for the boarding pass (TSA number, frequent flyer number, gate number, etc.)*
- *Other acceptance criteria*: *barcode displayed*

Elaboration happens *just-in-time* in the adaptive life-cycle approach. You don't want to elaborate too soon or the user stories not assigned to the next iteration may not get assigned at all.

Applying the Right Level of Robustness

We discussed how the life-cycle approach can influence the detail level of your techniques (progressive elaboration) and how BAs need to stay on top of realizing when more detail is needed. In this section, we will discuss the right level of robustness in terms of what drives the decision as to *how much* detail is needed. For example, different industry types may have different needs for more detail—industries that are:

- Heavily regulated would have audit requirements requiring more details to be exposed
- Global and/or moving toward outsourcing of work where there might be a disconnect in translation would require more clarity and less ambiguity
- Risk averse would require more due diligence at exposing and managing risks
- Quality focused or promoting internal process consistency and reusability would require certain levels of depth

The message here is that *yes*, there are many influencers. Some of the industry influencers have been listed, but how the life-cycle approach can influence the detail has also been discussed. There is one other aspect of robustness that should be addressed, which can be described using the terminology *low-fidelity* versus *high-fidelity*.

Low-fidelity is a term that was originally used in terms of the reproduction of sound or images. Low-fidelity means that there might be some distortions or imperfections, while high-fidelity conveys more realism or accuracy in comparison to the original. So, when we think of the techniques we use, low-fidelity (lo-fi) may be partially complete and more of a simulation (or not as real looking) and likely to have less technology involved. It can be produced quickly, cheaply, and is simple to understand. But it does not allow for much complexity, does not allow the *iterative*-ness needed to continue the exploration over time, and does not provide a better feel for reality, which may limit the ability to uncover issues. High-fidelity (hi-fi) moves toward more realism. The best way to demonstrate this is with prototyping. Figure 8.4 shows how prototyping can go from lo-fi, paper-based to a hi-fi, full simulation.

The paper-based prototype relies heavily on freehand drawing (whether on paper, whiteboard, or flipchart). For this lo-fi type of prototype, my personal preference is to use butcher paper sprayed with adhesive and placed on the wall with the ability to place plain white sheets of paper that are marked up. Paper-based is best for uncovering missing requirements as early as possible by doing some role play scenarios: "Sara, can you pretend you were filling out this form on paper, while Joe pretends he is the computer validating it? Are we asking for the correct information? Are the business rules for validating that information correct?" In addition to uncovering missing requirements, a role play like this one can also determine desirability or stimulate future thinking. This type of lo-fi prototype is likely to be a throwaway since it is done very early in the life cycle (leveraged for the information you obtain, but not retained as a design that evolves).

Another type of lo-fi prototype is storyboarding, which is used to understand the step-by-step flow of user's work that would be reflected with showing the sequence of screens. This type is

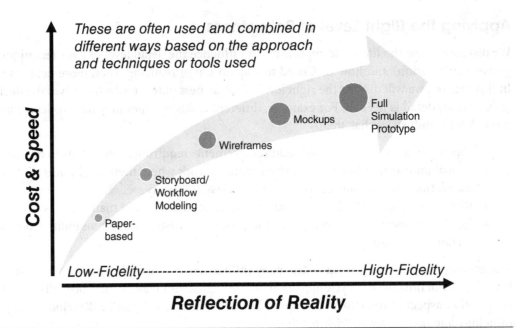

Figure 8.4   Prototypes: reflection of reality

often used for early acceptance of the future state: "Sara, can you tell me what comes next? Does this outcome address your needs?" Storyboards are a great way to demonstrate how a solution might address the business requirements, and because it shows sequence, it can also help provide depth in a particular area (vertical prototype) or show how all functions interact across the breadth of the initiative (horizontal prototype).

Going back to Figure 8.4, you will see that wireframes are more of a middle-level fidelity or *mid-fi*. Think of wireframes as a type of *blueprint* for a mobile device or web page. It is a static look (not interactive) at what the design might be, but does not go into the detail of fonts, photos, colors, etc. The focus is on what the layout looks like: "Sara, would it be better to move the search to the top of the screen?" It can also be useful to show adherence to design standards: "Stacey, can you verify that this is the proper design layout for the 'logon screen standard' that you sent me?" For the BA, the layout addresses usability and data requirements that focus on what content is on the screen.

Moving toward hi-fi design and closer to reality, mockups introduce static displays of visuals as the wireframe does, but with the focus of having more color schemes, font, style, etc. It prepares the prototype for the final simulation by providing the right look and feel: "Sara, do you want to leverage the use of larger fonts on the areas that are most important for our investors, and maybe use different colors to show the contrast between the investment areas?" Keep in mind that visual looks can be tied to user requirements. For example, highlighting specific content (such as an alert) may be shown with a larger font and in a different colored box (like using red to draw the end user's attention).

Full simulation is the highest fidelity—closest to reality and reflects an interactive final design. This prototype can demonstrate the solution and helps validate a variety of requirements in an evolutionary manner, meaning that it can be continually enhanced to become a workable product. Keep in mind that it is likely to progressively get to a full simulation by going from a lo-fi to a hi-fi prototype, but it is not a requirement to do so.

So, what is the right level of robustness? Well, it depends. The *right* level of robustness is more of an art than a science, but the BA (with practice) will know how deep to go. Often, it is a collaborative decision with stakeholders, so if you sense confusion, you elaborate a little more. In the adaptive life-cycle approach, the decision to dive deeper is always preceded by asking, "Is this enough to move us forward?"

Estimate Variations

Your estimating approaches can vary, but the assumptions you make can justify whatever estimates you provide based on the variations discussed in previous chapters (life cycles and other uniqueness considerations). The estimates requested can be based on cost, effort, duration, number of full-time equivalent (FTE) resources, or size. Here are a few examples of estimating variations:

- The sponsor of a business case for an enterprise-wide initiative using the predictive life-cycle approach is concerned about *FTE* estimates from their IT organization as input to overall *cost* estimates.
- The project manager (PM) of a vendor package implementation using a hybrid life-cycle approach is concerned about vendor *total cost of ownership* and *duration* estimates per each solution alternative and spending for each future release.
- Your agile team is discussing the story points for a user story during a sprint planning session and they are concerned about the estimated *size* of the user story.
- You helped the product owner build the product backlog for a one-year initiative with user stories elicited from a stakeholder workshop. Four iterations later, the product owner wants a story point estimate of the user stories that are left in the product backlog to determine how many more iterations are left to do (*duration*).

Review your work breakdown structure (WBS) and determine what tools and techniques you will use. Estimates will be much more accurate if you can start with a list of assumptions regarding tools and techniques. Another example of a WBS is shown in Figure 8.5. In this example, the techniques used are explicitly identified. Regarding the tools and techniques when estimating, any assumptions should be made visible in order to manage expectations.

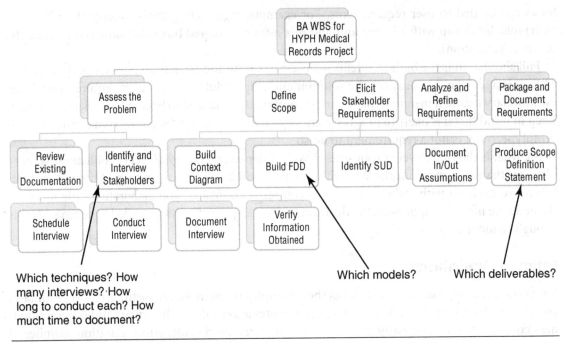

Figure 8.5   WBS with techniques

Estimate influencers to consider include:

- Complexity of the task or the feature
- Risks
- Number of features
- Dependencies
- Capabilities of the resource
- Part-time effect
- Life-cycle approach
- Number of stakeholders and diversity
- Activities, tools, and techniques

Here is a scenario where you have a task in your WBS to elicit stakeholder requirements. You have already determined that you will conduct interviews. To estimate this task, you need to assume how many stakeholders you plan to interview, and how long each interview will take to prep, conduct, and finalize. If your best guess at this time is that you will interview 10 stakeholders, and you expect that it would require four hours total for each stakeholder, the combined time of the interviews would be 40 hours of effort. To be safe, you also decided to add some contingency time for the risk that some stakeholders may require follow-up interviews to dig deeper. Based on your previous experience, you build in an additional 20% of time spent on follow-up interviews with stakeholders. That makes the total estimate 48 hours.

This estimating technique is called parametric estimating, because per unit (interview) it takes four hours, and you added risk buffers to the estimate (20%). With 10 interviews and the buffer, you estimated a total of 48 hours. What if the scope doubled and you suddenly have 20 stakeholders to interview? It becomes much easier to justify another 48 hours of effort because you made the assumptions clear regarding a *per interview* effort of four hours and a baseline of 10 interviews. What if it is *critical* that the duration remain the same? You just had an increase in interviews and an additional 48 hours of effort, yet the duration cannot change. You must look at other options. You can make a change to your assumed technique to see if that would save time. So instead of the four hours per interview, what if it wasn't an interview? For example, you could have a discussion with the PM about the possible impact of conducting a workshop for some of the stakeholders or group them in some way to conduct multiple meetings with more than one stakeholder. Running a workshop may shorten the overall interview time, but how feasible is it? Are the stakeholders geographically dispersed? Do they represent very different areas? How would it impact your effort versus the stakeholder's effort?

Leveraging the Diversity of Tables

Have you ever tried to communicate requirements that were so complex that you had to explain them over and over again and then you start to wonder whether you really understood them yourself? Those requirements need other techniques of analysis—alternatives—both for you and for your audience. Of course, modeling can help, but our focus in this section is to look at tables as an alternative technique for requirement analysis and solution analysis.

Decision Tables

Decision tables can make complex information easier to read and can help uncover errors or omissions. These tables are an especially good alternative to complex business rules. With decision tables you would need to consider the conditions and variables that will trigger decisions. Table 8.2 is split up into three conditions and five actions. Different combinations of conditions and actions make up the scenarios. Scenario 2, if written into a textual business rule, would be stated this way: "If the customer is an employee, then the customer must receive a 15% discount on Product X, a 10% discount on Product Y, and additional discounts would also apply." Each scenario represents a textual statement (seven, plus one that is missing in the table). By reviewing each scenario, you have the opportunity to *visualize* the problems and point to them. For Scenario 3, you might ask if it was intended *not* to give a customer who is over 65 *and* an employee the extra 5% on Product X. You might ask more about why Scenario 4 is an error, if they considered the differences for active versus inactive versus retired employees. Or you might notice there is a missing scenario and ask about it. Having visuals such as models and tables can help with these types of discussions, as well as finding missing requirements.

Table 8.2   Decision table to visibly analyze business rules

Condition	Scenario 1	Scenario 2	Scenario 3	Scenario 4	Scenario 5	Scenario 6	Scenario 7
Customer an employee?	N	Y	Y	Y	N	N	Y
...................over 65?	N	N	Y	Y	N	Y	N
.......vendor or special?	N	N	N	Y	Y	N	Y
Action							
15% Discount prod X		X					
10% Discount prod Y		X					
10% All products			X		X	X	
Addl discounts apply		X			X		
Error				X			X

N = No, Y = Yes, X = Applicable

Morphological Box

Morphological analysis was devised by astrophysicist Fritz Zwicky in order to address problems that were nonquantifiable by looking at different possible relationships and combinations. The uniqueness of the morphological box, the result of applying the technique, is that it helps the BA to look at different elements of a problem or the solutions of the problem in different combinations coming up with new solutions that you may not have thought of. It not only organizes the features of a solution, but it also compares and contrasts these elements to uncover useful alternative combinations. I often use this technique in workshops when we struggle in finding a viable solution to meet the conflicting demands of stakeholders. Table 8.3 provides an example of a morphological box looking at the parameters of cost, fit with strategy, ability to scale for growth, quality impact against the build, and timeline rank. This is compared to each of the solution options of build, buy, and work-around, with a last column for other alternatives. We could look at the combination, and after some discussion, decide to look at a new combination, for example: buy + build long term (internally build two critical features not addressed by package) and include the short-term work-around. The feasibility and quality issues would require additional discussion. It is a more simplistic way to present complex information to come up with other solution ideas. Another option to include as an alternative would be a cloud solution for the buy that may be a better fit to address scalability for growth.

We have only looked at two example tables, one that is ideal for documenting complex business rules and another for evaluating solutions and generating additional solution options. Tables are often preferable for organizing information in different ways. If one way doesn't work, try a different way: turn around a few columns and rows, add a column to add more information, show relationships between information, etc. Tables are a valuable technique to keep in mind when facilitating with executives or sitting at your desk digging in deep to analyze large amounts of data.

Table 8.3 Morphological box: solution options

	Build	Buy	Work-around	Other options
Cost	Highest: 1.2–1.5 m	Medium: 500k–800k	Lowest: 50k	Options to keep us under 1m?
Fit with strategy	100%—fully customizable to strategy	75% fit—two critical features not addressed	Fits with current model, not for long-term strategy	Buy + build for two features?
Ability to scale for growth	Constrained by capital budget	Constrained by capital budget	Short term only	Cloud?
Quality impact	Quality checks fully integrated with Six Sigma intiative	1% defect industry standard with this product (50% improvement to baseline)	Will not improve quality issues	Can buy option configure in some Six Sigma requests?
Timeline rank (1 = shortest)	3	2	1	Add work-around for short term to all options?

BUSINESS ANALYSIS TOOL TYPES

One area that the organizational assessment (discussed in Chapter 7) addresses is the use of technology to improve BA productivity. As with any role, automation can reduce effort and defects. In business analysis activities, especially for larger initiatives, tools are of great importance. Figure 8.6 shows the different levels of tool sophistication. Will a simple desktop tool suffice or do we need to go out and purchase an end-to-end (a.k.a. full life-cycle tool) that addresses requirements from business case to post-implementation evaluation? As with the introduction of any tool, it is critical that the organization is ready for it. If you don't have the individual competencies for business analysis, haven't practiced business analysis for a while, or don't have the capabilities to apply business analysis to your projects successfully, a fancy new sophisticated tool will end up being *shelf-ware*—a waste of an investment.

Homegrown and Single-Purpose Tools

As the organization matures, it is best to start with simple tools and then improve from there. As seen in Figure 8.6, you can always start with a homegrown tool. It could be a simple relational database that you got someone in IT to put together for you as a favor or other in-house tools that were built to address a specific purpose (especially since you probably weren't able to justify *purchasing* anything yet because your organization doesn't recognize business analysis for its value).

Often, when I am brought in to help a client in the area of business analysis, no tools exist—or if there are tools, they aren't using them. If they do happen to be using their tools, it is typically not consistent across their teams. To deal with all of the different environments that you may

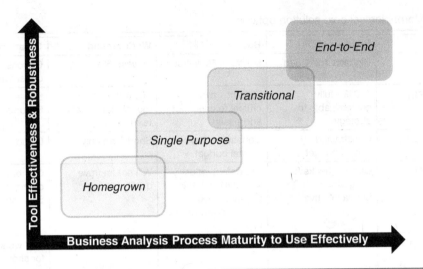

Figure 8.6   Business analysis tool maturity

encounter, a simple spreadsheet works well as both a personal BA workbook and a repository of information to leave behind (after some cleanup) with the client. This simple spreadsheet works well for these reasons: because most everyone has spreadsheet software; they can use it reasonably well; and if they do use a different tool later, it can likely import data from the spreadsheet. As a consultant, what I recommend is to keep a spreadsheet file for each life-cycle approach. The tabs within the spreadsheet become my worksheets, and while they are *works-in-progress*, they contain all of the information that I need in order to be organized and prepared when creating last-minute deliverables or when a stakeholder asks, "Which release is that requirement in?"

The predictive life-cycle spreadsheet file has many tabs (which should make sense). Remember, it is a worksheet for you, *not* a deliverable—but the content can be used to create needed deliverables. Here is an example of some of those tabs set up for the predictive approach:

- Initiative profile (vision or problem statement)
- Business requirements
- Stakeholder profile
- Documents inventory
- Scope and estimating assumptions
- Outstanding questions
- Requirements (stakeholder, solution, and business rules—includes traceability and re-quirement attributes)
- As-is models (you can draw in the spreadsheet or cut/paste)
- To-be models

- Gap analysis
- Data model
- Data dictionary
- CRUD
- Responsibility matrix
- Permissions matrix
- Supporting use cases

Here are some tabs set up for the adaptive approach:

- Vision and roadmap
- Business epics
- Stakeholders
- Personas
- User story template
- Product backlog
- Sprint backlog(s)
- Light models
- Story board
- Supporting use cases

BAs should not be template driven, so any similar tool should be tailored for the work you will be doing.

We looked at the lowest level of tool maturity, homegrown tools. Let's look at the next level, single-purpose tools. You want to do a diagram? Use a diagramming tool. You want to do use cases, use a use case tool. These are tools that exist for specific functions or may be used across disciplines and have standard features across the industry. But what if I want to link the data in the use case tool to a diagram in the diagramming tool? The challenge with single purpose tools is that they require more effort to connect the information between them dynamically. You might be able to export from one and import to another, but the transition can lose information, and unfortunately, every change would require going through that process again.

When coaching BAs, the most simplistic tools were found to be the best approach with which to start. It is easier to learn and introduce features a little at a time. Assessing BA capabilities, you may suggest the use of transitional tools or suggest a tool with which they have not taken full advantage of (or have never used at all). Once they become familiar with these simpler tools, the transition to a more sophisticated tool becomes much easier. As BAs, we need to practice what we preach. This is an iterative approach that is being applied to business analysis activities. As a mentor, I often think of BAs as my customers who just so happen to be users of business analysis processes and tools that automate certain processes.

Transitional Tools

The next level of tool maturity consists of transitional tools that help make connections or build bridges to other tools. But transitional tools have limitations since they were originally meant for another purpose. For example, let's say you use the fictitious tool, *product test*, as a testing tool in your current quality assurance group. Finding out that *product test* has a requirements module, you realize you can use this tool to trace your requirements to test cases. Awesome! It is better than what you are doing today, which is using a spreadsheet to manually trace the test case number to the requirement. The quality assurance group already use it and love it, so you don't have to convince them to help with tracing to test cases. It was a cheap way to get started on traceability. But that is about all it does. This worked great for a while, but we are getting better at what needs to be done in business analysis and know that there is more out there that can help address our needs.

Transitional tools are often used in more informal life-cycle approaches, such as agile. Agile tools that initially came out were developed to address the challenges of using agile in a geographically diverse environment. At first, it was more about the ability to share information as a team (such as kanban boards), and in some ways, it still is. You don't need to retain information or link it together because iterations are very short, and the information is short-lived. So, tools in the adaptive life-cycle approach may remain as transitional tools with a mix of several single-purpose tools. For organizations that go adaptive across the enterprise, they may find that an end-to-end tool specifically made for the adaptive life cycle may be quite useful—but again, the maturity in business analysis processes (even the adaptive approach) needs to be more advanced.

End-to-End Tools

End-to-end tools are all about scope. Are we talking full solution life cycle (SLC) or the business analysis domain (based on business analysis activities only)? Much of what a BA does is touched by many other activities within a life-cycle approach. Even though the bulk of business analysis activities are in analysis, the role has *threads* of activities through all phases. So, what I consider an end-to-end tool is one that address the SLC phases. The advantage of an integrated SLC tool is the interoperability among components and shared information. But even in these SLC tools, there are varying levels of how well they:

- Integrate with business strategy and architectures
- Adapt to life-cycle variations in processes and techniques
- Flow between modules and processes
- Integrate and share data
- Link between components
- Allow for customization (such as notations)
- Address varying techniques

- Can transform information from one presentation to another (such as graphics from matrices)
- Allow for reuse of components

My initial exposure to these tools was back in the late 1980s. Computer-aided software engineering (CASE) tools were some of the first automated end-to-end software development life-cycle tools. The *upper-case* part of the CASE tool addressed the idea of analysis and design being independent of technology. The *lower-case* part of the CASE tool addressed development of structured code, implementation, and testing. These tools also included project management (planning), an integrated repository, and the ability to track maintenance. It took four months of training to be effective using the CASE tool. So, there was often a huge investment, not only in the tool but also in the training and in the maintenance of that tool.

Most end-to-end life-cycle tools are used in large, more complex initiatives, which are either predictive or hybrid life cycles. If an organization makes the investment, many can be adapted for use in smaller projects, but adaptive life-cycle approaches have enough uniqueness in their activities that they typically have their own suite of single purpose or transitional tools, and therefore, the need for integration is less.

TECHNIQUE CHALLENGES AND OPPORTUNITIES

Transferable Techniques

Many BAs can (and do) perform in multiple roles at once or are likely to transition from role to role depending on the approach to allocating resources in their organization. Something exciting about performing in another role is the amount of knowledge that can be applied, but with a twist. For example, having been both a BA and PM, I found several techniques that can be used in both roles, yet in slightly different ways. Three that come to mind are the context diagram, decomposition, and the responsibility matrix.

The context diagram is used to define scope, but it can be used multiple ways. There are two scopes: product and work. Figure 8.7 provides a look at both. The BA is responsible for defining the system under discussion (SUD) for the current state—the boundaries of what is in scope to analyze. Using the context diagram, the center circle is the SUD and what surrounds the circle are the entities that provide input to the SUD and receive the outputs from the SUD (in other words, both direct and indirect users and interfaces to other systems). In contrast, the PM may use the context diagram to define the project boundaries. The center circle would be the project, and the entities surrounding the circle would be the stakeholder groups that would provide input to the project or receive output from the project, or in other words, the stakeholders (see example in Figure 7.4 for a mentoring program).

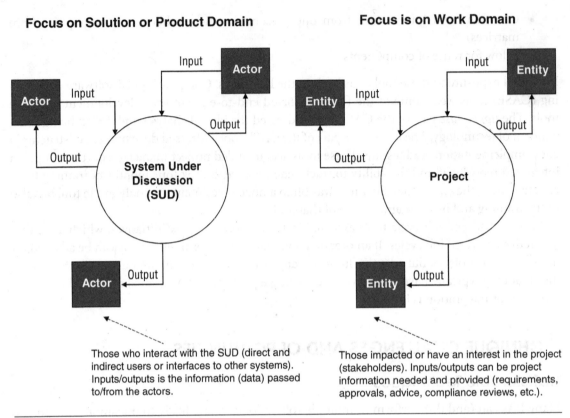

Figure 8.7   Context diagram variations

Decomposition is a technique that is used to break down a component and that component could be the SUD. The SUD breaks down into functions within the scope of the SUD, and functions (or subsystems) break down into processes and steps (use cases). An example of this was provided in Figure 4.3. Looking at it from a project perspective, the same technique can be used to show the WBS Decomposition and can also be applied to any other type of hierarchy—organization, capabilities, etc.

In project management, responsibility matrices are most often used to assign responsibilities to deliverables. If we listed a deliverable—*Business Requirements Document*—you would then identify in the matrix who would be:

- *Responsible* for creating the deliverable
- *Accountable* for the approval of the deliverable
- *Consulted* for advice or help
- *Informed* about the deliverable and its content

A responsibility matrix containing these four components is called a RACI chart and is very useful for assigning responsibilities for deliverables or other work-related activities for the project.

But now, let's look at how this could be used from a product or solution perspective. The BA may want to determine the process responsibilities for stakeholders rather than deliverables. If you took the functions from a *functional decomposition diagram*, you could build a RACI chart based on the functions or processes. If we listed a functional process (e.g., accounts payable), you would then identify in the matrix who would be:

- *Responsible* for providing the requirements for that process (source)
- *Accountable* for approving the requirements for that process (owner)
- *Consulted* for validation or additional input for that process
- *Informed* about changes to the process for possible interest or impact

As you see, this would still be a RACI diagram, but it would look at the product or solution (processes) rather than deliverables.

As demonstrated, these three techniques (context diagram, decomposition, and responsibility matrix) focus on the product or solution scope from the business analysis perspective, whereas they focus on the work scope from the project management perspective. Many of the same techniques that you learn as a BA can be used in many other roles, such as a change agent, data architect, strategist, quality manager, product owner, Scrum master, solution architect, etc., so the more techniques that you are able to expose yourself to, the easier it will be to perform in these other roles.

Technique Conflicts

Are there situations when techniques can't be swapped in/out? There are some techniques that are embedded in a life-cycle approach. This is where a deliverable outcome is based on using a specific technique. One that comes to mind is the use case and the user story. It appears that once there is a commitment to use one, the other is abandoned because they are closely associated with specific methodologies (more specific than a life-cycle approach, such as using use cases and scenarios in the Rational Unified Process). Can user stories and use cases co-exist?

There was one situation where there was a bit of chaos happening at a client site. The IT group was told that they had to convert all the use cases to user stories. They had been using use cases for years and they had to go agile. They asked me how the two were related and how to convert them. User stories and use cases are managed very differently. The intent of user stories in an adaptive life-cycle approach is to only be a place holder for the intended conversation in the assigned iteration and not a documentation method. In comparison, use cases are often used for documentation in hybrid life-cycle approaches because they are more likely to be retained for: reuse as part of current state process documentation (especially for business architecture assets and outsourcing), quality assurance documentation, or documenting vendor package scenarios. What would you do in this situation?

First, consider the consequences of why the use cases were retained and if they are still providing value to stakeholders? If so, how will that value be changed by converting use cases to user stories—will they still get the same value? Second, as user stories populate new product backlogs and are then assigned to iterations, could the use cases help in splitting user stories or in defining acceptance criteria? Taking the time to think of the *value* of what we are doing and determining the trade-offs we have to make should be an important part of the decision-making process. This situation is a case of reacting to a leadership request, but they suspected a problem and made the attempt to gather information in order to help them approach the situation in a better way. BAs need the courage to collect and present the information to help leadership make the best decision at the time—that's leadership.

SUMMARY

- Try to keep an open mind when applying techniques with one life-cycle approach. Many techniques can not only be applied across the different life cycles but also various types of initiatives and industries.
- Techniques such as process modeling can be used in different life cycles, but there may be some variations in how they are presented. For example, different life-cycle approaches use different notations for their models.
- Content breadth and depth, or model views, can vary depending on stakeholder interests and concerns.
- For any modeling technique, a *lightweight* version can be applied for the adaptive life-cycle approach.
- Techniques can evolve into more detail (progressive elaboration) as you move through the life cycle. An example is the use case that can start as a brief statement (header), progress to the basic steps, and finally move on to the exceptions and alternate path.
- The lo-fi to hi-fi technique addresses how closely a prototype technique relates to reality. Examples go from paper-based to fully interactive simulations.
- Estimates requested can be based on cost, effort, duration, number of FTE resources, or size. How each of these are estimated and the assumptions behind them can vary.
- Tables are a great alternative method in which to present complex requirements, observe relationships between information, find missing information, evaluate solution alternatives, or use for generating solution ideas.
- Business analysis maturity and tool maturity have a relationship. Business analysis tools can be homegrown, single-purpose, transitional, or end-to-end.
- Many of the same techniques that you learn about as a BA can be used in many other roles—thus, the more techniques you are exposed to, the easier it will be to perform in other roles.

QUESTIONS

1. Review the Glossary of Techniques in Appendix B.2 and determine which combination of techniques you would use and how you might use them for the following two elicitation scenarios.

    a. *Your sponsor is preparing a business case with you (adding new features to an existing product) and suggests that you elicit initial thoughts and attitudes toward two solution alternatives from a group of users.*

    Techniques: _____

    _____

    _____

    b. *You are in the middle of an iteration and the team is discussing the acceptance criteria for a user story. After asking some probing questions around data requirements, it was determined that there was a lot of discussion but a lack of true understanding of what the requirements were. You needed to pull out some of your techniques to help the team get on the same page. What techniques might help?*

    Techniques: _____

    _____

    _____

2. Figure 8.3 shows a few processes that need further analysis for process improvement. Name at least two techniques you would recommend.

    Techniques: _____

    _____

    _____

3. Based on your answer to #2, list two of the techniques and determine your estimating approach and assumptions for each.

    Techniques: _____

    _____

    _____

    _____

4. Name two techniques that are used in both business analysis and project management but in different ways.

    _____

    _____

5. Why might a BA use a transitional tool?

    _____

    _____

    _____

    _____

NOTES

1. OMG is a not-for-profit international technology standards organization. For more information about their notation standards go to their website at: www.omg.org.
2. The Open Group is a global consortium with a diverse membership of vendors, suppliers, academics, consultants, and customers. For more information about their architectural standards, go to their website at: www.opengroup.org.

EPILOGUE

Business analysis and the business analyst role will continue to evolve. Yesterday's latest trends will slowly fall more and more behind us, and new ones will take their place, but the core concepts of business analysis are unlikely to change. Will you always have to uncover requirements *before* deciding on a solution? Very likely. Will you have to determine boundaries and assess the impact of change? Surely. Will you always have to manage stakeholders' expectations? Probably. Will you always have to keep an eye on value? Absolutely. But how you perform business analysis in the most efficient way to provide the most value to your stakeholders is where business analysts can be an example to others by bringing passion and the art into their business analysis roles and careers. Can you master versatility? My hope is that this book has started you on that path, but only you can practice the mastery. Those that have done so, please share with others! Those that want to, please learn and keep trying! Those that don't want to, ask yourself if you are on the right career path.

Going back to Chapter 1, consider that not every cook wants to become a chef. But for those of you who do want to continue on this path of learning and discovery, consider mastering business analysis versatility's seven steps:

STEP ONE—MOVE TO AN ENTERPRISE MINDSET

"The chef not only knows about the inner workings of the kitchen, but also understands the importance of the vendors who supply the fresh ingredients, the need to follow the community's food service regulations, the obligation to know the tolerances of the restaurant owner, the significance of the geographical location, and even the cultural impacts of taste preferences, etc."

STEP TWO—ADAPT TO THE LIFE-CYCLE APPROACH

"Although the chef and the cook both start with an initial recipe, the chef's expertise allows for the creation of a full menu by making necessary changes and adaptions based on elements such as customer feedback and tolerance for changes to the menu, customer cost constraints, the need for innovation, available equipment, etc."

STEP THREE—CONSIDER UNIQUENESS

"Although the chef and the cook both start with an initial recipe, the chef's expertise allows for the creation of a full menu by making necessary changes and adaptions based on elements such as customer feedback and tolerance for changes to the menu, customer cost constraints, the need for innovation, available equipment, etc. But the owner and chef may identify many smaller changes that can be done incrementally, such as modifying a menu item each week to check the reaction with a small focus group of patrons."

STEP FOUR—ADJUST BASED ON RISKS

"As the chefs, we as business analysts should have the confidence to adapt and make changes, to make substitutions if needed, and know what we have available to us to make it work. We may have even predicted this and have a backup plan. Our advanced preparation in anticipating change gives us the courage to make the needed adjustments without a fear of failure because we are ready to improvise. We are willing to take on the risks for the rewards."

STEP FIVE—ALWAYS FOCUS ON VALUE

"To be a master chef is to go beyond the doors of the restaurant. It is about looking at food trends and new opportunities; constantly reviewing our menus, cooking processes, and techniques for potential improvements; evaluating the customer's response to changes in our menu items; and making the needed adjustments to provide more value to not only the restaurant patrons, but to the restaurant owner as well."

STEP SIX—BRIDGE THE CAPABILITY GAP

"A true master chef networks with other chefs to share ideas, pursues new certifications and award opportunities, and writes and shares recipes with the community."

STEP SEVEN—BUILD UP THE TOOL CHEST

"Finally, in order to be that master chef, the chef must mentor others in their mastery by ensuring that they at least know the basic techniques of food preparation and that they can grow to be creative and innovative in combining different techniques and even creating techniques of their own—all in an effort to keep their knowledge fresh and to be innovative in their passion."

Appendix A

Templates, Checklists, and Examples

A 2.1

FEASIBILITY STUDY TEMPLATE

A deliverable that provides an assessment of alternatives to see if they are technically possible within the constraints of the enterprise or organization.

FEASIBILITY STUDY
FOR [   ]

Presented to {Steering Committee or Board}
Presented by {Submitting Organization}
{Date of Submission}
{Version 0.1 DRAFT}

Prepared By _____ Dated: _____

For acceptance {Document Owner and Contact Info}

Accepted By _____ Dated: _____

For Version {Version #} {Sponsor and Contact Info}

[Table of Contents]

Revision History

Date	Revision	Author	Changes

Document Reviewers/Approvers

Name	Position	Reviewer or Approver?	Signature of Approver	Version Reviewed	Sign-Off Date

Executive Summary

<Summarize why the study is being conducted, the results, and any recommended actions. This section should be no more than one page. Consider what information your key high-level stakeholders would need to know to make their decision moving forward.>

Business Problem and Opportunity Statement

<Include information uncovered during the current state assessment and any external research activities. This may include strategic alignment and objectives for business units under study. It may also include other impacted areas such as physical locations, infrastructure, information, processes, markets, or regulatory environments.>

Feasibility Study Requirements

<Describe who conducted the study and who was involved, why it was conducted, what the expectations were for the study, the methods and techniques that were used, challenges when conducting the study and how they were addressed, and when it was completed.>

Feasibility Study Results

<Describe potential solutions using visuals and full descriptions. Describe the methods for reviewing each alternative (ranking and scores) and the final results. Address the feasibility from the following perspectives and constraints: resources (availability and capabilities), technology, operational impacts, economics, market demand, legal, safety, regulatory, existing physical environments, etc. Tolerance to risks in each of those areas should also be addressed. A recommended solution can be identified with an explanation as to why it is recommended.>

Solution Alternative 1 (Recommended)
Solution Alternative 2
Solution Alternative 3

Assumptions

<It is critical to document assumptions that were made when assessing the solutions and making any recommendation. They are those things that you consider to be true but could not validate.>

Appendix

<Appendix may include supporting information such as resources used vendor information for solutions, industry studies, governance standards used, surveys conducted, vendor responses, etc.>

A 2.2

BUSINESS CASE TEMPLATE

The business case provides a close look at the proposed initiatives for an enterprise or organization. Business cases must show how the enterprise or organization will get a return on their investments (ROI).

BUSINESS CASE
{INITIATIVE NAME}

Presented to {Steering Committee or Board}
Presented by {Submitting Organization}
{Date of Submission}
{Version 0.1 DRAFT}

Prepared By _____ Dated: _____

For acceptance {Document Owner and Contact Info}

Accepted By _____ Dated: _____

For Version {Version #} {Sponsor and Contact Info}

[Table of Contents]

Revision History

Date	Revision	Author	Changes

Document Reviewers/Approvers

Name	Position	Reviewer or Approver?	Signature of Approver	Version Reviewed	Sign-Off Date

Executive Summary

<Most people will only read the executive summary. It should summarize the document and be able to stand alone as a logical, clear, and concise summary of the points within the document. Write this section last.

The executive summary should be a summary of findings that focus on the reasons behind the recommended go-forward approach. The writer should consider the audience. Include a statement of the business need, relationship to strategic goals and initiatives, summary of options, costs, and benefits, and finally, the recommendations. Do not include assumptions, analysis, reasoning, or details.>

Introduction/Background

<Keep this section as brief as possible. The intent is to put the situation into perspective for the reader.

This is a brief statement to introduce the business problem with past and current information to set the stage for the reason behind developing the business case at this time.>

Overview

<Keep this section very short.

   Initiative title (long and short names). Initiative objective. Description of the product, service, or other solution that is expected to deliver. Organizational objectives. Relationship between this initiative and the corporate strategy.>

The Business Case

<This section focuses on the reasons why resources were assigned to do the business case. Describe the purpose of the business case (e.g., business need, obtain go-forward approval, obtain funding). Describe the sponsor of the business case development. Describe the intended audience.>

Problem/Opportunity Statement

<This section is where details are presented. Results of analyses may be included in the appendix and referenced in this section. The problem statement must meet expectations of business case stakeholders. Provide a very clear statement of the problem. Description of the relevant internal and external factors. Assessment of how the business needs are currently being met, or not. Analysis of the gap between the current situation and the stated objective(s). Initial priorities expectations.>

Assumptions and Constraints

<This section includes all assumptions made prior to and during the business case development process. Other sources of assumptions may include: proposal brief, strategic planning documents, service management contracts, and relevant vendor proposals. List of assumptions and constraints organized in relevant categories.>

Analysis of Options

<This section reflects a high-level analysis of possible alternatives that could be employed to bridge the gap between the current situation and proposed solution. This section is usually somewhat subjective. The degree of analysis should reflect the significance of the decision and the expectations of decision makers. Identification of options should include a minimum of: (1) do nothing, (2) option that achieves the results, (3) the preferred option. Comparison of options includes method of analysis with appendices showing details; for example, the decision criteria and scoring of each option displayed in a table. Ways of how results were assessed and a detailed risk analysis are also included as appendices.>

Benefit/Cost/Risk Analysis

<This section details the <u>recommended option</u> only and the level of detail is dependent upon the expectations of the sponsor.

Include the benefits, one-time costs, direct costs, recurrent costs, total cost of ownership, increased revenues, decreased expenses, asset conversions, and the major risks and the cost of risk minimization. Costs include risk and quality management costs.>

Implementation Strategy

<This information forms the basis for the project and clearly defines the project scope based on the recommended solution.

Include an approach roadmap and implementation strategy (break into smaller projects or address as one project?). Include any known constraints on the timeline of deliverables and targeted outcomes, involvement of key stakeholders, related projects/initiatives impacting implementation, organizational impacts, risks affecting the approach, resource availability (internal or external), recommended methodologies for solution development and delivery.>

Glossary and Appendices

<Use this section to help the document flow better by putting detailed analysis of options into the appendices. List of terms and acronyms used throughout the document may be included as an appendix.>

Net Present Value Analysis—Option 1

BALANCE SHEET	Year 0	Year 1	Year 2	Year 3
Capitalized expenditures				
INCOME STATEMENT				
Revenues				
• Cost of sales				
• *Gross margin*				
• Operating expenses				
• Depreciation				
• Operating income				
• Taxes				
• *Net income*				
STATEMENT OF CASH FLOWS				
• Net income				
• Plus: depreciation				
• Net cash flows				
• Discount factor (@ 8% rate)				
• Discounted cash flows				
NET PRESENT VALUE				

Net Present Value Analysis—Option 2

BALANCE SHEET	Year 0	Year 1	Year 2	Year 3
Capitalized expenditures				
INCOME STATEMENT				
Revenues				
• Cost of sales				
• *Gross margin*				
• Operating expenses				
• Depreciation				
• Operating income				
• Taxes				
• *Net income*				
STATEMENT OF CASH FLOWS				
• Net income				
• Plus: depreciation				
• Net cash flows				
• Discount factor (@ 8% rate)				
• Discounted cash flows				
NET PRESENT VALUE				

Risk Management Plan—Option 1

1. (Column A) Identify the risk
2. (Columns B, C, D, and E) Assess the impact, quantify the weight of the impact, quantify the probability, calculate the severity
3. (Column F) Determine response options and list recommended actions—consider, avoid, mitigate, transfer, accept, or if a contingency may be needed depending on impact

Risk (Column A)	Why Is It a Risk and What Is the Impact if Realized? (Column B)	Impact (1–5) (Column C)	Probability (1–5) (Column D)	Severity (prob x Impact) (Column E)	Communication Action or Additional Controls Needed (Column F)

Risk Management Plan—Option 2

1. (Column A) Identify the risk
2. (Columns B, C, D, and E) Assess the impact, quantify the weight of the impact, quantify the probability, calculate the severity
3. (Column F) Determine response options and list recommended actions—consider, avoid, mitigate, transfer, accept, or if a contingency may be needed depending on impact

Risk (Column A)	Why Is It a Risk and What Is the Impact if Realized? (Column B)	Impact (1–5) (Column C)	Probability (1–5) (Column D)	Severity (prob x Impact) (Column E)	Communication Action or Additional Controls Needed (Column F)

A 2.3

BUSINESS MODEL QUESTIONS: CURRENT STATE—TRAINING COMPANY

Adapted from Business Model Canvas, www.strategyzer.com

1. *Customer Segments* (CS)

Current state: how are customers categorized based on what value is being provided or by other business criteria (e.g., special services for certain types of accounts)?

2. *Key Partners* (KP)

Who do we interact with externally that helps us to save money, make money, reduce risks, add to our capabilities or get the needed resources to do all those things? They could be vendors, suppliers, educational institutions, support organizations, etc. They can be generic entities or be specifically named.

3. *Key Activities* (KA)

What are the things that we do to support, sell, create, or deliver training? These activities can be described as processes (verb/noun). They can also include external activities performed by key partners (#2).

4. *Key Resources* (KR)

What are the resources needed to perform those activities (the step-through list in #3)? Resources could include people, equipment, material used for products, organizational assets, etc.

5. *Value Proposition* (VP)

What value do we provide to each training customer segment (could facilitate with #1)? What problem or past pains are we trying to solve? Does each customer segment have unique needs to address?

6. *Customer Relationship* (CR)

What are the expectations from our training customers (see #1) and what has been established uniquely for them? Do we have any processes in place to help retain existing clients? Do we have any special programs for specific customer segments that spend a lot of money with us (such as large accounts)? Do we have any programs for clients that have been doing business with us for a long period of time or have done repeat business over the years?

7. *Channels*

Which channels do we use to sell our training products and services? Which work the best or are the most cost effective? Which ones are used only for awareness? Which ones are used for sales and purchases? Which ones are used to obtain feedback? Which ones are used to deliver? Which channels are the most effective for certain customer segments?

8. *Cost Structure*

What are the key costs associated with our product and services, including resources and activities (#3 and #4)? What is the bulk of training product or service costs?

9. *Revenue Stream*

Which training products and services provide us with revenue? Which provide us with the most revenue? Which provide us with the most net profit? How do these products and services relate to the customer segments? Are certain customer segments purchasing the most profitable products?

Note: Future state questions should be specific to vision and goals.

A 2.4

REQUIREMENT MANAGEMENT PLAN (RMP) TEMPLATE

The purpose of requirement management is to establish a common understanding of how requirements will be addressed between the customer and project or organization, within the project or organization, and throughout the life cycle. The goals of requirements management are to ensure that requirements are controlled to establish a baseline for development, acquisition, or management; and to ensure that the plans, work products, and activities are consistent with the requirements. The RMP template establishes an orderly method by which the goals of requirements management will be achieved. The plan also communicates essential information to project participants and helps newcomers get up to speed. Consequently, the plan is a living document, which needs to be updated and supplemented throughout its life.

1. Version Control

All documents should include some form of version history that includes version numbers, dates for the revision, why it was revised, and if there were any reviews or approvals.

2. Applicability to a Specific Project, Program, or Organization

This requirement plan is needed for <this project, program, or organization> because . . .

The benefits of having this plan are . . .

3. Target Audience for the RMP

Describe those who need to review, approve, or agree to the content of the RMP. This may include project team members, vendors, other business analysts (BAs), or any others that may be involved in the requirements management process.

4. Risks and Issues

Project constraints pose these business analysis challenges . . .

The project approach impacts these business analysis activities . . . .

Stakeholder risks in obtaining requirements are . . .

5. *As-Is* Requirement Processes

This section describes the approach to identifying, developing, maintaining, and managing requirements. Discuss inputs, processes, outputs, timing, entrance and exit criteria, events, and other information. Describe how participants will interface with each other.

Provide an overview of the processes relative to the life cycle; structure the processes or activities and phases by the model you are following (CMMI, PMP, etc.). This can be done graphically.

6. Documenting Requirements

Explain how requirements will be described and captured.

6.1. *Requirement Attributes*

Describe the information that will be associated with each requirement and establish who will be responsible for collecting the information.

Example:

Requirement Attribute	Use	Captured By
Change history	Change control and audit	Analyst
Unique ID	Traceability matrix	Analyst
Priority	Implementation planning	Assigned owner
Source	Traceability to requirement source	Analyst
Owner	Approver and decision maker	Analyst
Implementation complexity	Estimating and release planning	Designer
Status	Initial draft, validating, final review being performed by SME, approved for design	Analyst
Volatility	Scale of 1–5, where 5 is very likely to change during the project and may cause rework	SME
Acceptance criteria	Measurability and testability of the requirement	Analyst

6.2. *Requirement Written Structure*

Use a consistent structure with sets of common verbiage to avoid subjective and ambiguous statements that may be interpreted differently based on the reader's experience, culture, or natural language exposure.

Examples:

1. Use imperatives: these are words and phrases that are used with the requirement statement that command that something be provided:
   a. *Shall* is used to dictate the provision of a functional capability.
   b. *Must or must not* is used to establish business rules, constraints, or quality service requirements
   c. *Are applicable* is used to reference standards or other documents
   d. *Will* is used to cite things that are operational
2. Use continuances to introduce lower levels: below, as follows, following, listed, and supports.
3. Use directives to point to an illustrative source: figure, table, for example, note.
4. Don't use options since they will loosen the specification and establish a basis for trade-offs (lower-priority requirements)—examples not to use: can, may, optionally. Use the priority requirement attribute instead.
5. Avoid weak words and phrases—examples: adequate, as a minimum, as applicable, easy, as appropriate, not limited to, if practical, normal, timely, good, nice, fast, quickly, real time, current, all, complete, approximately, excellent, flexible, many, maximize, robust, sometimes, user-friendly.
6. Use consistent verbs in functional requirements and use cases—examples: access, analyze, answer, ask, adjust, allocate, allow, approve, assign, authenticate, authorize, benchmark, confirm, consult, calculate, calibrate, choose, classify, conduct, configure, decide, define, deliver, discover, display, distribute, eliminate, enter, evaluate, export, extend, find, forecast, format, identify, import, inform, invoke, list, measure, merge, mobilize, monitor, notify, post, prepare, promote, provide, queue, query, record, refresh, request, schedule, search, select, send, specify, stabilize, submit, synchronize, take, upgrade, validate, view.

6.3. Categorization, Numbering Convention

A hierarchical numbering scheme with no more than three levels and with the following prefixes should be used. Define code structure here.

Example classifications and unique ID (partially follows BABOK® classification):

Classification	Description	Unique Identification Code
Business requirements	Goals, objectives, benefits. Highest level from the business perspective.	BS999 (business requirements)
Stakeholder requirements	Aligned to business requirements and from the perspective of those who interact with the system under discussion (current state) or those that will (future state). They can be in textual format, a described high-level process, a business capability, documented as a user story, or as a use case.	SR999 (textual stakeholder requirement) US999 (user story) UC999 (use case) PR999 (process) CP999 (capability)
Solution requirements	Aligned to stakeholder requirements and from the perspective of the system or solution—how the stakeholder requirements will be addressed. They can be further classified as design constraints, functional requirements (includes data requirements), quality attributes, and data entities and attributes (data dictionary).	DC999 (design constraint) FR999 (functional requirement) NR999 (nonfunctional requirement) QA999 (quality attribute) DE999 (data entities) EI999 (external interface)
Business rules	A specific directive under control of the business; may be aligned to a process (behavioral rule) or data entity (operational rule).	BR999 (business rule)

6.4. Reports

Requirement reporting may be necessary based on organizational needs, but also depends on the amount of control needed to manage requirement risks. For example, if this was a project that is very likely to change before completion, there may be a set of requirements that need to be tracked differently, reporting on their volatility (see requirement attributes). Requirement statistics can help project managers (PMs) assess the need to change the project approach.

Example requirement reports:

- *Traceability matrix—such as use cases and associated test cases*
- *Unallocated requirements*
- *Requirements by risk*
- *Requirements by priority*
- *Requirements by qualification method*

- *Requirements status*
- *Cumulative changes*
- *Requirements statistics (% of volatile, % within each priority, etc.)*

6.5. Requirements Deliverables

6.5.1 Work Products

Work products are interim deliverables that do not get reviewed or approved. They are needed by the BA to conduct their analysis. They may be retained for individual future use as examples.

Examples: interview notes, analysis databases, checklists, spreadsheets, prototype guidelines, tool evaluation worksheet, etc.

6.5.2 Formal Deliverables

Deliverables can be listed as shown in the following table, or a responsibility matrix could be created to show roles and responsibilities for each deliverable.

Examples:

Deliverable	Description	Applicability/ Responsibility	Reviews/ Approvals
Business case	The BA may be involved in the creation of the business case for larger initiatives that may take a significant investment from the enterprise. This would involve identifying initial business needs with associated benefits, costs, risks, and results assessments.	NA	
Project request, charter or project design document (PDD)	In a more project-driven environment, you may have a formal way of defining and initiating projects. The PM and the sponsor would typically create this initiating document that defines the project scope and an initial understanding of solution scope.	The project charter was already created by the PM and includes a scope statement by the functional area BA.	Already approved.
Scope definition statement	Once a BA is assigned, a scope definition statement may either be included in the initiating document (such as the project charter) or can be a separate document to describe what is known regarding solution scope.	NA—included in project charter.	

Continued

Deliverable	Description	Applicability/ Responsibility	Reviews/ Approvals
Business requirements definition or document (BRD)	If there is a separation in organizations between the business and the delivery organization (such as IT, engineering, or an outside vendor), then there is typically a document that identifies requirements from the business and user or stakeholder's perspective. This deliverable content can also be used for package evaluations. Use cases are a bridge between the BRD and SRS and can appear in either or both.	The BA from the functional organization will create this document.	Approval from product owner required. Reviews to be conducted by functional area BA with sponsor, IT service delivery team, and QA team.
System, software, or solution requirements specification (SRS)	For requirements to be effective enough to build a solution, you need to get to the solution requirement level that includes the functional and nonfunctional requirements. These are described in the SRS with the inclusion of models, diagrams, and tables that provide context around the requirements and further define them. Note that in some organizations the SRS is split between functional and nonfunctional deliverables.	The SRS will be created by the BA in the IT organization. Requirements must be aligned to business requirements and traced to test cases.	Approval from product owner and appropriate process owners. Reviews conducted by IT and BA, with IT service delivery team and QA team.
Technical specification document (TSD)	The solution needs to be further specified with careful consideration of nonfunctional requirements (especially constraints). Further definition focuses on the technological environment (infrastructure, databases, etc.). The BA may be involved in the creation of the more conceptual design of solution components before a more physical design is developed.	The TSD will be created by the systems analyst.	Approval from architecture group and security group. Reviews by IT, BA, and QA team.
Business analysis approach	This deliverable plans the business analysis activities and associated techniques that will be used. Each project is unique. Depending on project size, complexity, risks, and volatility, the approach may vary. Therefore, it is necessary to collaborate with all those involved in these activities to ensure proper estimating based on solution ideas and a well-documented set of assumptions. A requirements management plan will likely be included with this approach document.	The BA in the functional organization and the BA in the IT organization will work together on an integrated business analysis approach.	Approved by PM. Created and agreed to by functional area BA and IT BA. Reviewed by project team.

7. Relevant Governance Processes and Procedures

Describe required procedures and other dependent processes that may affect the requirement management processes, such as change control, organizational change management, enterprise architectural procedures, approval checkpoints, template use directives, etc.

8. Current Requirement Tools

Describe the tools that will be used for requirements. Tools may include commercial software packages for the requirements repository, computer-aided software engineering (CASE) tools, test tools, project planning tools, issue management tools, estimating tools, as well as non-automated tools such as diagrams and storyboards. If a tool has not been selected, provide the requirements for selecting it.

Example:

Tool	Version	Use
Requirement tracker	Custom built	To document work-in-progress requirement gathering, analysis, and reporting
Action tracker	Custom built	To document issues and actions (includes requirement issues)
MS project	MS product 20xx	To document requirement management tasks—requires integration with overall plan owned by the PM

9. RMP APPENDIX

9.1. Glossary of Terms

9.2. Verification and Validation Methods

9.2.1. Reviews

Examples:

- Peer desk-check
- Round-robin or pass-around
- Walk-through

Example SRS walk-through review preparation checklist:

- Have clear objectives and a defined scope of the review
- Determine appropriate rate and timing (e.g., coverage of six pages per 30 minutes)
- Know your participants and their roles (author, moderator, reader, recorder)
    - Does everyone know each other?
    - Will the reporting structure of participants influence the ability to provide feedback?
    - Have roles been agreed to?
    - Who presents and for what purpose?
- Provide entry criteria (has been validated against standards, all issues documented with status, known defects documented with status, peer inspection completed, etc.)
    - Prepare a checklist that will help you define the exit criteria

- Were all issues and risks addressed?
- Expected deliverables completed? Who is responsible for updates and distribution?
- Any impact to previously created and/or approved deliverables (rework)?
- Action items listed and assigned?
- Pick the appropriate collaboration tool and approach
- List any considerations for dealing virtually and globally (time zones, language, etc.)
  - Will cultural differences impact the ability to get feedback from all participants?
  - Will there be any language barriers that will need to be addressed?
  - What time of day is best, considering all participant time zones?
  - Could a cultural liaison assist?
- Is there a team orientation package that can provide guidelines?

Distributed team review (virtual and global) considerations:

- Use the project charter for *shared goal* alignment
- Use a project's team orientation package (TOP) for project procedural alignment and to establish common project guidelines (promotes fairness and a *shared culture*)
- Use the RMP for requirements processes and tools; use consistently for more effective requirement collaboration (*shared process*)
- Use the responsibility charts and swim lanes to show touchpoints and roles within the process (*shared responsibility*)
- Give permission to all team members to question requirements through asynchronous means. Use tool features to collaborate and record sessions for replay (*enabling technology*)
- Use the following facilitation and collaboration techniques:
  - Round-robin: allow each person to speak
  - Individualized opinion: ask a group for feedback where only you should get the reply
  - Silent brainstorming: everyone makes their own list silently; have one individual compile the information and then evaluate it as a group
  - Walk through templates and examples *before* reviews of final deliverables

Example virtual review template

Objectives and Outcomes	Deadline for Completion	Scope of Discussion (priority order)	Participants and Role in Session	Entry and Exit Criteria
Review business rules for validation against audit requirements. Interpretation and final approval from compliance auditor and understanding of business rules from offshore liaison.	One week before design phase starts. Four hours allocated for review.	Sarbanes Oxley 35 Rules 8m/rule	BA (author, moderator). Compliance auditor (reader). Offshore liaison (recorder).	Entry criteria: business rules reviewed by lead BA and all questions or issues provided to participants 24 hours before the review. Exit criteria: requirement changes documented in matrix and SRS updated.
Follow-Up Meetings	**Virtual/Global Needs**	**Medium**		**Additional Comments**
Possible inclusion of lead developers.	Time of day— consider time zone differences.	WebEx		Offshore liaison is in the role of designer and also represents the·developers.

9.2.2. Inspection Checklist

Example requirement evaluation checklist:

Evaluation Criteria
1. Is associated to a test case or other deliverable for validation and acceptance (testable and verifiable)
2. Is understood by affected parties (e.g., SME, developers, testers) and intended for a global audience (reason why it is in natural language)
3. Unacceptable words (jargon, abbreviations, acronyms), phrases, and vague terms (TBD) are absent (e.g., adverbs, adjectives, as appropriate, at a minimum)
4. Adheres to defined terms in the requirements glossary
5. Must be able to interpret it only one way—this is very difficult in natural language (unambiguous)
6. Conforms to standard verbiage and format
7. Appropriate level of detail for its position in the hierarchy
8. Has the associated information required by the RMP
9. Within scope as defined in the project charter
10. Avoids specifying a design or solution
11. Realistic within the constraints of the project
12. Written in the imperative (shall)
13. Cross-references are specific, so the information can be easily located; the reference is located in the project document library if it is external to the requirement

Continued

Evaluation Criteria
14. Can be traced to its parent or driver
15. Unrestrictive; can be implemented by more than one solution or design
16. Expressed in an active (not past tense) voice
17. Multiple statements used to break down complex or compound statements
18. Quality attributes are quantified
Evaluation Criteria—All Requirements
1. Consistent with each other
2. Addresses each type of requirement (business, rules, external interfaces, etc.)
3. Most important attributes documented (status, volatility, etc.) based on type of project
4. Address user interfaces
5. Nonfunctional requirements are addressed
6. Assumptions and dependencies for requirements are stated
7. Address system and user error conditions
8. Trace to their parent or driver (no dropped traceability)
9. Interfaces are specified (internal/external)
10. Inputs and outputs are specified
11. Organized for additional clarity and a good basis for design decisions

9.2.3. *Templates*

Use Case Template (Fully Dressed)

Fully-Dressed Use Case Template

Use Case ID:

Name:

Primary Actor:

Secondary Actors:

Includes:

Pre-condition:

Post-condition:

Trigger (Optional):

Stakeholder Interest (Optional):

Basic Flow:

Extensions (Exceptions and Alternate Paths):

Assumptions:

A 3.1

SYSTEM USE CASE

Template

Use Case ID: (*unique identifier*)
Use Case Name (Goal): (*described as verb/noun, like a process*)
Description: (*optional—brief statement*)
Primary Actor: (*person or automated software performing the process—their goal*)
Secondary Actors: (*optional—person or automated software that supports the primary actor to achieve the goal*)
Trigger: (*optional—could be first step or in pre-condition*)
Pre-Condition: (*assumptions made—can be dependencies, state of the environment, the place in the process before the first step can be conducted*)
Post-Condition: (*the state once the last step is completed to success*)
Minimal Success Guarantee: (*optional—minimal that must be done if all steps are not completed to success, such as tracking all transactions for an audit trail*)

(*A low-fidelity use case, a.k.a. use case brief, will stop here—with just the header above*)
(*A high-fidelity use case, a.k.a. fully dressed use case, will include all the sections below*)

Basic Flow Steps: (*single column format, includes interaction between primary actor or secondary actors and the system under discussion*)
1)
2)
3)
4)
5)
6)

7)
8)
9)
10)

Extension Steps: (*exceptions and alternate or variation flows*)

Example

<u>Fully Elaborated Use Case</u>

Use Case ID: *UC2-21*
Use Case Name (Goal): *Enroll in weight loss program—free version*
Description: *Enroll as a member of an online weight loss program to take advantage of available resources to improve health. Registration information will be provided and the system (WLP) will return with a list of available resources based on zip code. Some resources will require an upgrade to a monthly payment version.*
Primary Actor: *Potential member*
Secondary Actors: *Sales system*
Pre-Condition: *Weight loss program open to introduction menu. Enrollment option selected.*
Post-Condition: *Registration code is sent to provided e-mail address and profile is sent to the sales system.*

Basic Flow Steps:
1) *WLP displays enrollment entry form*
2) *Potential member enters enrollment profile information*
3) *WLP validates enrollment profile information*
4) *WLP displays enrollment information entered and asks for e-mail confirmation*
5) *Potential member validates information entered and confirms e-mail*
6) *WLP with list of available resources based on zip code and asks if potential member would like the list e-mailed*
7) *Potential member does not want list e-mailed*
8) *WLP sends registration code to potential member's e-mail*
9) *WLP sends profile information to sales system*

Extension Steps:

5) *Information is incorrect*
5.1) *Potential member corrects information*
7) *Potential member wants list e-mailed*
7.1) *WLP sends list to potential member's e-mail*

A 3.2

PERSONAS TEMPLATE

Who is the kind of person who would interact with the product or solution?

Template

(*This template shows an elaborated version of a persona*)

(*Add a picture or drawing to seem more real*)

(*Name should not be a role, it should be a specific instance of a user or actor with a name to make it personalized, a primary persona's goals would be top priority*)

Product or Solution: _____

Persona Name: _____ Primary? Y or N

(*Relevant description may include demographics, personal background information, work environment, skill or experience in using similar product or solution, attitudes, or other behaviors*)

Relevant Description of Persona:

_____

_____

_____

_____

_____

(Goals should describe their expectations, needs, what they are trying to solve, and features they may want and why)

Goals of Persona:

_____

_____

_____

_____

_____

Examples

Progressively elaborated personas through a life cycle.

Brief: Version 1

(Can be created during product backlog build or during stakeholder analysis with only short description)

Product or Solution: ___ATM Book-of-Stamps Offering___

Persona Name: ___Gina Leela___   Primary? Y or ~~N~~

Gina is a Midwest retired consultant in her late 50s who still likes to mail cards for all different occasions and is a frequent ATM user.

Elaborated: Version 2

(Can be elaborated during requirements analysis)

Product or Solution: ___ATM Book-of-Stamps Offering___

Persona Name: ___Gina Leela___   Primary? Y or ~~N~~

Gina is a Midwest retired consultant in her late 50s who still likes to mail cards for all different occasions. Gina volunteers at the local food bank three days a week and watches her granddaughter on the other two days. She spends time making greeting cards with her granddaughter that they mail out for family special occasions. She is a frequent user of ATMs and online banking. She's only been inside a bank once this year—to pay off a loan.

Detailed: *Version 3*

(*After more research on the user, the persona can be elaborated during iteration conversation, use case scenario discussions, acceptance criteria discussions, or solution option discussions*)

Product or Solution: ATM Book-of-Stamps Offering

Persona Name: Gina Leela   Primary? Y or ~~N~~

Relevant Description of Persona:

Gina is a Midwest retired consultant in her late 50s who still likes to mail cards for all different occasions. Gina volunteers at the local food bank three days a week and watches her granddaughter the other two days. She spends time making greeting cards with her granddaughter that they mail out for family special occasions. She is a frequent user of ATMs and online banking for both her checking and savings accounts. She's only been inside a bank once this year—to pay off a loan. She has at least five ATMs available to her within a three-mile radius—two within walking distance and one with a mailbox next to it that she walks to every Wednesday to take money out.

Goals of Persona:

Gina has been frustrated that the hours at her local post office have been changed and that the small post office is in jeopardy of being closed. Gina was hoping that her bank would be adding this new Book-of-Stamps offering very soon so she could get stamps any time she'd like. She'd like to have at least a variety to select from so they are aesthetically pleasing for her cards and would like to buy more than one book at a time. There is an expectation that this feature will be added soon, at least before the holidays, since her friend has that ability now at a competitor's bank. Gina's friend has been nagging her for quite some time to change to that bank, but she loves the proximity of her bank's ATMs and would prefer to stay.

A 3.3

SAMPLE LIST OF COMPLEXITY QUESTIONS

---

1. When reviewing requirements with team members, have the team members done anything like this before?

    (Replies to questions can be put on a scale. Example scale: 4 = no experience, 3 = some with consultant guidance, 2 = once before, 1 = more than once)
2. Does the team have any experience building such a solution? How much experience?
3. Are any of the solutions planned to be outsourced? How many vendors/contracts? What type of contracts?
4. How many stakeholders are impacted by the requirement?
5. Are the impacted stakeholders in various geographical locations? How easy is it to get access to them?
6. Are there any political or other external influences impacting the requirement?
7. Can you predict how many types of users would interact with the solution to this requirement?
8. Does the requirement impact user skills?
9. How old is the existing system that the requirement impacts?
10. How complex is the existing system process that the requirement impacts?
11. Are there any outstanding defects or other changes affecting the impacted existing process?
12. How confident are we regarding its scope of work and function?
13. How many assumptions are we making as a team around this requirement?
14. How likely is the requirement to change during its solution development?
15. Will the speed with which the requirement must be fulfilled impact the quality or the acceptance of the requirement?
16. Do functions have to cross different platforms or types of technology (different hardware requirements)?
17. Are there communications between different vendor products?
18. Are there different business events or triggers?
19. Are there any dependencies with other solutions not yet implemented?

20. Are there external interfaces required? How many? What types?
21. Is this requirement related to other requirements? What kind of relationship exists (shared information, within the same process, parent-child, etc.)?
22. Is it possible that when this requirement gets implemented it might break something else?
23. How drastic will the effect of the implemented requirement be on job procedures?
24. Does the team have some pre-built modules that can be reused to address a portion of the new requirement?
25. Can the requirements be broken down into smaller, less complex components that can be implemented more iteratively?

A 4.1

EXAMPLE RFP SCORING WORKSHEET

Key Features	Weight	Product Ratings (R)/Score (S)					
		Vendor A		Vendor B		Vendor C	
		A(R)	A(S)	B(R)	B(S)	C(R)	C(S)
1. Requirements Elicitation							
1.1 Real-time rules-based requirements auditing	4	4	16	3	12	3	12
1.2 Advanced requirements sorting and filtering	5	2	10	3	15	5	25
1.3 Visual scenario capture							
1.4 Spell checking							
1.5 Glossary of terms							
2. Requirements Documentation and Validation							
2.1 Resource and reference attachment							
2.2 Track requirement detail using standard and user-defined attributes							
2.3 Visual storyboard execution and simulation							
2.4 Hierarchical structure for organization							
2.5 Customized templates and masters							
2.6 Captures use cases at various levels							
2.7 Image file attachment to requirements							
2.8 Comparison analysis of documents							
2.9 User-defined classification of requirements							
2.10 Captures requirement attributes (rationale, owner, volatility, etc.)							
2.11 Captures requirement status							
2.12 Checks quality and consistency							
2.13 WYSIWYG previewing (what you see is what you get)							

Continued

Key Features	Weight	Product Ratings (R)/Score (S)					
		Vendor A		Vendor B		Vendor C	
		A(R)	A(S)	B(R)	B(S)	C(R)	C(S)
3. Requirements Management							
3.1 Multi-dimensional traceability with project life-cycle artifacts							
3.2 Real-time impact analysis							
3.3 Calculates development risk based on requirement attributes							
3.4 Centralized repository (supports distributed access)							
3.5 Sharing across projects							
3.6 Advanced measurement and reporting							
3.7 Change tracking and notification							
3.8 Configuration management with baseline, check-in/out, and locking features							
3.9 Roll back to previous versions (at least 3)							
3.10 ID re-numbering							
4. Application Life-Cycle Integration							
4.1 Visual scenario and requirements synchronization							
4.2 Generates and traces test cases							
4.3 Provides sample projects							
5. Import and Export Capabilities							
5.1 Import requirements from existing documents							
5.2 Edit requirements offline							
5.3 Requirements to UML transformation							
5.4 Requirements to BPMN transformation							
6. Architecture							
6.1 Both desktop and network use							
6.2 Evaluation copy available for free							
6.3 Compatible with existing desktop and network software							
6.4 Capable of handling multiple users							
6.5 Multitasking							
7. Interfaces							
7.1 Microsoft Visual Studio Team System® integration							
7.2 Eclipse platform							
7.3 Web client							
7.4 Microsoft Visual Studio®							
7.5 Windows client							
7.6 Inter-tool communications							

Continued

Key Features	Weight	Product Ratings (R)/Score (S)					
		Vendor A		Vendor B		Vendor C	
		A(R)	A(S)	B(R)	B(S)	C(R)	C(S)
8. Support and Warranty							
8.1 Technical phone support 24x7							
8.2 Free upgrades for first year							
8.3 Free online training							
8.4 User groups							

Weights

Vendor Response Rating

Note: Weights are typically not provided to the vendor. They are used during the evaluation process for final scoring.

5—In current environment, highly critical
4—In current environment, moderately critical
3—In current environment, noncritical
2—Future consideration, critical
1—Future consideration, noncritical
0—Not considered for this RFP

5—Exceeds requirement
4—Fully fulfills requirement
3—Partially fulfills requirement (> = 50%)
2—Minimally fulfills the requirement
1—Does not fulfill requirement, alternative or free enhancement
0—Does not fulfill requirement

A 4.2

BUSINESS ANALYSIS WORK BREAKDOWN STRUCTURE (WBS) CONSIDERATIONS

SLC Stage > / Initiative Type V	Concept Definition	Requirements Analysis	Conceptual and Physical Design	Acquire or Build Solution Through Evaluate and Support Solution
Mostly Predictive				
Enterprise-wide	Leverage business architecture views to assess impact; develop cost/ benefit and roadmap showing approach integration; and supplement BA plans to manage risk, change, communications, and the requirement process.	Use visual modeling and decomposition techniques to break down large processes for clarity, assign process owners, facilitate workshops across business units to reduce conflicts, re-evaluate cost/ benefit for alternate solutions to get to a decision, and coordinate proof-of-concepts to address high risk areas.	Build conceptual data model and swim lanes to identify interfaces for complex areas, communicate gap analysis (impacts) to solution users, apply change management practices, and identify requirements to transition to new solution.	Allocate requirements to solution components, assist in package configurations, identify localization differences, include end-to-end validations, support live validations, and liaison between stakeholders and QA team to facilitate validation across solution components

Continued

SLC Stage > / Initiative Type V	Concept Definition	Requirements Analysis	Conceptual and Physical Design	Acquire or Build Solution Through Evaluate and Support Solution
Process-driven	Determine impacted organizations and assess or create *as-is* process models identifying areas of opportunity, visually show through process models various solution options considering any needs for a release structure, and identify process performance metrics.	Document stakeholder and functional requirements through use cases associated with models, elicit additional requirements from use case reviews, further decompose process models to validate assumptions and uncover additional requirements, and identify additional applicable process attributes (actors, volumes, cycle time, value-added time, non-value-added activities, etc.).	Communicate gap analysis (impacts) to solution users and apply change management practices; assist in applying use cases and process definitions to user procedures and training; leverage use cases to build test cases, storyboards, and prototype scenarios.	Coordinate to assure user or process owner continued involvement, assist in allocating use cases and processes to appropriate architectural layers and solution components, and evaluate process metrics.
Mostly Adaptive				
User-focused	Conduct user experience research, understand different user classes (business vs. consumer, demographics, etc.), build primary personas, and identify design constraints and standards for user experience.	Identify user stories and usability requirements, identify areas of complexity where use cases can uncover more requirements, leverage low-fidelity usability testing (paper-based navigation) to uncover additional requirements and validate existing requirements, and coordinate more formal horizontal prototype for user experience validation.	Emphasis on designing navigation and consistent look and feel across functionality for the user, use various lightweight navigation, identify and address user skill gaps for transition to new solution, and validate site requirements have been addressed in design.	Coordinate user representation during iterative building, facilitate adherence to communicated design standards for usability, usability testing included in acceptance tests, observe users interacting with the system, bring user experience experts in for evaluations, evaluate ongoing user feedback.

Continued

SLC Stage > / Initiative Type V	Concept Definition	Requirements Analysis	Conceptual and Physical Design	Acquire or Build Solution Through Evaluate and Support Solution
Small Enhancement and Maintenance	Ad hoc involvement, perform root cause analysis for problems and define as high-level user stories (epics), identify dependencies and alignment to strategies or other roadmaps, and rank with product owner into product backlog to schedule into iterations for active systems or group into themes (releases/projects) for less active systems.	Extract top-ranked elaborating user story during iteration planning for maintenance fixes, group into small agreed-upon iterations and identify additional requirements (business rules, nonfunctional, data, etc.) during acceptance criteria discussion, conduct storyboarding, and assist in release coordination.	Provide design constraint information from architecture teams, use lightweight models (a.k.a. model storming) in a low-fidelity form (paper or whiteboard) during iteration conversations.	Informally assist in translation of requirements, assist in demo and iterative changes, assist in testing with any external QA teams, and participate in retrospectives.
Mostly Hybrid				
Vendor Package	Request for information: focus on high-level requirements; design/architectural constraints and alignment to strategy to help narrow long list; and consider solution options: single product, product with custom build, multiple products from one vendor, multiple products from multiple vendors.	Focus on stakeholder requirements/features, quality attributes, data requirements, and vendor capabilities to define weighted criteria for request for proposal (RFP); evaluate based on quantitative vendor responses; assess solution fit and narrow list to two solutions; re-evaluate cost/benefit for two solutions and facilitate decision; coordinate conference room pilot (product prototype) with procurement for user education or proof of concept and assist in building test scenarios.	Map requirements to product capabilities and identify unique configurations or customizations and additional interface or reporting requirements; communicate gap analysis (impacts) to solution users and apply change management practices; identify requirements to transition to new solution—especially population of tables and other data; assist in complying with security; and control requirement and building test scenarios.	Conduct conference room pilot and re-evaluate baseline, assist in configuring acquired product, update product documentation, facilitate integration test validation, facilitate focus group of users for validations, monitor service level agreements, provide vendor feedback on product, and continue to monitor external user group evaluations of product releases.

Continued

SLC Stage > / Initiative Type V	Concept Definition	Requirements Analysis	Conceptual and Physical Design	Acquire or Build Solution Through Evaluate and Support Solution
Data-Driven	Identify high-level business scenarios (problem, concerns, benefits gained) from stakeholders requiring information for decision making and assess or create *as-is* data models, evaluate data models to identify views needed from each viewpoint to address concerns, and leverage process models to better understand how information is used.	Identify how information will be used by stakeholders; identify information sources, quality, and forms of delivery; identify business rules: how information will be inferred, derived, be factually based, and any actions to be taken based on conditions; and define how data will be transformed (conversion, cleansing, integration, aggregation) and any associated nonfunctional requirements.	Build and run business scenarios through prototype dashboards, reports, or other business intelligence visuals to identify missing requirements; extract data requirements from stakeholder requirements to identify initial entities; build data models to facilitate physical design; and determine if more data marts may be required to address nonfunctional requirements.	Build permission tables for access to information, test quality of sources and transformation processes, facilitate validation of outcomes with stakeholders, evaluate nonfunctional requirements to access information (e.g., performance) in live environment, and evaluate ongoing stakeholder feedback on information use for decision making.
Technology-Driven (infrastructure migration example)	Leverage technology architecture to determine standards and constraints, assess connections to business architecture to assess business impacts, evaluate alignment to business strategy, and determine value proposition and costs of *doing nothing*.	Assist in inventory of components being moved and their disposition, determine transition requirements and facilitate proof-of-concepts for tools used in migration, identify nonfunctional requirements to be validated, and identify impact of data to be migrated and whether structures are changing.	Prepare for transition, compare points to ensure business continuity, and assess any security impacts.	Make sure to make connection between the technology changes and the business impacts during validation, during acceptance and regression tests validate that functions that worked before are still working, post-transition evaluation to assure stakeholders of *no impact*, and assist in retiring old platform.

Web Added Value™

Appendix B

Answers to End-of-Chapter Questions

Business Analysis Techniques Glossary

B 1.1

ANSWERS TO END-OF-CHAPTER QUESTIONS

CHAPTER 1

For the following scenarios 1–4, determine which leadership skills will help you prepare. What should be your course of action?

1. You have been following your business analysis approach and have finished eliciting the requirements from over a dozen stakeholders. You have captured the statements, but still must conduct some analysis activities to ensure you didn't miss anything and that stakeholder conflicts are resolved. This will take another week, just one day more than estimated. The Project Manager (PM), Suzzy, wants you to stop now since the designers and developers are ready to start—and the PM feels you are just analyzing too much anyway. You set up a meeting to discuss this with Suzzy.

    Leadership skills: *Answer*—Courage and negotiation

    Course of action: *Answer*—Find the data and have the courage to state your case. Ask why she thinks you are analyzing too much and dig deeper to understand if there are any other concerns. Discuss the impacts for both alternatives. Consider options.

2. Jamie is one of your stakeholders for a major strategic project and has volunteered to represent all the customer representatives. Based on some initial research, you found out that Jamie is new to the organization and has only been active with the customer representative organization for a few months. But, you also know that this stakeholder does have extensive industry knowledge from another company. You fear that Jamie does not have the organizational and business domain knowledge to represent that group as the

key business owner and decision maker. Additionally, fearing that assumptions will be made regarding how processes are performed here, Jamie has agreed to meet with you to validate your concerns, understand how important this assignment might be for her, and ensure the proper representation of a very important group.

Leadership skills: *Answer*—Courage, influence, and trust

Course of action: *Answer*—Be open and honest about fears, ask if the role is understood and what is expected. Explain the importance of the representation and the expectations of representation. If it is challenge, offer to help find some solutions.

3. During initial stakeholder meetings, you noticed a lot of resistance and a lack of cooperation from your key stakeholder, Terry. You recently worked up the courage to confront the issue and find out why. It took a while, but after discussions with others, you found that in prior experiences working with IT, the customers were disappointed—promises not kept, lack of user involvement, IT didn't listen, etc. Without solid customer cooperation, this project will have a very limited chance of succeeding.

    Leadership skills: *Answer*—Trust and influence

    Course of action: *Answer*—Set up meeting with Terry to discuss involvement. Encourage sharing of concerns (understand root cause through questioning), listen actively, take action by asking what you can do right now to address them. Build credibility through influence: who you are, what you have done in the past, etc.

4. You have been working for seven months on a project that is doing very well. But, last week after an acceptance testing validation walk through, Lambra, the user group representative, suggested how the software could be improved. In your opinion this was outside the scope of the defined requirements for this project. This scope increase would require rework and would delay the project by 30 days. You thought you were done with this project and have already been assigned to another project in a few days. Lambra asked to meet for further discussion.

    Leadership Skills: *Answer*—Negotiation and accepting change

    Course of Action: *Answer*—Be prepared with data to show how the scope increase will delay the project and the impact it will have on her, the user group she represents, and others. Listen to why the scope increase is important to her, the value it brings, how it aligns to business requirements, and the impacts if not included. Maybe the delay is worth the value it brings. Determine who should be making the final decision. See if there is a win/win. Think of solutions together. Present to decision maker(s). Example options: Could the scope increase be broken down into specific features or functions that can be prioritized—maybe just a specific portion must go in now and some can go in later. Agree to bring in a group to review the change and facilitate a consensus on a plan.

5. I am trying to influence a client to select my solution by convincing them that the economic conditions will change and that the solution will help stimulate business under those conditions, but they need to act now in order to be ready in time. What is the influence technique I am trying to use?

> *Answer*—Scarcity

6. True or false

a. Be *flexible* with your interests and *assertive* with your options.

> *Answer*—False, it is the reverse. Options are your solutions and they should be flexible. Interests are typically not compromised, but they can be prioritized.

b. Scarcity is an influence technique that should be used often.

> *Answer*—False, scarcity must be used carefully or you will lose trust in the relationship if it turns out not to be true.

CHAPTER 2

1. What key elements would be in your requirements management plan (RMP) (Appendix A2.4) for the following scenario?

> *You are the lead BA for a large program that has three BAs reporting to you, all co-located with their stakeholders in Milwaukee. The solution designer role is assigned to an offshore liaison systems analyst. The solution designer is stationed in Milwaukee with your team. The builders of the software are in India, while the testers are in China. The solution designer, builders, and testers all work for the same new contracted vendor. This is the first major project your company has conducted with this vendor. Assume an integrated team relationship.*

> RMP Elements:

> *Example answer*—RMP Elements: Assuming the relationship is one of an *integrated team*, there is a greater need to manage expectations to ensure the team is in sync with how the requirements will be communicated, allocated, traced, verified, and evaluated in the solution. Because of the team's diversity and being distributed, all sections would be relevant. Content may vary depending on vendor best practices and tools. A meeting to go over the RMP with the offshore liaison is highly

recommended to *sync up* expectations. The life-cycle approach used will influence what and how the requirements will be communicated.

2. a. Table 2.1 shows a simple communication plan. After reviewing the plan, what type of relationship do you think the business analyst (BA) has with the vendor? Please justify your answer.

Vendor relationship options are: staff augmentation, turnkey, integrated team, managed partnership, and enterprise partnership.

Answer—Turnkey, because this was likely a purchased product request for proposal (RFP) that required installation of software and configuration).

b. How might Table 2.1 look different if the relationship was different? Give an example.

Example answer—Integrated team, the plan would likely communicate with a vendor *installation team*, *test team*, or *offshore liaison*.

3. Provide one potential risk for each asset category:

Physical assets:
Financial assets:
Customer assets:
Employee assets:
Organizational assets:

Example answers—

Physical assets: floods, hurricane damage
Financial assets: market crash
Customer assets: competitor
Employee assets: safety problems
Organizational assets: hacker

4. Table 2.6 shows various business scenarios. Select one scenario example from the table and consider what knowledge (diagrams or matrices such as organization charts, process maps such as value streams, and models such as data models) might be needed from the business architecture that would help stakeholders in decision making.

Example answer—(business scenario) Healthcare, new product: It is important to provide a way to present information on multiple devices used by physicians—PDAs, laptops, iPads, etc. We currently have several projects in progress to move us to electronic medical records.

Example knowledge assets that might be needed from the business architecture for this scenario assuming they exist within the business architecture are:

- Data model view of information to define the boundaries and to present for validation
- Business rules for what information can/cannot be shared on certain devices
- Physician information in order to determine access requirements
- Connection of information to other enterprise layers and business processes to assess impacts

5. For a staff augmentation relationship, BAs should first present challenges they face with that resource to the:

a. Sponsor or whoever is paying for the resource
b. Resource's vendor management
c. Procurement or whoever is managing the contract
d. PM or whoever is managing their work

   Answer—d

6. Using Figure 2.2, *Business Model Canvas Example: Training Company*, and the five asset categories (physical, financial, customer, employee, organizational assets), name two enterprise risks and their impacts on business scenario: "Currently we offer business analysis and project management training, but within two years we plan to expand our training to deliver technology organization content, such as training for software development tools (purchased or licensed)."

   Example answers—

   Enterprise risk (1): We don't have organizational capabilities to sell or teach technology training.

   Impacts (1): Employee assets—capabilities of staff (sales, marketing, etc.); customer assets—different segments and value propositions.

   Enterprise Risk (2): Unable to fulfill profit expectations without a cost/benefit analysis.

   Impacts (2): Physical assets—cost of software/hardware to conduct that type of technology training, cost of facilities that can handle that type of training, cost of internal support for technology (resource cost), and cost of content/licenses. Organizational assets—more complex setup requirements, more prep time (resource cost), and additional materials. Positive impacts—compliments several university certificates, brings in new job roles to programs, allows *full package* selling for *big account* clients.

CHAPTER 3

1. If your project had the following characteristics, which life-cycle approach would be the best fit and why? Would you consider any variations to the approach and why?

   - Unknown legal requirements
   - Global initiative with users in five different countries and three languages
   - Takes 18 months
   - Has an enterprise impact

   Answer—The mostly predictive life cycle mostly works here because of the complexity and breadth of impact. Would likely add a prototype and several pilots (hybrid) because of the diverse local differences and users.

2. In the predictive life-cycle approach for the evaluate solution stage, what are some of the challenges that were identified in the example for Company X?

   Answers—(1) gaps in PM and BA knowledge for such a complex project, (2) stakeholders' inability to commit to measures of success, (3) lack of vision—what they might need from the solution in the future.

3. Identify the life-cycle approach that would most likely use this form of a written requirement:

   a. Use case
   b. User story
   c. SMART business requirement
   d. Business epic
   e. Decision table for business rules
   f. Alternate paths and exceptions

   Answers—

   a. Use case: hybrid
   b. User story: adaptive
   c. SMART business requirement: predictive/hybrid
   d. Business epic: adaptive
   e. Decision table for business rules: predictive

f.   Alternative paths and exceptions: hybrid (within use case)

4.   (a) Which combination of prototype types, see Figures 3.7 and 3.8, would be best for the following scenario:

> *Sally is running a workshop with a small group of stakeholders from the sales team and Joe, one of the developers. She decided that it would be best to show the sales team how some of their requirements might be addressed in the new system. She plans to step through several PowerPoint drawings of web pages that she worked on with Joe.*

> *Answer*—Horizontal, throwaway

(b) Could you apply all four types of prototypes in one hybrid life cycle?

> *Answer*—It depends . . . Not at once, but they can have various iterations throughout the project life cycle. For instance: (1) early in the life cycle you might do a horizontal/throwaway during a requirement workshop to uncover initial requirements; (2) do the vertical/throwaway during individual interviews to simulate a specific feature with a stakeholder by drawing it out on the board; (3) use a horizontal/evolutionary prototype by starting with a high-level persona (let's say airline passenger) with associated user stories, and then breaking those down based on further breakdown of personas (frequent fliers, children traveling alone, etc.); and (4) possibly a vertical/evolutionary by building out each one completely as you go (very *agile-like*).

5.   Explain how the requirement volatility might affect the solution design.

> *Answer*—Knowing that requirements might change, the solution may be designed in a way that would allow for less costly changes for those types of requirements or more flexibility to make changes, such as user-driven external tables or user-defined fields in software.

CHAPTER 4

1.   What are the core concepts that every BA should be aware of when assessing their work?

> *Answer*—Contexts, changes, stakeholders, value, needs, solutions

2.   (a) Why should the BA create a work breakdown structure (WBS)? (b) Who do you review it with and why? (c) Would you create a WBS for an adaptive life-cycle approach?

Answer—(a) The WBS will assist the BA to achieve buy-in, access impacts on project scope, uncover risks, make deliverable responsibilities clear, and improve the accuracy of estimates. (b) You need to review this with the PM to assess impacts and dependencies to other areas. (c) Yes, but not formally. It may be used for team discussion of roles/tasks, especially if new to the adaptive approach.

3. For process-driven initiatives, name three unique business analysis activities.

   Answers—

   (1) Current state to future state gap analysis
   (2) Decomposition of process
   (3) Process modeling

4. For data-driven initiatives, name three unique business analysis activities.

   Answers—

   (1) Uncover definitional business rules
   (2) Create or modify data dictionary
   (3) Create or modify data modeling

5. For user-focused initiatives, name three unique business analysis activities.

   Answers—

   (1) Create personas
   (2) Observe users
   (3) Assess user skills

6. Locate a specific example of an industry provided in this chapter and do some domain knowledge research using the business model canvas. What characteristics might influence your business analysis approach and how?

   (For discussion purposes only.)

CHAPTER 5

1. For each situation, identify three risks (this may require you to do some research online) and determine how you might adjust your business analysis approach to respond to those risks.

    a. You are working for a bank and you are implementing a Cloud solution package for your HR benefits organization. It is the first time a Cloud solution will be used for your company.

    Answer example for risks—

    - Lack of in-house capabilities regarding use of this new technology; must assess skill gaps (people risk)
    - Security or other business policy risks (such as data protection) that we typically can have more control of in-house; must assess these policies and address solution weaknesses (business risk)
    - Stability of the Internet and other infrastructure needed to support the new technology; identify current state technology constraints and address gaps (technology risk)
    - Having only one point of failure—one service provider we are dependent upon; clearly define quality attributes to include in a service-level agreement (vendor risk)
    - Not having control of when and where upgrades to the system will be done; include vendor communication plan in agreement (vendor risk)

    b. You are working for a training company that currently does all instructor-led workshops and will be implementing the first all eLearning program to sell as a solution for their clients.

    Answer example for risks—

    - Lack of in-house knowledge for building and designing eLearning (people/vendor risk); if the PM brings in vendor resources with the right competencies, add time to activities to communicate requirements to vendor and add time for you to also learn about eLearning solutions
    - Lack of in-house infrastructure to track and deliver training with limited intervention (technology risk); add activities to perform analysis on current state and future state of infrastructure to support new environment
    - eLearning accessibility from different platforms

2. For the following risk scenario, identify why you would want to respond to the risk and name three different strategies to respond to the risk.

> *Sally is planning to parachute jump out of a plane for her 40th birthday. There is a risk that her parachute may not open properly.*

Why respond:

Answer—The probability might be low, but the impact is too great (life threatening)

Three risk strategies:

Answers—

1. Avoid: don't go—Sally's son may influence this decision
2. Share: jump with an instructor—might be required for new jumpers
3. Mitigate: inspect the parachute—might be a regulation to dictate this process

3. Name three key considerations for identifying risks specifically associated with a requirement.

Three key considerations:

Answers—

1. Risks not required for every requirement
2. Assess specific requirement risks associated with cost, scope, schedule, etc.
3. Review with PM for impact to overall solution

4. In an adaptive life-cycle approach, which user stories are likely to not be addressed for risk?

Answer—Those at the bottom of the product backlog. Why address these when they may age off and never get to the top for iteration planning?

5. For the following two scenarios, identify the risk(s) and provide a response to the risk(s).

a. *When wrapping up the interviews, you realized that 80% of stakeholders were consistent with their needs, but 20% were conflicting. You are pressured to move forward, but you **do not** feel confident that this should be passed on to design this way.*

Answers—

Risk: the 20% that is conflicting may end up remaining that way, which may cause rework of design and build with larger delays and project costs if changed again later.

Response: What is the overall strategy? Should it be left that way? There is a possibility that the differences could be designed into the solution. You would need to validate whether that is allowed and possible to do. Otherwise, you would need to *sell* the fact that it would be much less costly to address conflicts now to ensure that they don't get built into the software this way and then having to *fix* them later causing rework.

Lessons Learned: if this risk could have been identified earlier, knowing there was an organizational need toward consistency, then a better approach would have been to run a requirement workshop to address conflicts and to drive toward consensus (with the decision-making process defined) instead of performing interviews.

b. *The PM is asking if the estimate for implementing the new system will be impacted based on the requirements you have gathered. You believe the estimate will be impacted, so you set up a meeting to go over the information captured so far. It looks like 60% of the requirements are identified as highly volatile requirements and about 20% are highly complex with a large business impact.*

Answers—

Risk: requirements constantly changing, highly complex requirement with large business impact.

Response: the risk for highly volatile requirements is that they may change during or after implementation. You would need to determine which by having further conversations around those volatile requirements. If this is during the life cycle, then a more iterative approach may be best to allow flexibility for changes, such as doing a more horizontal and evolutionary prototype. If it is post-implementation, then the design would need to be flexible so maintenance of changes will be easier to implement later (such as to not embed business rules into code).

Lessons learned: consider a more vertical prototype such as a proof of concept when you have highly complex requirements with large business impacts. Consider a pilot or build those highly complex requirements first for a *fail-fast* approach.

CHAPTER 6

1. What is the difference between solution value and business analysis work value?

    Answer—Solution value is based on the outcome that provides value to the receivers of that outcome, whereas business analysis work value is based on the process that produces the outcome, such as the business analysis activities.

2. In the following scenario, what are some value challenges that should be considered? How might you determine which is more important to address if all of them cannot be accomplished?

    The company's "Green" team wants environmental waste reduced by 20% by reducing the use of a particular material—QBGOOD—and replacing it with a better environmental material—QBOK. Marketing wants to do a holiday promotion of a new product by reducing the price by 35% for a two-week period. Evaluation of customer feedback says that customers love the new QBGOOD material and are willing to pay more for the product to get that feature. The CEO wants to increase profits the next quarter by 20% and is hoping the new product will help reach that target.

    Answer—The challenge is that there are several conflicting values. Changes cannot all be implemented without one group of stakeholders being impacted. The reducing of the price by marketing might help in the long run to promote the product, but it may impact the profits for the next quarter. Replacing the material because of environmental issues for a customer-preferred material in the product will also impact sales.

3. Write a value proposition for the following scenario:

    You were mapping the features of a financial software package to the stakeholder needs. You noticed that 30% of the features were unmatched and most affected the procurement area. These features could be fully addressed by interfacing to a procurement software package that you knew about from your previous employer. After a brief discussion with the boss, you think it could reduce the time to procure equipment by 10%.

    Value proposition: *Answer*—Procurement could reduce the number of unmatched features to the new financial software package because of implementing an interfacing procurement software package. Based on the information provided by the vendor and benchmarking, the value of implementing this package could reduce the time of ordering procurement of equipment by 10%.

4. Based on your answer to #3, what would be some measures that you would want to make more tangible?

   Answer—Reduce the time of ordering procurement of equipment by 10%. I would want to see if this could be translated into dollars; metrics might include cycle time by type of order, types of order problems that cause delays and by how much, historical metrics to benchmark to (pre- versus post-implementation), etc.

5. In the role of value manager, what can you do to ensure potential value becomes real value?

   Answer—Use an enterprise mindset by leveraging the balanced scorecard and business architecture, being involved in business case creation and portfolio management (moving from intangible to tangible), addressing requirement-level value through traceability and requirement validation, and evaluating the solution at multiple opportunities pre- and post-implementation.

CHAPTER 7

1. What is the impact to your business analysis approach if your organization does not have any consistent project management processes in place if they use predominately predictive life-cycle approaches?

   Answer—If in a predictive life-cycle approach, you are likely to take up some of those activities that a PM would do such as identify work and activities surrounding the definition of management of work scope. See the interactions with project management processes in Figure 7.3. Also, the RMP is more important to use as a communication tool to explain the requirements management process.

2. As a volunteer business analysis mentor, you are to meet your BA mentee for the first time in a few days. What should you do to prepare?

   Answers—

   a. Prepare with interview questions to understand goals/objectives and education/experience
   b. Prepare a sample approach, identify stakeholder, and ensure you have ongoing agendas/meetings for review and agreement
   c. Prepare to have the learning growth plan and assessment tool to walk through with them

3. What types of competencies are likely to be transferable to other roles?

   Answer—Soft skills and techniques

4. Name five benefits of having a BACC established at your company.

   Answer—Consistent best practices, consulting and coaching BA services, maintaining repository of templates and artifacts, providing quality checklists and procedures, and acquiring capable resources.

5. What is the difference between mentoring and coaching?

   Answer—To mentor you should be an expert who can share that knowledge with others, whereas a coach does not need to be an expert but must be good as a motivator who will encourage others to meet their goals. A mentor can also be a coach.

CHAPTER 8

1. Review the Glossary of Techniques in Appendix B.2 and determine which combination of techniques you would use and how you might use them for the following two elicitation scenarios.

   a. *Your sponsor is preparing a business case with you (adding new features to an existing product) and suggests that you elicit initial thoughts and attitudes toward two solution alternatives from a group of users.*

   Techniques: *Example answer*—Create a *focus group* consisting of pre-qualified users of the existing product to provide feedback, initially by *survey* or by using *kano analysis*. To dig deeper, continue with *interviews* of the focus group or facilitate a focus group *workshop* with a low-fidelity (screen shots) horizontal *prototype* of the two solution alternatives. During the *workshop* activities you should obtain reactions using *kano analysis* or informally using *brainstorming* or *brainwriting*. Formally, you can distribute a *questionnaire* (similar to survey).

   b. *You are in the middle of an iteration and the team is discussing the acceptance criteria for a user story. After asking some probing questions around data requirements, it was determined that there was a lot of discussion but a lack of true understanding of what the requirements were. You needed to pull out some of your techniques to help the team get on the same page. What techniques might help?*

   Techniques: *Example answer*—The interaction between the user and the solution can also show the data that flows in the interaction. *Use cases* are very good at showing that flow, but you need to be aware that it is from a primary actor (user) perspective and it may not make supporting data requirements visible. A *data flow diagram* will show the flow of data and data stores, and the scope can be as far out as you want it. You would want to keep it simple and just draw it on the board, maybe take a picture (lightweight). That would be good for discussion and to help capture the data requirements as part of the acceptance criteria. A partial *data model* could also be created to ensure the associated business rules are also captured.

2. Figure 8.3 shows a few processes that need further analysis for process improvement. Name at least two techniques you would recommend.

   Techniques: *Example answer—Use observation* to get a better understanding of the process and draw out a *data flow diagram* or a *use case* to confirm understanding; *business capabilities mapping* to see how our own capabilities to conduct those processes must be improved; and an *assessment* of the volumes (data) to determine work load issues.

3. Based on your answer to #2, list two of the techniques and determine your estimating approach and assumptions for each.

   Techniques: *Example answer—Observation* would depend on location and determination of how much of the cycle time needs to be observed. The estimate would be based on the identification of specific tasks involved and estimating each of them (bottom-up) assuming the following tasks: (1) *prep time*—selection of the users and where, when, how long, what will be observed (breadth and depth) and how they will be observed (passive or active); identify constraints (willingness, environment); obtain needed permissions; install any needed tools or equipment; prepare observation sheets; conduct a preliminary interview; and review any existing documentation; (2) *conduct observation*—explain reason for observation, manage expectations, explain rules of engagement, and ask permission for pictures or recording; (3) *conclude observation*—address questions, summarize items to share, compare to existing documentation, identify issues or gaps, create data flow diagram or other models for validation, send note of thanks, and follow up with other needed techniques (interviews, prototypes, etc.).

4. Name two techniques that are used in both business analysis and project management but in different ways.

   Techniques: *Answer*—Context diagram, responsibility matrix

5. Why might a BA use a transitional tool?

   Answer—(1) To take advantage of existing tools, (2) easy to start up with tool right away, (3) others already know the tool, and (4) it's an adaptive life-cycle approach where there are smaller iterations and less traceability needs

B 1.2

BUSINESS ANALYSIS TECHNIQUES GLOSSARY

Glossary of Techniques

Technique	Description (related to business analysis)	Most often used when:
1) Affinity Diagram	Displays a diagram with groupings by categories and subcategories showing things that have a relationship to each other; similar to using a spreadsheet to group data together to make it easier to analyze.	Finding missing components and relating different types of requirements, processes, releases, etc.
2) Assumptions and Constraints Analysis	Validating assumptions and constraints through the life cycle.	Uncovering solution risks, transitioning assumptions to requirements, and defining scope.
3) Benchmarking	Compares measures and metrics of specific functions to external systems.	Improving processes and identifying gaps or capabilities.
4) Brainstorming (Brainwriting)	The problem is written visually to be seen by the group; group shouts out ideas and they are listed without critique; then discussion occurs. (Brainwriting variation—ideas are done in silence on sticky notes and then reconciled visually in front of group).	Generating quick lists of solution ideas allowing for more *thinking time* for group ideas (less self-editing).
5) Business Capabilities Analysis	Defines and evaluates organizational resource abilities to perform work. Can be shown as affinity diagram, nested boxes, or decomposition.	A benchmark is needed to measure future organizational performance; mapped to other business architecture components or initiatives for business decision making.
6) Competitive Analysis (Market Analysis)	Evaluates information and identifies gaps regarding external entities (could include markets) that might threaten or expose weaknesses of the organization.	Devising strategies and justifying initiatives in business cases.
7) Context Diagram (Scope Diagram)	Defines the boundary for the system under discussion (SUD), its inputs and outputs, and those that interact with it (actors).	Defining scope for current state or future state.

Continued

Technique	Description (related to business analysis)	Most often used when:
8) Cost-Benefit Analysis (Financial Analysis)	Financial analysis weighing costs of an opportunity to its benefits.	Evaluating solution options and for initiative justification.
9) Data Flow Diagram	Shows the movement and the transformation of data in a visual form with externals (outside the system), data stores, processes, and the data flows between them.	Defining scope, connecting data models and process models, and identify interfaces.
10) Data Modeling	Visualized data entities, their relationships and definitional rules; may be conceptual, logical, or physical models.	Visualizing and uncovering data requirements, defining business intelligence views, defining physical database structures—a consistent and agreed upon view of data is needed.
11) Data Dictionary	Provides detailed data requirement information and supports the data model.	A glossary is needed to define data and data structures; a consistent and agreed-upon view of data is needed.
12) Decomposition (Hierarchical Charts)	Breaks down components into smaller chunks in a visual, hierarchical diagram.	Breakdown is needed of organizations (organizational charge), work (work breakdown structure), functions (functional decomposition diagram), use cases, capabilities, feature model, etc., for clarity or to define scope.
13) Decision Analysis	Depending on evaluation criteria used, the outcome value may vary, such as a financial value, a score, risk assessment, etc. Can be shown in a matrix or a decision tree.	Facilitating a solution selection, make-or-buy decisions, or reducing political or emotional choices.
14) Decision Table	Provides a visible means of analyzing different combinations and choices.	Simplifying the communication and analysis of complex business rules.
15) Document Analysis	Review of documents that may include job procedures, standards, previous project deliverables, vendor support information, etc.	Uncovering requirements, gaining domain knowledge, validating existing requirements, and preparing for stakeholder elicitation.
16) Delphi (Wisdom of the Crowd)	A group technique where ideas are elicited using brainwriting, ideas are summarized, and additional rounds of feedback are performed until an agreement on the assumptions has resulted in a consensus.	Uncovering scope assumptions that may not be consistent across the group because of their diversity in experiences or culture, and used in adaptive life-cycle approaches for estimating story points or using planning poker.
17) Feature Injection	After determining business value (purpose alignment/Kano analysis), the minimal set of features required to deliver the expected value is determined and then elaboration happens only on those few features.	Prioritizing and assessing different solution options.
18) Feature Scoring (Weighted Ranking)	Applies quantitative methods to requirements or features for use in prioritization or ranking.	Evaluating vendors or to facilitate solution selection.

Continued

Technique	Description (related to business analysis)	Most often used when:
19) Flow Charts	A diagram that shows the sequence of steps with boxes and decisions with diamonds.	Defining a simple flow for understanding a process for collaboration and verification.
20) Focus Groups	Potential solution users selected as a testing group to try out the solution and provide feedback.	Validating a solution horizontal prototype or live alpha tests.
21) Gap Analysis	Performing a comparison of the current SUD and the future solution (asking what you will *keep, remove, add,* or *change*); compared components can vary.	Communicating to those affected by the change to identify transition requirements.
22) Given-When-Then	A structure used for writing acceptance tests for user stories.	Writing acceptance tests from acceptance criteria.
23) Interviews	Direct communications with individual stakeholders that can be structured or unstructured using active listening and questioning techniques.	Defining a problem, assessing stakeholder interest and involvement, clarifying current state, uncovering requirements for future state, and addressing stakeholder concerns.
24) Interface Analysis	Identifying the connections between solutions or solution components and associated requirements.	Defining scope boundaries and identifying stakeholders.
25) Kano Analysis	Analyzes features of products from a customer perspective, such as satisfaction and delivery.	Evaluating how current users of a product might view a future feature; will help the team prioritize features.
26) Lessons Learned (Retrospectives)	A look back at business analysis activities to uncover (1) what worked, (2) what didn't work and, (3) what could be improved in future work.	At the end of a project, stage, or iteration.
27) Morphological Box	Relates different parameters to possible solutions to uncover different combinations and more solution options.	Finding viable solution alternatives.
28) Multi-voting (Nominal Voting)	Narrows large list of ideas or solutions (generated by other techniques such as brainstorming), allowing for each stakeholder to have a specific number of votes (= number of ideas / 3) that can be distributed across the list; solution ideas with the most votes are discussed and more rounds may be conducted after discussion to progress toward a final decision.	There are long lists of ideas or solutions and many stakeholders, requiring the list to be prioritized and narrowed for selection.
29) Observation	Users are observed within their environment. It can be active, where interruptions and questions are allowed—or passive, where no interruptions are allowed.	Gaining understanding of current process—especially exceptions and work-arounds.

Continued

Technique	Description (related to business analysis)	Most often used when:
30) Prioritization (MoSCoW, Ranking)	Using criteria (such as value) and classifications (such as *Must, Should, Could or Won't*) for requirements to identify areas of focus.	Determining what to work on next, defining scope, working within constraints, or grooming product backlog.
31) Process Modeling (Function Modeling)	Visually displays processes in various notations (such as Unified Modeling Language or Business Process Model and Notation). Various information about the process may be displayed such as flow of information, cycle time, value-added time, volumes, or who or what performs the process (actor).	Describing current or future state, specifying requirements and validating requirements, providing simulations, identifying exceptions, and dealing with quality initiatives and process improvement opportunities.
32) Prototypes (Exploratory Prototype)	A simulation of the solution across all functions (horizontal) with more breadth, or for one function (vertical) with much more depth. It can also be a temporary prototype (throwaway) or an evolving prototype (evolutionary).	Uncovering requirements or validating requirements when they are considered to be volatile—where horizontal is used for usability evaluation and demonstrations of future features and vertical is more for uncovering the feasibility or the unknown requirements of one feature or function.
33) Purpose Alignment Model	Assesses features against strategies determining whether the feature is a market differentiator (low/high) and mission critical (low/high).	Determining the value of a feature, and also helps with prioritization.
34) Responsibility Matrix (RACI)	Assigns responsibilities to roles or organizational entities for processes or other elements.	Clarifying and communicating business analysis and requirement management responsibilities.
35) Reviews	Activities or meetings to inspect or demonstrate life-cycle work products.	Tracing requirements to solution components, evaluating a solution or solution alternatives, validating scope boundaries, having a show and tell session.
36) Risk Analysis	Identifying, assessing, and treating uncertainties in an initiative that can affect its value.	Uncovering uncertainties in the business analysis work or from establishing the requirements.
37) Root Cause Analysis (Fish Bone Diagram, 5 Whys, Cause & Effect, Interrelationship Diagram)	Root cause isolates each element of what may have caused an identified problem, which can be diagrammed out as a fish bone or interrelationship diagram or used in conversation by asking the five-why probing questions.	Problem solving; uncovering requirements when a solution is suggested first will help get to the requirement.
38) Rule Models	Visually display complex business rules in decision tables or trees, showing conditions and actions to be taken.	Communicating business rules to vendors, testers, and other team members who need clarity for building and testing the solution.

Continued

Technique	Description (related to business analysis)	Most often used when:
39) Stakeholder Analysis (Stakeholder Mapping, Stakeholder Assessment)	Analyzing stakeholders for the interests, concerns, authority, and involvement by using maps, matrices, or diagrams.	Building stakeholder profiles for requirement elicitation, identifying users, creating personas (mostly adaptive life cycle), building actor/goal lists (mostly hybrid life cycle), defining scope, and assessing organizational impacts.
40) State Transition (State Table or Diagram, State Model)	Shows how entities can move through a life cycle and change the state that it is in depending on a triggering event (such as a process output or business rule change).	Uncovering missing processes or missing data.
41) Story Points	A method of estimating the relative size and complexity of a user story.	Uncovering user story scope, assumptions, and tasks during iteration planning.
42) Surveys (Questionnaires)	A set of questions, often with rated responses, that is used to gather information from a large group.	Handling anonymous responses, working with a very large group of users, or you need a quick and inexpensive source for information.
43) SWOT Analysis	Analyzes internal strengths and weaknesses against external opportunities and threats.	Evaluating solutions, assessing objectives, or identifying risks.
44) Timeboxing	Sets a fixed time for tasks to curb procrastination, analysis paralysis, or perfectionism.	There is a need to constrain activities in workshops, prototypes, and iterations.
45) Tracing Requirements (Traceability)	Tracks requirements that may also include use cases or user stories: (1) back to sources and business requirements, (2) within requirements, and (3) forward in the life cycle to solution life-cycle stage components (models, design elements, build components, acceptance tests, etc.).	Validating (1) customer acceptance, (2) benefit realization, and (3) vendor contractual obligations.
46) Use Case (Systems Use Case)	Shows how the goal of an actor using the solution (system) is accomplished by describing the interaction between them and the outcomes; it can be written in textual steps or shown graphically.	Uncovering stakeholder requirements, functional requirements, and various scenarios (mostly used in hybrid life cycles).
47) User Story	A short sentence describing a user need and the value to the user.	Ranking needs, grouping into iterations, or inviting conversation and elaboration.
48) Vendor Assessment	Assessing the vendor's and product's ability to meet the needs and agreements of the organization.	Finding the *right fit* for outsourced or packaged solutions.
49) Workshop (Requirement Workshop, Facilitated Workshop, Joint Application Delivery or Design)	Based on a structured agenda with stated objectives, a facilitator assists participants in collaboration toward meeting those objectives (meeting outcomes).	Eliciting requirements from a group, addressing conflicting stakeholder requirements, uncovering current state knowledge, defining the future state, evaluating a prototype or vendor package, and making group solution decisions.

Appendix C

BA Competency and Capability Development Tools

C 7.1

BUSINESS ANALYST COMPETENCY AND CAPABILITY SELF-ASSESSMENT

Name: _____ Completion date: _____ Revisions: _____

Manager: _____ Review date: _____

Ratings:
0 = No exposure	1 = Awareness and some knowledge	2 = Some training or coaching
3 = Knowledgeable and some practice	4 = Knowledgeable with extensive experience	5 = Considered expert and shares knowledge

Current rating is based on your exposure and experience today
Tactical capability target is where you think you should be specific to current or upcoming initiatives and varies based on organizational goals
Strategic capability target is where you think you should be specific to individual career goals
Review notes should provide actions to address any gaps or changes based on manager review

When reviewing statements, keep in mind that:
- An initiative could be any size, such as an iteration, release, project, or program
- A requirement could be in any form, such as textual, user story, or use case

Competency	Current Rating	Tactical Capability Target	Strategic Capability Target	Review Notes
Example 1: Understands overall guiding principles, strategies, policies, and regulations to assess impact on business analysis approach	2	2	4	*Opportunity in next year as team lead on larger project*
Example 2: Assesses needs of audiences for work products to match the correct tool, level of detail, language, etc.	3	3	3	*No change needed, but opportunities exist to assist in presentations*
General Competencies				
1. Understands overall guiding principles, strategies, policies, and regulations to assess impact on business analysis approach				

Continued

Competency	Current Rating	Tactical Capability Target	Strategic Capability Target	Review Notes
2. Assesses needs of audiences for work products to match the correct tool, level of detail, language, etc.				
3. Volunteers to facilitate business analysis meetings to address requirement conflicts, solution discussions, decision making, etc.				
4. Aware of interactions across business areas				
5. Shares knowledge to improve team and organizational competencies				
6. Assists team in the facilitation of stakeholder support for the initiative				
7. Develops and maintains current and future state business architectures				
8. Facilitates and documents vision or problem statements and high-level business needs				
9. Facilitates prioritization and takes into account critical needs of the customer				
10. Communicates and negotiates mitigation strategies for business risks				
11. Takes ownership of every requirement through the life of the requirement and recalls status				
12. Seeks opportunities to assist in solution idea generation				
13. Communicates role changes and gaps in competencies				
14. Builds an ongoing trusting relationship quickly with stakeholders				
15. Applies negotiation and influence techniques to assist in stakeholder collaboration				
16. Ensures right people are involved to reduce over-promising and to manage expectations				
Business Analysis Specific Competencies—Planning				
17. Stays abreast of best practices, industry domains, and IT-enabled business solutions within the business analysis area				

Continued

Competency	Current Rating	Tactical Capability Target	Strategic Capability Target	Review Notes
18. Identifies and assesses stakeholders				
19. Defines and negotiates business analysis roles and responsibilities specific to initiative or initiative types				
20. Provides initial solution scope options				
21. Assists in financial evaluation of options (business case)				
22. Identifies business analysis activities according to characteristics of initiative and integrates those activities with program or initiative manager's overall plan				
23. Adapts approach to requirement processes based on risks and initiative or initiative types				
24. Collaborates with program or initiative manager regarding requirements management activities and their impact to the overall plan				
25. Creates and gains agreement on a common set of requirements management processes, procedures, and guidelines				
26. Facilitates requirements management knowledge sharing and best practices across the team				
27. Proactively develops a communication plan to keep process owners and requirements stakeholders informed				
28. Prepares to monitor value by determining solution metrics				
29. Identifies process of how changes to solution scope will be managed				
30. Anticipates and mitigates requirements risks and risks to business analysis work				
31. Considers plans for data conversion and business transition				
32. Estimates business analysis activities and supports those estimates with a visible list of assumptions				

Continued

Competency	Current Rating	Tactical Capability Target	Strategic Capability Target	Review Notes
33. Determines and verifies how to monitor solution value measures throughout life cycle and post solution implementation				
34. Determines and verifies business analysis work measures				
35. Develops a requirements management plan when needed for communicating the requirements process to the team and/or vendors developing the solution				
Business Analysis Specific Competencies—Elicitation				
36. Conducts competitive analysis and benchmark studies				
37. Shows diplomacy and fairness in requirements elicitation				
38. Ensures organizational protocols are followed during elicitation activities				
39. Facilitates consensus where requirements conflict across stakeholders				
40. Avoids getting to solution decisions until requirements are well understood by using probing techniques				
41. Facilitates requirement decision making and approvals, yet avoids own participation and leading questions				
42. Prepares by reviewing existing information before eliciting from stakeholders				
43. Documents assumptions when constraints (such as time) are imposed on the elicitation process				
44. Conducts various elicitation techniques (such as interviewing, prototypes, reverse engineering, etc.) depending on audience, risks, and type of initiative				
45. Considers impacts to both the current and future processes				

Continued

Competency	Current Rating	Tactical Capability Target	Strategic Capability Target	Review Notes
46. Ensures that all types of requirements are considered in the elicitation process (such as business, user, functional, business rules, quality service, etc.)				
47. Uses multiple sources to obtain and confirm requirements				
Business Analysis Specific Competencies—Analysis				
48. Verifies previously established assumptions (such as those documented within a business case) that may transition into additional requirements				
49. Identifies requirement attributes appropriate for the initiative (such as requirement ownership, priority, impact to business, stability, etc.)				
50. Verifies requirements with both technical and business stakeholders				
51. Validates requirements are attainable and feasible within the technical and operational environments and initiative constraints				
52. Performs initial validation of a subset of requirements with peers				
53. Performs a gap analysis (such as between current and future process states or between data entities and processes)				
54. Writes requirements in appropriate structure and at the appropriate level of detail for the audience and risks				
55. Uses analysis techniques appropriate for the culture and initiative, such as business process analysis and data analysis				
56. Develops packages of requirements for releases or iterative development				
57. Establishes package boundaries depending on system interfaces, user interaction, themes, work distribution (such as to a vendor), priorities, etc.				

Continued

Competency	Current Rating	Tactical Capability Target	Strategic Capability Target	Review Notes
58. Assists in the development of a request for proposal (RFP) when a commercial off-the-shelf (COTS) solution is considered				
59. Traces requirements backward (business requirements) and forward (design, build, and test components) to the extent necessary for the initiative				
60. Considers requirements for reuse according to policy or for own use				
Business Analysis Specific Competencies—Communications				
61. Stays in contact with customers throughout the business analysis process through both formal and informal communication channels				
62. Regularly communicates accurate accounts of solution scope and manages expectations of stakeholders				
63. Translates both business and technical information into a language that can be easily understood by all customers				
64. Uses various tools to communicate and validate requirements across cultures (business modeling, use cases, scenarios, etc.)				
65. Proactively provides clarification of business analysis process steps to the business				
66. Creates work products to validate understanding (agendas, meeting notes, sketches for contextual understanding, matrices, etc.)				
67. Creates or assists in the creation of other deliverables to support the systems development life-cycle effort (user manuals, presentation slides, user stories, training materials, test cases, etc.)				
68. Participates in formal walk throughs of systems development life-cycle deliverables to validate requirement traceability				

Continued

Competency	Current Rating	Tactical Capability Target	Strategic Capability Target	Review Notes
69. Specifies and visually diagrams requirements to provide insight into process improvements				
Business Analysis Specific Competencies—Solution Assessment				
70. Develops solution alternatives, including COTS solutions				
71. Ensures requirements are allocated to the solution(s)				
72. Assists in the solution evaluations				
73. Facilitates selection of solution among stakeholders				
74. Communicates solution, its benefits and impacts, to the business				
75. Identifies requirements to transition to the new environment once a solution has been identified				
76. Supports usability and implementation of the solution by ensuring that the business makes the transition to the new business process				
77. Evaluates solution performance according to previously identified solution metrics				
78. Conducts a post-implementation assessment to document improvement and enhancement opportunities				
Professional Skills and Techniques				
A. Analytical				
79. Benchmarking				
80. Business process engineering, business modeling				
81. Decomposition/splitting (user stories, processes, features, work)				
82. Document analysis				
83. Focus groups				
84. Gap analysis				
85. Interface analysis				
86. Observation				
87. Problem solving and tracking				

Continued

Competency	Current Rating	Tactical Capability Target	Strategic Capability Target	Review Notes
88. Prototyping				
89. Root cause analysis				
90. Scope definition				
91. Self-learning				
92. Stakeholder mapping				
93. Survey and questionnaires				
94. System thinking				
95. SWOT analysis				
96. Tracing requirements				
97. User analysis (such as personas)				
98. Work flow analysis				
B. Management				
99. Business and industry domain knowledge				
100. Change organizational impact management				
101. Coaching				
102. Conflict resolution				
103. Cross-cultural understanding				
104. Decision making				
105. Estimating (delta, parametric, story points, etc.)				
106. Ethical policy knowledge and adherence				
107. Financial valuation				
108. Interviewing				
109. Issue management				
110. Lessons learned and retrospectives				
111. Motivating				
112. Negotiating				
113. Organizational knowledge				
114. Planning (work breakdown structure)				
115. Presentation of solutions				
116. Prioritizing and ranking				
117. RACI matrix				

Continued

Competency	Current Rating	Tactical Capability Target	Strategic Capability Target	Review Notes
118. Risk management				
119. Solution knowledge				
C. Communication and Facilitation				
120. Brainstorming and/or brainwriting				
121. Guiding to consensus				
122. Influencing participation				
123. Listening				
124. Managing objectives to allocated time				
125. Meeting/workshop planning				
126. Multi-voting and nominal				
127. Questioning				
128. Translating				
129. Technical writing and documenting (both textually and graphically)				
130. Uncovering hidden assumptions				
131. Visualization				

This book has free material available for download from the
Web Added Value™ resource center at *www.jrosspub.com*

C 7.2

BUSINESS ANALYSIS ORGANIZATIONAL CAPABILITY ASSESSMENT

This tool assesses the organization's ability to support business analysis activities for successful outcomes through its people, processes, and technology. This assessment provides the opportunity to identify where gaps exist with organizational support. Two examples are provided below.

0 = No capability
1 = Capability isolated and based on individual performance
2 = Capability isolated and based on team performance
3 = Capability repeated across organization
4 = Capability is measured and continuously improved
5 = Capability is optimized; considered best practice in industry

	Today	Tactical Target	Strategic Target	Review Notes
Support Individual Business Analyst Competencies and Capabilities				
EXAMPLE 1: Collaboration with human resources defines a career path for BA positions	1	3	3	Job position career paths are very long term—perhaps 5 years out. Focus will be on individual performance rewards as part of annual management objectives.
EXAMPLE 2: Formal BA job descriptions exist for each level	2	3	4	Job descriptions are by business unit today, but consideration is to have consistency across the enterprise and have some measurements. A focus group of BAs will be launched to address this and several other gaps.
1. Collaboration with human resources defines a career path for BA positions				
2. Formal BA job descriptions exist for each level				
3. A competency framework exists for each BA level				

Continued

	Today	Tactical Target	Strategic Target	Review Notes
4. Training opportunities are provided to improve business analysis performance that address various job levels and are delivered in various ways (self-paced eLearning, instructor-led virtual, etc.)				
5. BAs are provided the opportunity to practice activities in a safe environment				
6. Expected behaviors to foster a trusting culture are clearly communicated				
7. Suggested performance measures are communicated				
8. Coaching opportunities are provided				
9. Knowledge sharing is rewarded, and tools are available to support it				
10. Ethics and fairness guidelines and examples are provided				
11. Resources to sustain successful performance are provided				
12. Allow learning time for new techniques and tools				
Support Business Analysis Process Capabilities				
13. Initiatives are justified (e.g., a business case) and prioritized to facilitate business analysis prioritization				
14. Business policy impacts are clearly identified and communicated				
15. Relationships, trust, and commitment to the requirements process are established to ensure needed cooperation				
16. Process and data owners are clearly identified and utilized for appropriate decision making and approvals				

Continued

	Today	Tactical Target	Strategic Target	Review Notes
17. Stakeholder expectations are managed by the organization regarding the need for trade-offs among resource cost, overall budget, schedule, and solution scope				
18. An environment is established to facilitate open communications of business and requirement risks				
19. Requirement management activities, deliverables, and roles are clearly defined and communicated				
20. Project management and solution life-cycle processes are in place with defined activities, deliverables, and roles to support business analysis activities				
21. Business analysis activities are well-known across initiatives and integrated into methodologies				
22. Business analysis estimating guidelines are provided to improve estimate accuracy				
23. Business analysis estimating history is captured to improve future estimates				
24. Requirement change control processes are clearly defined based on various delivery approaches				
25. Recommended tools and techniques help facilitate the gathering and validating of requirements in virtual and global environments				
26. Minimum standards for business and technical approvals are defined and enforced				

Continued

	Today	Tactical Target	Strategic Target	Review Notes
27. Minimum standards for documentation (such as for audit purposes or certifications) are clearly identified				
28. Analysis tools, techniques, templates, and checklists are recommended (organizational process assets)				
29. Minimum standards for traceability are enforced with clear roles and responsibilities for maintaining traceability				
30. Escalation procedures are well communicated for addressing requirement conflicts				
31. Formal communication procedures are provided to guide the BA in managing stakeholder expectations and for communicating requirements at the appropriate level of detail				
32. Minimum standards for communications and touchpoints between roles (such as BA to tester) and between organizations are enforced				
33. Release planning processes are clearly defined and communicated				
34. Repositories of reusable business analysis assets are regularly populated and maintained				
35. Processes to ensure proper transition and warranty monitoring are clearly defined and communicated				

Continued

	Today	Tactical Target	Strategic Target	Review Notes
Increase BA Productivity with Technology				
36. Standards are provided for home-grown tools and single-purpose tools such as notations standards and templates				
37. Added modules or features for transitional tools such as adding a requirements module to a testing tool are easily requisitioned				
38. Tools for virtual meetings support elicitation activities				
39. Tools for visuals such as business modeling tools are provided to support analysis activities				
40. Tools to perform prototyping such as wireframe tools are provided to support solution verification				
41. Tools that support the extensive effort of tracing requirements to other components are provided				

C 7.3

BUSINESS ARCHITECT COMPETENCY
SELF-ASSESSMENT

Name: _____ Completion date: _____ Revisions: _____

Manager: _____ Review date: _____

Ratings: 0 = No exposure   1 = Awareness   2 = Best practice understanding
         3 = Some experience   4 = Best practice understanding + experience   5 = Others seek my advice

Current rating is based on your exposure and experience today

Target rating is based on where you think you should be for your current or future role (this column can be split if you feel your role there may change)

Review notes should address any gaps or changes based on manager review

NOTES: Extent of competency level needed for application to projects will vary based on type and structure of the project, defined responsibilities within the organization, and the organizational culture.

Competency	Current Rating	Target Rating	Review Notes
I. Enterprise Analysis			
1. Makes an effort to understand overall guiding principles, strategies, policies, and regulations			
2. Stays abreast of best practices, industry domains, and IT-enabled business solutions within the business analysis area			
3. Awareness of interactions across business areas			
4. Conducts competitive analysis and benchmark studies			
5. Facilitates strategic planning sessions			

Continued

Competency	Current Rating	Target Rating	Review Notes
6. Develops and maintains current and future state business architectures			
7. Facilitates and documents vision or problem statements and high-level business needs			
8. Facilitates solution options			
9. Provides initial solution scope options and helps prepare the business case			
10. Assists product, program, and project managers in identification of assets for reuse			
11. Ensures proper metrics in place to measure success			
12. Facilitates prioritization and takes into account critical needs of the customer			
13. Communicates and negotiates mitigation strategies for business risks			
14. Has a clear understanding of organizational environments (politics, hierarchy, user skill levels, stakeholder categories)			
15. Assists in the development of a request for information (RFI) when an enterprise-wide commercial-off-the-shelf (COTS) solution is considered			
16. Advises on new opportunities through analysis of architectural assets			
17. Evaluates solution performance			
18. Conducts a post-implementation assessment to document improvement and enhancements			
19. Supports usability and implementation of the solution by ensuring that the business makes the transition to new business processes			
II. Business Architecture Planning and Monitoring			
20. Identifies and assesses stakeholders			
21. Assesses needs of audiences for work products to match the correct tool, level of detail, language, etc.			
22. Anticipates and mitigates business analysis risks			

Continued

Competency	Current Rating	Target Rating	Review Notes
23. Adapts approach to business analysis processes based on risks and project types			
24. Fosters a common and shared team atmosphere by creating and agreeing on a common set of business analysis processes, procedures, and guidelines			
25. Socializes business analysis processes, procedures, and guidelines			
26. Facilitates business analysis knowledge sharing and best practices across the team			
27. Collaborates with project manager regarding requirements management activities and their impact to the overall project plan			
28. Proactively develops a communication plan to keep stakeholders informed			
29. Assists in the management of changes to initiative scope			
30. Considers plans for business transition			
31. Identifies business architecture activities			
32. Estimates business architecture activities			
33. Defines business architecture roles and responsibilities			
34. Determines metrics to monitor business analysis work			
35. Integrates business analysis activities with the systems development life cycle			
36. Adheres to governance processes			
III. Professional Skills and Techniques			
A. Analytical			
37. Benchmarking			
38. Business process engineering, business modeling			
39. Business, structured, or object-oriented analysis techniques			
40. Decomposition			
41. Document analysis			
42. Focus groups			

Continued

Competency	Current Rating	Target Rating	Review Notes
43. Gap analysis			
44. Interface analysis			
45. Observation			
46. Problem solving and tracking			
47. Prototyping			
48. Root cause analysis			
49. Scope definition			
50. Self learning			
51. Stakeholder mapping			
52. Survey and questionnaires			
53. System thinking			
54. SWOT Analysis			
55. Tracing requirements			
56. Work flow analysis			
B. Management			
57. Business and industry knowledge			
58. Change organizational impact management			
59. Coaching			
60. Conflict resolution			
61. Cross-cultural understanding			
62. Decision making and analysis			
63. Estimating			
64. Ethical policy knowledge and adherence			
65. Financial valuation			
66. Interviewing			
67. Issue management			
68. Motivating			
69. Negotiating			
70. Organizational knowledge			
71. Planning (work breakdown structure)			
72. Policy making			
73. Presentation of solutions			
74. Prioritizing and ranking			
75. RACI matrix			
76. Risk management			

Continued

Competency	Current Rating	Target Rating	Review Notes
77. Socialization of information			
78. Solution knowledge			
C. Communication and Facilitation			
79. Brainstorming and/or brainwriting			
80. Guiding to consensus			
81. Influencing participation			
82. Listening			
83. Managing objectives to allocated time			
84. Meeting/workshop planning			
85. Multi-voting and nominal			
86. Questioning			
87. Translating			
88. Technical writing and documenting (both textually and graphically)			
89. Uncovering hidden assumptions			
90. Visualization			

C 7.4

BUSINESS ANALYSIS COACHING: INDIVIDUAL GROWTH PLAN

Growth plan for: _____

For the following period: _____

Last update: _____

Summary of short-term goals to accomplish by _____:

```
┌─────────────────────────────────────────────────────────────┐
│                                                             │
│                                                             │
│                                                             │
│                                                             │
│                                                             │
│                                                             │
│                                                             │
└─────────────────────────────────────────────────────────────┘
```

Summary of long-term goals to accomplish by _____:

```
┌─────────────────────────────────────────────────────────────┐
│                                                             │
│                                                             │
│                                                             │
│                                                             │
│                                                             │
└─────────────────────────────────────────────────────────────┘
```

Competency and Goal/ Value Improvements identified in self-assessments, from team learning plans, input from coach, input from manager, or other areas of interest	Short-Term Objective	Target Date	Complete Date	Long-Term Objective	Lessons Learned and Future Considerations
Business modeling as identified in the team learning plan. Will be performing process modeling of current processes on project starting in two weeks. Manager also sees me as becoming an expert in this area to help other teams and BAs.	Create one swim lane model using notations and techniques learned during coaching session and have it reviewed by a peer within one week of project start. In that same week, do a second one and have that reviewed by the coach. Also validate by the process owner.	4/14/20xx	6/30/20xx	Gain enough experience and confidence so I can coach others on our team within one year. Also gain enough experience so I can estimate how long it takes me to create a model so that it can be estimated within a 20% accuracy goal.	Make sure to label diagrams with *as-is* or *to-be*. Make sure to add a legend to each diagram so process owners don't need to be educated every time. Allow some flexibility on notation as to not bog down discussions. Remember to focus on the *happy path* first before digging into exceptions (slows process down).

Resources Used:

Reviews

Conducted With:	Date:	Comments:

INDEX

Page numbers followed by *f* indicate figures and those followed by *t* indicate tables